THE STRUCTURE OF
THE MEAT ANIMALS

17

THE STRUCTURE OF
THE MEAT ANIMALS

A GUIDE TO THEIR ANATOMY AND PHYSIOLOGY

17

BY

RODERICK MACGREGOR

F.R.C.V.S., M.R.S.I., M.I. OF M.

636

REVISED BY

FRANK GERRARD

M.B.E., F.INST.M., M.INST.R., M.R.S.I.

ILLUSTRATED BY A. P. BURTON

LONDON
THE TECHNICAL PRESS LTD.

First published in 1952
2nd edition revised 1965

PRINTED IN GREAT BRITAIN
BY PHOTOLITHOGRAPHY
UNWIN BROTHERS LIMITED
WOKING AND LONDON

FOREWORD

I FEEL that it is a great privilege to have the opportunity of writing a brief foreword to this volume. Whereas the engineer has a fairly accurate knowledge of the raw material of his craft, until recently the same could not be said of the butcher. In his case a knowledge of anatomy, the structure of the animal, of physiology, the way the body works, its composition, as influenced by nutrition and growth, are just as important as the structure, hardness and strength of a bar of mild steel.

I feel confident that not only the butcher, but also the potential meat inspector, will find in this book the sound basic principles which can be applied to their everyday work. Without the notes on physiology it is difficult to acquire the reasons for the shape, position and functioning of the various organs. A thorough knowledge of physiology implies a sound basis of biochemistry, a subject which is outside the scope of this work, but doubtless the really keen student will obtain such knowledge from some of the excellent books dealing specifically with this subject.

I am sure that the Author will not consider it a criticism of his work if I stress the fact that book-learning *must* be supplemented by personal experience, and the reader should take every opportunity to correlate his theoretical attainments with the practical knowledge, which can be gained only by handling the live animal, the carcase and its organs.

FRANK GERRARD.

PREFACE TO SECOND EDITION

IT was unfortunate that my good friend, the Author, died prior to the preparation of the second edition of this book. Of recent years there has been an increasing interest in Meat Technology, the standards of training have improved and the Institute of Meat Examinations cover a much wider field than previously. It is with this in mind, and an appreciation of his work for the student, which has prompted me to undertake willingly the task of revising and preparing a second edition of his book.

F. G.

LIST OF PLATES

ACKNOWLEDGEMENTS

Fig. nos. 5, 6a, 6b, 6c, 7, 8, 10, 11, 12, 18, 20, 21, 22, 23, 25, 26a, 31, 48a, 48b, 48c, 49a, 49b, 51a, 51b, 51c, 51d, 51e, 51f, 54, 55, 56a, 56b, 57 were made from figures in 'The Anatomy of the Domestic Animals', by Septimus Sisson, S.B., V.S., D.V.Sc., revised by James Daniels Grossman, G.P.H., D.V.M. Due acknowledgement is made to Messrs. W. B. Saunders & Co. Ltd. for permission to reproduce them. Fig. 3 is taken from C. G. Trew's " Figure and Animal Drawing ", and the Author is indebted to Messrs. A. & C. Black Ltd., 4-6 Soho Square, London, W. 1, for permission to copy it.

CONTENTS

CHAPTER I

BIOLOGICAL PRINCIPLES

Connective Tissue ; Trabeculae and Parenchyma ; Cells ; Vegetative and Master Tissues; the Shape of the Body; Summary.

As a preliminary to undertaking a detailed study of the structure of animals, take a piece of meat and examine the various tissues of which it is composed.

Red meat or ' Red Muscle Tissue ' consists of parallel fibres of red, fairly soft material.   The uncut surfaces are covered with a transparent membrane that is moist and glistening if the meat is fresh.   The cut surfaces show that this membrane is continued throughout the muscle substance, running between the red fibres like a lattice work and forming the ' marbling '. This membrane is called ' Connective Tissue '.   Fatty tissue is also covered with a similar membrane of connective tissue which also runs like a lattice through the whole piece of fat. Globules of pure fat can be picked out of the spaces in this lattice of connective tissue, or it can be melted and strained off, leaving behind the connective tissue which forms the ' cracklings '.   Bone is also covered with a membrane of connective tissue which can be peeled off with tweezers, and there is also a lattice work running through the bone tissue itself, but in this case it will need a microscope to detect the actual strands.   If, however, a piece of old dried bone be fashioned into a cup and water placed therein, it will seep out fairly rapidly through minute holes in the bone.   These holes contained the strands of the lattice of connective tissue when the bone was fresh.

The viscera or internal organs have a similar structure. The lungs, the spleen or milt, the liver and kidneys each has a smooth, glistening, outer surface formed by a membrane of connective tissue, and this membrane continues as a lattice-work throughout the substance of the organ.   This lattice can be clearly seen in a cut surface of a piece of lung or spleen, but it may be necessary to use a reading glass or pocket lens to see it in the liver or kidneys.

1

It is obvious, therefore, that connective tissue forms a large part of every organ and tissue of the body, and some further description of it is, therefore, necessary, and it will help if certain technical names are applied to it. The connective tissue covering an organ is called the ' Capsule ' of that organ. In the organs mentioned, lungs, spleen, liver and kidneys, the capsules cover the whole organ, forming a bag or ' sac ' with only one opening, the 'hilus', through which large blood vessels and tubes or ' ducts ' pass. The lattice work in the substance of the organ is called ' Trabeculae ', the Latin for a lattice or trellis. The tissue supported by trabeculae that does the actual work of the organ is called its ' Parenchyma ', the Greek for moulded material. The parenchyma of the liver is the brown liver material ; that of the red muscle is the soft red material mentioned in the second paragraph of this chapter; that of the fatty tissues is the globules of pure fat. Hence it can be stated that every organ or tissue in the body consists of a capsule and trabeculae of connective tissue supporting a parenchyma of ' functioning ' or working tissue. The connective tissue is similar in all organs, but the parenchyma differs according to its functions.

It is usually possible to obtain unborn or ' foetal ' calves from abattoirs as they are cut out from the wombs of slaughtered cows and discarded. Such a foetus, about 3 inches long, that is to say, in the second or third month after its conception, is easily recognisable as a calf. It has a calf-like body, head and legs but is hairless and soft, and can be twisted out of shape. On opening it, it will be found that each bone and muscle and all the viscera have been modelled in connective tissue.

Connective tissue, when magnified about 100 times, is seen to consist of interwoven fibrils or minute threads, with a transparent yellow liquid, the ' *Lymph* ', flowing between them. It is this lymph that gives fresh meat its moist appearance. When the fibrils are closely woven, leaving only minute lymph spaces between, it is called ' Fibrous Connective Tissue ', and when they form a loose lace-work with large lymph spaces, it is called Areolar (area covering) Connective Tissue. Two kinds of fibrils can be seen, though they vary in their relative frequency. Some are very fine, branched and colourless or *white* and rather brittle, and the others are thicker, unbranched, *yellow* and elastic.

On raising the magnification to about 400 times, each fibril is seen to consist of a tube or ' Wall ' containing a jelly-like material, the ' Cytoplasm '; and a central spot or ' Nucleus '. A body consisting of these three parts, wall, cytoplasm and nucleus, is called a ' cell ' or ' cyte ', and connective tissue therefore consists of interwoven white and yellow fibril cells. The cytoplasm of the white fibril cells is soluble in hot water and forms gelatin; that of the yellow fibril cells is insoluble in most liquids. The nucleus governs the activity of the cell and, if the tissue has been long dead, will have disappeared.

In addition to the fibril cells, connective tissue contains flat, square or polygonal cells, called ' Endothelial Cells '. These lie side by side without visible lymph spaces between them and form membranes to retain the lymph and other fluids. Usually these membranes are rolled up to form minute vessels, the ' Capillary Vessels '.

In the capillary blood vessels spherical blood cells may be seen, with wall and cytoplasm, though for reasons which will be explained later, most of these blood cells have no visible nuclei. Examination of any parenchyma shows that it also consists of cells, having walls, cytoplasm and nuclei, though their shape, colour and size will be different in each organ. In fact, the whole body is entirely built up of cells which are therefore the ' units ' of life. Each of these cells lives its individual life, sucking nutriment from the lymph in the lymph spaces, and discarding into that lymph the used up material from its cytoplasm; in much the same way as the microscopic animals living in slimy water take in their nutriment from the water around them and discard into it the material they have used. The microscopic animals, however, live independently of each other, but the cells that build up a large animal's body cling together and work in co-operation, under the influence or direction of a ' Psyche ' or ' Soul '. When this psyche ceases to direct them, we say that the animal is ' dead '; the cells cease to co-operate and each one therefore dies soon afterwards.

This individual life of the cells may be observed if we watch the body of a recently killed animal.   The legs will move with a running action as long as the muscle parenchyma cells continue alive; but there is no object or purpose in their movement, as the body does not try to rise and escape.   Similarly the skin will sweat, although the air around is cold, and the eyes will open, although the light is bright.   The cells in all these parts are still living, but they have no central guidance and their actions therefore cannot help each other.   So one by one they die from lack of the mutual help by which alone they can exist. It is perhaps best to compare a living animal to a hive of bees. Each bee has a definite task to perform in the hive and each cell has a definite function in the body; but, if the queen bee or controlling influence in the hive is destroyed, the bees are thrown into confusion and finally die off one by one; and when the Psyche ceases to control the body the cells no longer function in unison and each cell gradually dies.

Occasionally, a group of cells will die as a result of injury or disease, though the rest of the body remains alive.   Such an area of dead cells in a living body is termed ' Necrosis '. A necrotic area can be detected either by its lack of function or activity, or, more readily, by its lack of ' tone '.   Living cells (with few exceptions) are always pulling slightly against each other and are therefore in a state of tension or ' tone ', hence living flesh is springy to touch, and, if cut, gapes open. Dead flesh pits somewhat on pressure and, when cut will not gape.   This tone of living flesh is of importance in detecting if a wound was made before, or after death, as well as in enabling a doctor to ascertain the extent of an injury to a living person.

Cells that perform identical tasks are similar in appearance and size in all animals.   The liver parenchyma cells are identical whether they come from a sheep, pig or ox, and the connective tissue cells of a new-born calf are the same size as those of a full-grown cow.   The difference in sizes of these animals is due solely to the number of cells that constitute their organs, and therefore, while the calf is growing, the cells must be increasing in numbers.   Now the simplest way in which this increase could occur would be for each cell to divide into two, and each half cell to grow to the full size of the undivided cell. This process occurs and can be seen in connective tissue, both in the fibrils and the endothelial cells. The nucleus divides first, then the cell splits down its length, and finally each half grows to its full size. Parenchyma cells, however, that are engaged on the actual work of the body, do not divide, as each one is formed from a half fibril cell split off a connective tissue cell. It is customary, therefore, to speak of ' Vegetative Tissues ', i.e. the connective tissue fibrils, the endothelial cells and certain others that multiply; and the ' Master Tissues ' formed for work only but incapable of further growth in themselves. When the animal is young, the vegetative tissues multiply rapidly and continually lay down more parenchyma and master tissue cells, thus increasing the size of the whole body. At maturity, the vegetative tissues lay down master tissues sufficiently fast to replace wastage, but no more, hence there is no more growth. In senility the wastage is faster than the replacement, and the animal becomes shrivelled and wizened in appearance.

Since cells of the vegetative tissues are increasing in number throughout the animal's period of growth, one would suspect that they all originate from one cell ; and this, in fact, is the case. Every animal starts its life as a single cell, the Germ Cell, formed by its mother and father during mating. Soon afterwards, the germ cell divides into two, then into four, eight, sixteen, and so on till a visible mass is formed. Thereafter, the cells assume their various shapes; ' spindle ' cells to form the fibrils of connective tissue yellow and white; ' round ' or biscuit-like cells to form the endothelium; and other shapes to form the other types of vegetative or growing tissue; and these will shape out the animal. Further detail of this will be given in the chapters on Sex and Reproduction.

Chemical analysis of the materials forming the cells of living bodies, both animals and plants, show that they all contain four classes of compounds; carbohydrates, fats and proteins and a considerable amount of water. Water, it is commonly known, is a compound of two parts of hydrogen with one of oxygen and this is usually written by chemists as ' H_2O '. The cells of the green plants can cause water to combine with carbon forming carbohydrates. There are many different kinds of carbohydrates, but those in an animal's body can be grouped as ' sugars ' or easily soluble carbohydrates with small molecules, and ' starches ' or less soluble carbo-hydrates with large molecules containing 30,000 or 40,000 atoms of carbon, hydrogen and oxygen each. The animal cells cannot make these carbohydrates but must eat plants or other animals that have eaten plants to acquire them. After eating carbohydrates the animal cells cause them to combine with oxygen which breaks them down into H_2O (water) and CO_2 (a gas breathed out by all animals).

Fats consist also of carbon and hydrogen with very little oxygen. They can be made both by animal cells and plant cells but both must have either carbohydrate or protein to make them. Hence to acquire fats the animal cells must again eat plants or other animals that have eaten plants. Fats can be oxidised like the carbohydrates forming H_2O and CO_2, or they may be stored to use in times of starvation. Proteins form the cell walls and the nuclei and often other parts of the cell, as well as part of the fluid material, such as lymph and mucus. There are many different proteins, but essentially they all consist of carbon, hydrogen and oxygen, and some other mineral such as calcium (lime), sulphur, phosphorus and others. These numerous different atoms are held together by sets of atoms of nitrogen and hydrogen called the Amide or Nitrogen group. Plants, especially the microscopic plants called bacteria, take these nitrogen groups from the soil and build them up into proteins. Animals eat these plants and break up the proteins into nitrogen groups and carbon, hydrogen, oxygen and minerals, and then re-assemble them to form proteins suitable for their own bodies. The animal cell thus makes its own protein but can only do so if nitrogen groups are provided in the form of other proteins. Proteins in the animal cell are broken down like the fats and carbo-hydrates into simple compounds, the CO_2 being returned to the air (so that the plants can again convert it into carbo-hydrate) and the nitrogen groups and water being returned to the soil as urine.

Thus plants build up carbohydrate, fat and protein, animals break them down into CO_2, H_2O and simple compounds of nitrogen.

The body itself may be considered as a tube made of bones and muscles with an outer layer of skin. Inside this tube are the organs that nourish the whole body, and these are regarded as lying in three cavities, or divisions of the tube, as follows:—

The Thorax or Thoracic Cavity (the Chest), containing the organs of respiration or lungs and the main organ of circulation, the heart.

The Abdomen, or Abdominal Cavity (the Belly), containing the main organs of digestion.

The Pelvis or Pelvic Cavity (the Hips) containing the main organs of excretion, the rectum or end of the gut and the urinary bladder.

The Head also consists of cavities which will be described later.

To avoid confusion arising when one is considering alternately an upright man, a horizontal quadruped, or a hanging carcase, the following terms should be used:—

Anterior meaning nearer the head.

Posterior meaning nearer the tail.

Dorsal meaning nearer the back of a man or upper portion of a quadruped.

Ventral meaning nearer the front of a man, or lower portion of a quadruped.

Medial meaning nearer the central line running from head to tail.

Lateral meaning further from the central line running from head to tail.

Upper portion of a limb meaning nearer the body.

Lower portion of a limb meaning furthest from the body.

SUMMARY

The body of every animal is built up of a mass of cells, each consisting of a cell wall, a cytoplasm and a nucleus; and each forming a living unit. Most living cells pull continuously against each other, thus giving the flesh ' Tone '. In the spaces between the cells is a clear yellow fluid, the lymph, that supplies them with nourishment and removes waste matter. Cells may be roughly divided as ' Vegetative ' cells, capable of multiplication by repeatedly dividing into two, and ' Master Tissue ' cells, incapable of further multiplication but specialised to perform other functions. Master tissue cells are all created by vegetative cells, and vegetative cells arise by repeated division from a single ' Germ Cell '.

The commonest vegetative tissue is the connective tissue, made up of mixed yellow elastic insoluble fibrils and white, brittle, soluble fibrils. Capillary vessels are made of endothelial cells; another vegetative tissue specialised to form membranes to retain fluids; and these vessels run throughout connective tissue.

Every organ in the body consists of a capsule of connective tissue surrounding it; a lattice work or trabeculae of connective tissue running through it; and parenchyma cells of some master tissue, performing the function of that organ. The organ is first modelled by the capsule and trabeculae and, later, is filled up with parenchyma. The capillary vessels in the connective tissue supply the lymph in the organ with the nourishment that the parenchyma needs. Thus, the connective tissue first builds up and then nourishes the organs.

CHAPTER II

OSTEOLOGY OR THE STUDY OF BONES

Bone Tissue, Marrow, Cartilage; the Development of the Skeleton;
Joints, Ligaments and Tendons; the Mammalian Skeleton;
Skeletons of Different Animals.

A PIECE of bone consists of the following tissues:—

'Compact Bone' Tissue. This forms the outer shell of all bones. In colour it is creamy-white, with a faint tinge of pink, and it is hard and brittle. Although it looks solid, it is, in fact, porous, being pierced with numerous microscopic canals carrying capillary blood vessels for nourishing the interior of the bone. These are the 'Haversian Canals'. Some bones are also entered by two or three larger, clearly visible, blood vessels which pass through 'Nutrient Foramina', or perforations of the bone corresponding to the hilus mentioned in the previous chapter.

'Cancellated' or 'Spongy' Bone Tissue. This is found inside most bones. It is made up of numerous small bony plates forming a labyrinth of small but clearly visible 'Medullary Spaces' which give it the appearance of a sponge. The shafts of the long bones of the limbs have no cancellated tissue within them, but form hollow tubes called 'Medullary Cavities' (Fig. 1).

'Medulla' or Marrow. The small medullary spaces in spongy bone tissue are filled with Red Marrow. This consists of a mass of spherical red cells that are strongly vegetative and multiply rapidly. As soon as each space is filled, the surplus drifts off in the capillary blood-vessels and becomes the red blood cells or corpuscles. Wastage of red blood cells is considerable, and the red marrow of the spongy bone tissue is always occupied in replacing them.

In a newly-born animal, the marrow in the large medullary cavities of the limb bones is also red, as it is occupied in making new blood; but as growth nears completion it has less to do and is gradually replaced by fat, turning orange and finally yellow at maturity.

9

'Cartilage' or Gristle. The ends of bones that would rub against each other are covered with cartilage, a pearly-white material, soft enough to cut with a knife and pliant and resilient, which forms a cushion to lessen the shock if the bones are driven together. In young growing animals areas of cartilage are found in the bones at places where rapid growth is taking place, notably the ends of the shafts of limb bones just below the head and just above the lower extremity. These 'Growth Bands' turn into bone when the animal is mature, and they thus form a useful guide as to the age of the animal providing the carcase. In newly-born animals, the entire skeleton is composed of cartilage (except the limb bones of the calf and foal) to allow it to be compressed while passing between the hip bones of the mother at birth, but 'ossification' or change of cartilage into bone starts early in infancy.

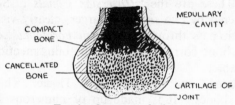

FIG. 1.—Structure of a bone.

Cartilage is also found in parts of the body unassociated with the skeleton, notably the trachea or windpipe and some of the larger blood-vessels. In both these places its function is to provide flexible tubes whose bore can be altered by bending the cartilage in or out.

'Periosteum' and 'Perichondrium'. The connective tissue membrane that covers all bone and cartilage, corresponding to the 'capsule' of other organs, is called the Periosteum, or 'surrounder of bone'. Strictly speaking, this word should be kept for the capsule of bones only, while that of cartilage should be called 'Perichondrium', but in actual practice, the latter word is rarely used. Periosteum can be peeled off fresh bone easily with a pair of forceps.

Development of the Skeleton. In the preceding chapter it was shown that the skeleton is outlined in the foetus in the form of capsules and trabeculae of connective tissue. The capsules remain for life, forming the Periosteum, but most of the fibrils of the trabeculae are converted into cartilage cells by becoming shorter and broader until they are oval or almost oblong in shape, and then thickening their walls at the expense of cytoplasm, until only a trace remains round the nucleus. Such cells lose their tension, and so cut cartilage does not gape open like other tissues and may seem lifeless; but the cells retain their powers of vegetation and can multiply rapidly, thus filling up the capsule and forming a parenchyma. Thereafter they cause the whole skeleton and body to grow. These oblong cells pack up close together, leaving only minute lymph spaces at their corners; thus, under the microscope, cartilage has the appearance of a structure of bricks, the centre of each brick being marked by the nucleus with a film of cytoplasm round it. On boiling, these films of cytoplasm dissolve out, and yield, in the aggregate, an appreciable quantity of gelatine, but there is little else of any nutritive value in cartilage. In the diet of carnivorous animals its most important role is that of 'indigestible matter' necessary for keeping the bowels open.

As stated above, the greater part of the skeleton must remain as resilient cartilage until after birth, but, in the foal and the calf a certain amount of ossification or hardening of the bones of the limbs, but only in the limbs, occurs before birth to enable the animal to stand soon after delivery. The process of ossification is somewhat complicated but may be summarised thus. Certain cells in the walls of the capillary blood-vessels extract various salts of calcium (lime) and magnesium from the blood and form them into minute sharp-edged plates. These plates are pushed edgewise into the surrounding cartilage and form a disc with a hole in the centre (Fig. 2). Layers of these discs with their holes in line form the Haversian canal. The process is continuous throughout life, the discs getting larger and encroaching more and more on the cartilage, so that, in old age there is very little cartilage left and the bones are correspondingly brittle and hard. Conversely, in youth, while there is still a considerable quantity of cartilage left uninvaded, the bones are softer and more resilient. In entire males, the bones normally become harder and heavier than those of females or castrates.

Cartilage cells that have been so invaded by the ossifying process, however slight, are no longer capable of multiplying.

Therefore, in the bones of a growing animal growth bands of pure cartilage are left, at which places the bones can lengthen by simple multiplication of the cells; but these growth bands disappear as the animal becomes mature, a state that is reached earlier in the female than the male. Growth in thickness is carried out by the periosteum which lays down on the outer surface layers of cartilage cells that start to ossify soon after they are formed, but they give the growing bones of a young animal a characteristic reddish look. Simultaneously, the endothelial cells of the capillary blood-vessels eat or dissolve away the centre of the bone, thus forming the medullary spaces and cavities. The same endothelial cells then multiply

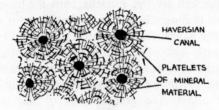

HAVERSIAN CANAL

PLATELETS OF MINERAL MATERIAL

FIG. 2.—Microscopic structure of bone.

and form a membranous lining to the cavities, called the Endo-osteum. The cells of the Endo-osteum give rise to marrow cells.

As a whole, bone is more nutritious than cartilage. Though there is less gelatine, the red marrow and marrow fat are highly nutritious and the lime salts are of great value. It is, however, usually necessary to grind bone into a fine flour before herbivorous animals will eat it. Naturally, no accurate figures can be given as to its value, for the constituents vary so much with age, as well as the nutrition and general health of the animal, but as a rough guide, it may be taken that in a 3-year-old ox one-third of the bone is cartilage, and the remainder mineral salts. These are roughly Calcium Phosphate 83 per cent., Calcium Carbonate 10 per cent. and other salts 7 per cent. The importance of ample calcium in the diet is thus well shown.

'Articulations' or the Joining of Bones. Two bones are said to be 'sutured' when they are joined by threads of yellow connective tissue fibrils. Such joints allow internal organs and the bones surrounding them to increase in size, but they do not allow for the bones to move relatively to each other. The bones of the skull are so joined as well as those of the hips and many others. It is common for sutured joints to 'fuse' in old age and sometimes at maturity. The connective tissue turns into cartilage and then ossifies.

When free movement is required, as in the limbs, a 'synovial' joint is formed. The ends of the two bones that might rub together are covered with a thin layer of cartilage that remains unossified through life. Surrounding the joint is a capsule of yellow connective tissue lined inside with an endothelial sac containing a form of lymph called 'Synovia' or 'joint oil'. In a healthy young animal, this synovia is sufficiently copious to keep the ends of the bones apart and so there is no detectable friction when they move. In a starved or very aged animal the synovia is less and the ends of the bones may actually be in contact. In such an animal the joints will 'creak' when moved. A dried and mounted skeleton always looks much smaller than the animal it came from, owing to the removal of the synovia between the joints.

The yellow connective tissue supporting the synovial membrane, is elastic and will stretch sufficiently to avoid rupture if submitted to a sudden strain. It merges with the periosteum of each bone and holds the two ends in apposition; but it is usually assisted by additional ligaments, or 'runners', which are bands of yellow fibrous tissue. They have no food value.

Tendons, that attach muscles to bones, are similar ropes or sheets, but of white, non-elastic tissue, since an elastic tendon would reduce the pull of the muscle. They run through 'Synovial Sheaths' or tubes containing synovia that ensures frictionless movement. Tendons will supply a large amount of gelatine, but have little other food value.

A tendon sheath is not, strictly speaking, a tube. It should be regarded more as an oblong water mattress folded round the tendon, so that down one side of the tendon a line remains marking the junction of the two edges of the mattress. The surface touching the tendon adheres to it and moves with it, rubbing against the outer surface of the 'mattress'. The synovia contained in the 'mattress' minimises friction as the two surfaces rub together. Similarly in synovial joints and bursae, the membrane of the sac adheres to the surrounding tissue, and, on movement, the inner surfaces of the sacs tend to rub together.

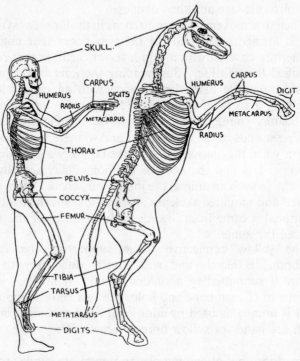

FIG. 3.—Mammalian skeletons. Human and horse.

At points where the bone comes close under the skin, as at the hip or the back of the head, there are small synovial sacs called ' Bursae '. These reduce friction between the skin and bone.

THE MAMMALIAN SKELETON

Certain technical terms are used in describing bones.
Foramen (plural *Foramina*). A perforation or hole in a bone.
Fossa. A deep depression not connected with a joint.
Process. A piece ' proceeding from ' or standing out from the main bone.

Tuberosity. A rough prominence to which muscles or their tendons are attached. Small tuberosities are sometimes called 'Tubercles'.

Articular Surface. The surface of the bone forming a synovial joint and therefore covered with cartilage and synovial membrane.

Facet. A more or less flat articular surface.

Glenoid Cavity. A shallow depression containing an articular surface.

Cotyloid Cavity or *Acetabulum.* A deep glenoid cavity.

Head of the Bone. The articular hemisphere at the upper end of a bone forming a synovial joint with a glenoid or cotyloid cavity. Such a joint is termed a 'Ball and Socket' joint.

Condyle. A curved articular surface somewhat cylindrical in shape.

Trochlea. A 'pulley shaped' articular surface.

The actual bones of a mammal should be examined and compared with the following descriptions.

The skeleton of a warm blooded animal, i.e. a mammal or bird, is based on the Vertebral Column (Fig. 4 (*a* and *b*)), commonly called the Spinal Column or Backbone. It consists of a number of separate bones, the Vertebrae, which, though differing from each other, have certain pronounced features in common, namely, a Body, an Arch, and seven Processes (Fig. 5).

The body is approximately a cylinder with the anterior end convex and the posterior end concave. It is surmounted by the arch, under which runs the Vertebral Foramen or Foramen Magnum. Where the arch joins the body there are a pair of Transverse Processes, and at the apex of the arch is the Spinous Process, frequently referred to as the 'Spine' for short. From the edges of the arch at its shoulders, the four Articular Processes protrude parallel with the body; the anterior pair being provided with facets on their upper surfaces that form synovial joints with similar facets on the under sides of the posterior articular processes of the adjacent bone. The bodies of adjacent vertebrae are joined by thin discs of cartilage sutured to each bone, the 'Intervertebral Discs'. In life, the vertebral foramina under the arches are in line, and together form the

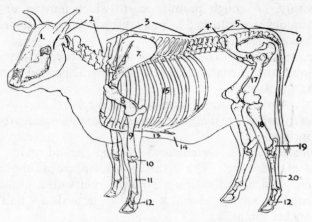

FIG. 4.—Skeleton of ox. (*a*) Standing.

1. Skull
2. Cervical vertebrae (7)
3. Thoracic vertebrae (13)
4. Lumbar
5. Sacrum
6. Coccygeal vertebrae

7. Scapula
8. Humerus
9. Radius and ulna
10. Carpus
11. Metacarpus
12. Digits
13. Sternum
14. Xiphoid cartilage
15. Ribs (13 pairs)
16. Pelvic bones
17. Femur
18. Tibia
19. Tarsus
20. Metatarsus

(*b*) Hanging carcase.

Vertebral or Spinal Canal, containing the Spinal Cord, a cord of nerves forming part of the Central Nervous System. Between the articular processes and the intervertebral discs are spaces called the Intervertebral Foramina, through which nerves pass from the Spinal Cord to all parts of the body.

A consideration of the joint between two vertebrae will show that, if the back is arched or twisted there is very little relative movement between the bodies of the vertebrae, and the elasticity of the intervertebral discs will allow for this; but

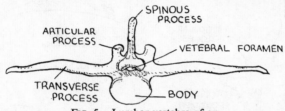

FIG. 5.—Lumbar vertebra of ox.

there is considerable movement between the articular processes; hence these are united by synovial, free moving, joints. If, however, the back is hollowed, the articular processes tend to press together and very little movement is possible in this direction. Actually, the farm animals as a whole have relatively small intervertebral discs and their backs are accordingly not very flexible. Cats, ferrets, and one may add, humans, have relatively large intervertebral discs, and consequently have more sinuous backs.

Although no two vertebrae are alike, they can be grouped in five classes: Cervical or neck, Thoracic or chest, Lumbar or belly or abdomen; Sacral or hip or pelvic; and Coccygeal or Caudal or tail. These five classes can be recognised in all mammals.

The Cervical Vertebrae are seven in number in all mammals; the differences in the length of the neck between, say, the camel and the ox being solely due to the different length of the individual bones. The first two cervical vertebrae are irregular, but from the third to the seventh the transverse processes are directed more downward than outward and are short but as broad as the body is long; the channel between them being occupied by the Longus Colli muscle (Fig. 6a). The base of

each transverse process is pierced by a ' Transverse Foramen '
running parallel to the spinal canal and found only in the
cervical vertebrae.   The spinous processes are directed forwards

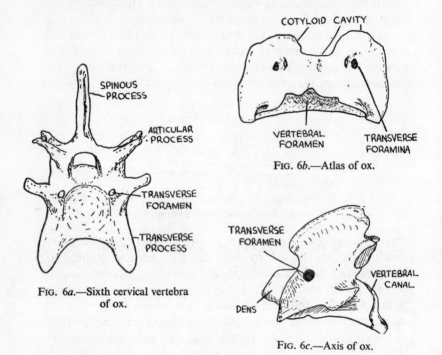

FIG. 6a.—Sixth cervical vertebra
of ox.

FIG. 6b.—Atlas of ox.

FIG. 6c.—Axis of ox.

and are short but increase gradually in length from the third to
the sixth and suddenly at the seventh in which this process is
twice the length of that of the sixth.   This bone is therefore
called the ' Vertebra Prominens ', and it also differs from the
other cervical vertebrae in having a pair of facets at the posterior end of the body for articulation with the head of the
first ribs.

The first cervical vertebra is called the *Atlas*, since in man
it holds up the head and in ancient times Mount Atlas in
Morocco was supposed to support the heavens (Fig. 6b).   It has
a very small body and no spinous or articular processes but
the transverse processes are broadened out and have the
appearance of butterfly wings;   hence the popular name

'Butterfly Bone'. The anterior edge has a deep cotyloid cavity which articulates with the condyles of the occiput (the posterior bone of the skull) and allows the head to nod. The vertebral foramen is large and is lined with an articular surface which is continued to the posterior edge of the bone. There are two Transverse Formina in each wing.

The second cervical vertebra is called the Axis, since on it the head pivots when turning from side to side (Fig. 6c). On the anterior edge is a process, the Dens (Tooth) or Odontoid (Toothlike) Process which enters the Vertebral Foramen of the atlas and forms a synovial joint which allows the pivotal movements. The spinous process has the form of a broad keel running the length of the bone and there are two very small transverse processes directed backwards. The posterior end of the bone resembles that of other cervical vertebrae.

Between the condyles of the occiput and the arch of the atlas are gaps above and below the Spinal Canal. A knife driven downwards against the back of the skull or upwards through the larynx (' Adam's Apple ') will slide into the canal, killing the animal by severing the spinal cord; a method of slaughter used in many large abattoirs in America and the Dominions. A similar gap occurs between the atlas and the axis, but is more difficult to find in the living animal, and so it is not used. In small animals, rabbits, hares and birds, it is easy to dislocate the cervical vertebrae and so crush the cord, causing death; but this cannot be done with any certainty in cattle, sheep or swine, though it sometimes occurs accidentally.

The Thoracic Vertebrae (or Dorsal*) are given as thirteen in the ox, fourteen or fifteen in the pig, and eighteen in the horse, but actually in all these animals variations of one, or even two, over or under these figures may occur. Extra thoracic vertebrae mean extra ribs and therefore extra chops and so are to be desired in all meat animals. Thoracic vertebrae (Fig. 7) have short bodies and very short transverse processes. The spinous processes are as a whole long, and increase in length from the first to the fourth or fifth and thereafter decrease gradually to the last which somewhat resembles a lumbar vertebra. Facets occur on all the transverse processes, for

* The word ' dorsal ' means, literally ' on or of the back ', and all vertebrae are therefore ' dorsal '. It is, however, customary to call the Thoracic Vertebrae the ' Dorsal Vertebrae '.

articulation with corresponding facets on the shafts of the ribs; and at each end of the bodies for articulation with the heads of the ribs. In the last thoracic vertebra there are no facets at the posterior end of the body.

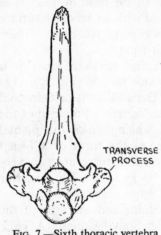

The Lumbar Vertebrae (Fig. 5), six or seven in number, are very similar to the last thoracic vertebrae, but have long transverse processes and, of course, no facets for articulation with the ribs. The anterior articular processes fold round the posterior processes of the adjacent bone, thus forming a very strong lock when the back is hollowed, and so rendering it possible for the animal to carry a considerable weight on a

FIG. 7.—Sixth thoracic vertebra of ox.

saddle resting on the long transverse processes. In old age, these joints tend to fuse and ossify, making it difficult for the animal to rise and lie down and, in cattle and horses, this gives rise to the fault of ' Sleeping Standing '. Such animals do not thrive, and are very liable to injure themselves by falling when asleep, so they are best slaughtered.

The Sacral Vertebrae (Fig. 8), four or five in number, fuse early in life forming one bone, the Sacrum. The first pair of transverse processes are long, and carry on their upper posterior side facets for articulation with the Pelvic or Hip Bones. The remaining processes, both transverse and spinous, fuse into ridges and get smaller towards the back. The Spinal Cord ends about half way down the sacrum, but the canal remains open for its whole length.

The Coccygeal or Caudal Vertebrae vary in number, both in the different species and in individual animals of the same breed. The first few resemble the posterior end of the sacrum, but thereafter they rapidly lose their processes, then the arches become incomplete, and finally cylinders of bone alone are left. These cylinders are slow in ossifying, and the last few never do so. Hence there is always great irregularity in the actual count when fully ossified bones alone are considered.

It is possible to pass a hypodermic needle into the spinal canal between the end of the sacrum and the first coccygeal bone, and as there is no spinal cord there, this may be done without fear of injury. Suitable drugs injected at this point will numb the hind quarters for an hour or two and enable difficult calving operations to be performed. This process is known as ' Spinal Anaesthesia '.

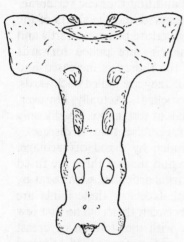

Fig. 8.—Sacrum of ox, ventral view.   Fig. 9.—Sacrum of ox, dorsal view.

The separate vertebrae are bound together by strong but elastic ligaments running between the processes, both transverse and spinous, and they form a fairly straight line, except at the neck and the front of the thorax, where the line dips downwards a varying amount. The outline of the back, however, is maintained level by the Ligamentum Nuchae, or ' Patwack ', a rope-like ligament running from the back of the head to the top of the fourth and fifth Thoracic Spinous Processes. This ligament tends to lock the neck bones together, and helps to support the head, and in the ox, horse and sheep it is sufficiently strong to enable the animal to sleep with its head nodding in the air. In other animals it is relatively weaker, and they prefer to rest their heads when sleeping. Thinner sheets of ligamentous material connect the Ligamentum Nuchae to the cervical bones.

The Thoracic Cage. This is the bony skeleton of the

thorax or chest, and consists of the thoracic vertebrae, already described, the ribs or 'Costae', the costal cartilages and the Sternum or breast bone.

The ribs are arranged in pairs corresponding in number to the thoracic vertebrae. Each rib has a curved shaft provided at its upper end with a facet that articulates with the transverse process of the vertebra behind it, and a head that articulates between the bodies of two vertebrae, the head of the first rib being between the seventh cervical and first thoracic vertebrae. The shaft of the first rib is slightly curved and the shafts of the others progressively more so, the curvature being outwards and slightly backwards, so that if the ribs are pulled forwards towards the first, the diameter of the thorax is increased and air is drawn in to the lungs, while if they are pulled backwards, the diameter is decreased and air expelled. Actually, however, this movement is negligible in animals at rest, and is usually only visible when they are panting from exercise, heat or disease.

The shaft of each rib is continued by a rod of cartilage, *the costal cartilages*. The first rib and the last three are fused to these cartilages, but the central ribs articulate with them by synovial joints. As, however, both facets of these joints are flat, there is very little movement between them. The first few costal cartilages articulate directly with the sternum or breast bone, and the corresponding ribs are therefore called ' Sternal Ribs', while the remaining cartilages are each attached to the cartilage of the rib in front by a loose connective tissue, and the corresponding ribs are therefore called ' Asternal ' * or ' False Ribs'. Occasionally, one or more pairs of ribs have no cartilages and these are called 'Floating Ribs'. Costal cartilage tends to accumulate salts in a manner similar to bone, and by the time the animal is adult, it may be almost as hard as bone, but it contains no medullary cavities or cancellated tissue and so can always be distinguished from true bone.

Although the ribs are generally regarded as forming a protective covering of the vital organs within the thorax, in actual fact they are comparatively weak bones and may be easily broken in a living animal that has been subjected to rough handling. The outer shell of compact bone is relatively thin and the cancellated bone within is scanty and contains

* ' A ' before a Greek or Latin word means ' without '.   E.g. Atheism ' A ' without, ' Theism ', belief in God.

fairly large medullary spaces although no actual marrow cavity exists. Fortunately, the muscular covering usually binds the broken ends of a rib in apposition until they knit together and recovery follows without appreciable disturbance to health. The swelling where the bones have knit will however remain and may be frequently seen in carcases.

The Sternum Brisket or Breast Bone really consists of separate bones, the *sternebrae* corresponding in number to the sternal ribs. Most of these are joined together by discs of cartilage fused with the bones, but the first bone, called the Manubrium, usually forms a synovial joint with the second, allowing free, though slight, movement. The last sternebra is continued behind the thorax and beneath the front of the abdomen as a circular disc of cartilage. This is the Xiphoid or Ensiform cartilage that protects and supports the liver. In the human being it is shaped like a dagger, hence the names Xiphoid or Ensiform, both of which mean ' sword shaped ', though in most animals it is·a circular disc.

The Forelimb (Figs. 15, 16, 17). In the meat animals, most of what corresponds to our upper arm lies within the skin of the thorax closely attached to the ribs by muscles, but the actual elbow joint is just clear. The forearm cannot be twisted (except by pigs) but maintains the hand with the palm facing backwards. The joint usually called the ' knee ' corresponds to the human wrist; there is only one large bone in the hand (except in pigs) and the animal stands, in effect, on the tips of the fingers. The forelimb contains the following bones:—

	Human	*Animal*
Scapula	Shoulder Blade	Blade Bone
Humerus	Upper Arm	Clod
Radius and Ulna	Forearm	Shin
Carpus	Wrist	Knee
Metacarpal Bones	Hand	Flat Shank or Cannon Bone
Digits	Fingers	In Hoof

The Scapula or Blade Bone is a flat bone, usually triangular in outline, lying over the ribs with the apex of the triangle facing downwards and forwards. This apex ends in a glenoid for articulation with the Humerus, and, in front of this is a small Bicipital tuberosity to which the biceps muscle is attached. The upper border of the bone, forming the base of the triangle, is prolonged by a sheet of cartilage, the ' Prolonging Cartilage', which can adapt itself to the curvature of the ribs when the arms are spread. The outer surface shows a ridge running parallel to the length of the bone, nearly in the middle but slightly closer to the front edge. This is the Spine of the Scapula. It terminates near the glenoid in a process, the Acromion Process.

The Humerus or ' Clod Bone ' is a long but massive bone having a large narrow cavity. Its upper end has a head, for articulation with the glenoid of the scapula, and in front of the head towards the outer side, a large tuberosity for muscular attachments. Beside this is the Bicipital Groove, through which the tendon of the biceps runs. The shaft of the bone has a wide ' Spiral Groove ' running downwards and outwards and then forwards. The lower end has, in front, a large condyle for articulation with the radius and, behind, the deep ' Olecranon Fossa ' into which the top of the Ulna fits.

The Radius, or **Shin,** is a long bone with a large medullary cavity. It is oval in section, with the back rather flattened, and has facets at each end, the upper one articulating with the humerus and the lower with the carpus. The bone has a slight forward convexity. **The Ulna** lies along the back outer edge of the radius. It projects above it as a large curved process, the Olecranon, which fits into the olecranon fossa of the humerus when the arm is held straight. At the junction of the olecranon and the radius, it also articulates with the condyle of the humerus forming the elbow joint. In humans, pigs, dogs and rabbits, the lower end of the ulna can rotate round the radius so twisting the wrist; but this is impossible in cattle and horses.

The Carpus or ' Knee ' consists of two rows of three cubical shaped bones in each, and a seventh ' accessory carpal bone ', shaped like a circular disc on the outer back edge of the top row. These bones all articulate with each other by synovial joints.

The Metacarpal Bones (or Shanks or Cannon Bones) are long and cylindrical, with marrow cavities. The top ends have facets for articulation with the carpal bones and the lower ends condyles for articulation with the digits.

The Digits consist of three bones each. The top one is the largest and is cylindrical in shape with a facet at the upper and a condyle at the lower end; the second is similar but shorter and the third resembles a claw or hoof as the case may be; but none of them have marrow cavities. Behind the joints of the digits are pairs of ' sesamoid ' (like ' sesame ' or ' bird seed ') bones that hold the tendons away from the joint itself and provide smooth ' bearings ' for them.

The Hind Limb (Figs. 18 and 19). None of the meat animals have the thigh entirely clear of the body as we do. In them, most of it lies within the skin of the trunk, and only the lower extremity is clear. This extremity takes part in forming the ' Stifle Joint ', corresponding to the human knee. The ' Hock Joint ' corresponding to the human ankle and heel, is permanently raised off the ground so that the animal, in effect, stands on the tip of its toes. The Hind Limb contains the following bones:—

	Human	Animal
Pelvic Bones	Hips	Aitch Bone and Rump
Femur	Thigh	' Silverside Bone '
Patella	Knee Cap	Cramp Bone
Tibia and Fibula	Leg	Leg
Tarsal Bones	Ankle and Heel	Hock
Metatarsal Bones	Foot	Round Shank or Cannon Bone
Digits	Toes	In Hoof

The Pelvic Bones, * Aitch Bone and Rump, forming the walls and floor of the pelvic cavity, really consist of two plate-like bones, the Innominate bones or Ossa Coxarum, which fuse together at the Pubic Symphysis or central line of the floor. Each has, on its outer surface, an Acetabulum for articulation with the head of the femur, and each is pierced by a large hole, the Obturator Foramen, which lightens the bone but does not give passage to any large vessels. Each of these bones is formed by the fusion of three separate bones, the Ilium, Ischium and Pubis and these are best considered separately, as they are often referred to in describing the position of adjacent organs.

The Ilium. A triangular bone with the base forwards and the apex continued as a shaft directed downwards and backwards. The outer angle forms the Angle of the Haunch, and the inner, the Angle of the Croup. On the lower face between

* Owing to the numerous different planes occupied by the surfaces of the pelvic bones, they cannot be satisfactorily illustrated, and the student should, therefore, make every effort to study the bones themselves.

these angles is a facet for articulation with the first transverse spine of the sacrum, but as both facets concerned are flat, very little movement is possible in this joint. The shaft gives attachment to the muscles of the Abdominal Wall and terminates as the anterior third of the Acetabulum. The Iliac bloodvessels and lymph nodes lie on the inner face of the Ilium.

The Ischium forms most of the side wall of the Pelvic cavity. It joins the ilium at the acetabulum, forming the posterior third thereof. This junction with the ilium forms the front outside corner of the bone ; the front inside corner joins with the Pubis, and the front edge between the corners forms the posterior edge of the Obturator Foramen. The anterior half of the medial edge joins with its fellow to form the posterior half of the Pubic Symphysis, but the posterior half diverges from its fellow to form the Ischial Arch,* round which, in the male, the penis turns forward after leaving the bladder. The Sciatic (a corruption of Ischiatic) nerve and lymph nodes are found in this region.

The Pubis is a flat bone, forming most of the floor of the Pelvic Cavity. It has the outline of a right angle triangle, with the hypotenuse forming the anterior edge of the Obturator Foramen; the shorter side joining with its fellow at the Pubic Symphysis and the angle at its end joining the ischium. The angle at the end of the longer side meets the ilium and ischium at the acetabulum, forming the middle third thereof, but the acetabular rim has a deep fossa between the Pubis and the Ischium into which the Central Ligament of the hip joint is fastened.

In the Female. The front edge of the Pubis is sharp and forms a continuous line with its fellow to give attachment to the muscles of the Abdominal Wall, thus forming a continuous seam with their attachment to the shaft of the ilium. The whole Pelvic Cavity is wide so as to contain the Uterus and Vagina, as well as the Rectum and Bladder; and the Ischium and Pubis form a fairly level floor.

In the Male. The front edge of the Pubis is rounded and blunt, and thickens near its junction with its fellow to form the Pubic Tuberosity. The muscles of the abdominal wall

* A large number of books on meat inspection have the Ischial Arch labelled as the ' Inguinal Canal ', an obvious error. The correct position of the Inguinal Canals, of which there are two, is given here.

are attached only to this tuberosity and the shaft of the ilium. Between the blunt edge of the Pubis and the muscles are a pair of gaps, the Inguinal Canals,* through which the spermatic cords pass from the Abdomen into the Scrotum. The Penis, after turning round the Ischial Arch, runs forward under the Pubic Symphysis between the two spermatic cords. The Pelvic Cavity of the male is much narrower than that of the female, since it has only the rectum and bladder to contain; and the floor formed by the Ischium and Pubis is markedly concave.

The separate bones, ilium, ischium and pubis are sutured together at birth, but fuse during adolescence. The pubic symphysis, however, remains as a sutured joint until maturity is complete, after which it ossifies. Females usually bear their first young before this ossification is complete and, in doing so, spread the bones further apart. Thus, a female who has borne young will have a wider pelvis than a barren one, except when the first-born was not delivered until growth was complete; a state of affairs that good farmers avoid, as it leads to constant trouble in subsequent parturitions.

The upper edge of the shaft of the ilium is bound to the transverse processes of the sacrum by a sheet of ligament, and the posterior end of the ischium is bound to the sacrum by a rope-like ligament. A few hours before parturition, these ligaments soften so as to be easily stretched when the young one passes through the pelvis. The farmer's term is ' her bones have softened ', and they take it as a certain sign that parturition is imminent.

The Femur or Thigh Bone is the strongest and most massive bone in the body. In life, it lies pointing downwards and forwards from the hip, but, in a hanging carcase, it is stretched back in line with the shaft of the ilium. The Head, which articulates with the acetabulum on the pelvic bone, has a fossa running from the centre to the medial edge for the attachment of the central ligament of the joint. Beside the head on the outer side of the bone are two tuberosities, the Trochanter Major behind and the Trochanter Minor in front. The shaft is rounded and smooth in front but flat and rough behind, and there is a large marrow cavity. At the lower end there is a Trochlea in front for articulation with the patella and two condyles behind with a deep fossa between them for articula-

* See footnote on previous page.

tion with the tibia. Confusion between the humerus and femur sometimes occurs owing to the weight of both bones, and a careful comparison should be made to memorise the points of difference, as follows:—

Humerus. One condyle at lower end. Tuberosities in front of head at upper end.

Femur. Two condyles at lower end. Trochanters beside head at upper end.

The Patella or Cramp Bone is a small, solid mass of bone, lying on the trochlea of the femur. It is strongly held to the femur and the tibia by ligaments and so prevents the stifle joint dislocating forwards, while the sides are prolonged by two wings of cartilage that embrace the trochlea and prevent sideward dislocation. The Vast or Quadriceps muscles in front of the thigh are inserted into the patella and, by pulling on it, move the leg forward and straighten out the stifle joint. No muscles pass over it to the front of the tibia.

The Tibia or Leg Bone. This bone has a long shaft with a large marrow cavity. The upper half is triangular in section with a prominent edge in front bent slightly outwards but the lower half is oval. The upper end shows two facets (for articulation with the condyles of the femur) separated by a short bifurcated spine which fits into the fossa between the condyles and prevents sidewards dislocation of the stifle joint. The lower end has two glenoids for articulation with the Trochlea of the Tarsus.

The Fibula is a thin sliver of bone with no marrow cavity. When it is complete, as in the pig, it runs from the outer angle of the head of the tibia to the outer side of the Trochlea of the Tarsus, but in most animals it is rudimentary and fused to the Tibia.

The Tarsal Bones. These are the Astragalus, a pulley-shaped bone that articulates with the glenoids of the Tibia; the Os Calcis, a solid block of bone pointing backwards and upwards behind the leg, and giving attachment to the strong Achilles tendon from the gastrocnemius muscle ('calf of the leg' in humans); and four or five disc-like bones below the Astragalus. All articulate together by ordinary synovial joints.

The Metatarsal Bones are usually longer and rounder in section than the metacarpals, but otherwise resemble them.

The Digits resemble those of the forelimb.

Certain joints of the hind limb are rather complicated and warrant further description.

The Hip or Femero-Pelvic Joint. This is surrounded with the usual capsular ligament but also has a strong central ligament running from the centre of the acetabulum of the pelvic bone to the centre of the head of the femur. To disarticulate this joint, it is necessary to cut round the capsule and then insert a thin bladed knife into the joint cavity to cut the central ligament.

The Stifle or Femero-Tibio-Patello Joint. On each facet of the tibia lies a ' Semilunar ' or ' Half-moon ' cartilage. In reality, these cartilages are crescent shaped, and lie with the points of the crescent touching the spine of the tibia, and the condyles of the femur resting on them. They appear to act as shock absorbers to lessen the vibration as the foot strikes the ground. A common synovial sac lies on the facets of the tibia below the cartilages, passes upwards by the spine, and spreads out over the cartilages under the condyles, finally extending upward to lie between the patella and trochlea. A sac of this size contains a considerable quantity of synovia, which is a favoured breeding material for the bacteria that cause ' Bone Taint '. Hence the frequency of the trouble in this region. Many slaughtermen open the joint to let out the synovia, and so lessen this risk. The operation is popularly called ' letting out the heat ', but its actual efficiency is often in doubt.

The Hock or Tarsal Joint. Most of the movement of this joint is at the tibio-trochlea articulation, and is a straight forward and backward movement, but animals such as pigs with complete fibulae can also twist the ankle outwards to some extent. The remaining articulations are to distribute pressures. The joint is best dis-articulated at the tarso-metatarsal articulation which is easily separated and leaves the os calcis firmly fixed in place to take the hanging hook. ' Ham stringing ' consists of cutting the Achilles tendon, so that the joint can no longer take a weight. A hamstrung animal cannot stand and must be slaughtered as the injury is incurable. A hamstrung carcase cannot be conveniently hung.

The Skull (Figs. 20, 21). The skull consists of some thirty bones sutured together, but there is no object in memorising the names and positions of all of them, as only three or four are normally referred to. It is, however, important to acquire a clear idea of the cavities that these bones surround.

The Cranium or Brain Box. This cavity is much smaller than is usually realised. It has the form of an oval cavity only some 4″ × 2″ in cattle and horses, lying at the back of the head with the long axis of the oval parallel to the line of the face. The front end reaches a line drawn across the face touching the tops of the orbits or eye sockets. The back end reaches the back of the head and is covered by only one bony plate, the occipital bone. Two condyles on the occipital bone articulate with the atlas and, between them is the Foramen Magnum, through which part of the brain passes to join the spinal cord. Most of the remainder of the head is made up of air-spaces, called Sinuses; and blows, or even shots on these that do not penetrate the cranium, will not stun the animal.

In front of the cranium is the *Frontal Sinus*, a labyrinth of air passages that communicate with the nose. It is principally covered by the *Frontal Bone*, which is thicker and stronger in entire males than in females or early castrates. The frontal bone is also wider in males, giving the large appearance to the male head, though actually the cranium and brain are similar in both sexes.

The Nasal Cavity or Nose lies in front of and below the frontal sinus, and is in communication with it. It is separated from the buccal cavity or mouth by the bony palate, and the two nostrils are divided for varying lengths by a septum or bony plate. Each nostril contains scroll-like rolls of delicate cancellated bone tissue with no compact shell, the *Turbinate Bones* or *Snuffles*. Fracture of these turbinate bones is extremely easy and causes copious but seldom serious bleeding. The back of the nasal cavity opens into the Pharynx.

The Buccal Cavity or Mouth lies below the palate and also opens into the Pharynx.

The Pharynx lies below the cranium, and is entered, in front, by both the nasal and buccal cavities, and behind by the Larynx or voice box and the Oesophagus or Gullet. These are supported in a stirrup of bone hanging on two cartilaginous rods, the **Hyoid** bone, or ' Adam's Apple '.

The Orbits or eye sockets lie in front of and below the cranium, and are each about twice the size of the eyeball. In a well-nourished animal they contain large quantities of fat. Close below and behind the orbits and sometimes forming part of them are the cheek bones or ridges in which the lower jaw or mandible hangs. The **Mandible** itself is shaped like a pair of ' L 's. The horizontal lines support the floor of the mouth, and the uprights terminate in hooks which articulate and hang from the cheek bones.

The Teeth. The teeth are modified forms of bone, devoid of periosteum, endo-osteum and Haversian canals.* Thus they are unable to repair themselves or resist disease, but, fortunately, injuries and disease of the teeth are comparatively rare. The foetus has no teeth visible, but soon after birth the temporary or ' milk ' teeth are cut. These are small and white, with a very noticeable lustre or shine. At varying times during adolescence they are replaced by permanent teeth, which are larger and duller in appearance. Each permanent tooth is cut immediately the temporary tooth drops out, and it grows rapidly, usually coming into wear about a month later.

Teeth (see Figs. 20, 22, 23, 25 and 26) are classified thus: The incisors in front, usually three on each side of each jaw are chisel like, with fairly sharp edges. They are often given the following names: First pair or ' Centrals ' lying together on each side of the central line; second pair or ' Medials ' lying one on each side of the centrals; third pair or ' Laterals ' lying on outer side of the medials, while if a fourth pair are present they are called ' Corners '. The Canines, tusks or ' eye teeth ', one on each side of each jaw, are pointed and cone shaped. The Premolars, three or four on each side of each jaw, are blunt and irregular. The Molars, three or four on each side of each jaw, are similar to the premolars, but are only permanent, i.e. there are no temporary molars. Molars and premolars are often classed together as ' cheek teeth '. Between the incisors and the premolars there is usually an ' Interdental Space ' in the middle of which the canine tooth grows.

It is convenient to use a formula for describing the dentition of an animal. The following is the dental formula for a horse:—

---

* Actually, the teeth are developed in the mucous membrane which covers the gums, not from connective tissue, as are true bones.

$$\text{T.}\ \frac{3\,(1)\quad 3\text{ or }4}{3\,(1)\quad 3}\ .\qquad \text{P.}\ \frac{3\,(1)\quad 3\text{ or }4\quad 3}{3\,(1)\quad 3\quad 3}.$$

The numerator represents one side of the upper jaw and the denominator one side of the lower jaw.   This formula indicates that on each side, a foal (T for Temporary) has 3 incisors, 1 canine, in males only (hence the (1) is placed in brackets), and 3 or 4 premolars in the upper jaw and 3 incisors, 1 canine, if male, and 3 pre-molars in the lower jaw.   The adult horse (P for Permanent) has the same formula except for the addition of 3 molars in each jaw.

The foregoing description applies to the skeletons of all the mammals, the group of warm-blooded, four-footed creatures of which the meat animals are species.   Actually, as is shown in Fig. 3, there is surprisingly little difference in the bones of the mammals, and they can usually be recognised easily even if the living animal from which they came is unknown.   The major differences in the skeleton of the meat animals are described in the next section, but it will be convenient if we group them in classes, thus:—

Ruminants, or animals that chew the cud, includes cattle, buffalo, sheep and goats, camel, deer and antelope.   Except where otherwise stated, the bones of all ruminants are similar in shape, though there will, of course, be differences in size.

*Swine.** The domestic pig is the only species in this group.

Horses and Asses.   The word ' Ass ' includes the ' Donkey ', which name should only be applied to small asses about 3 feet high.   Many breeds of asses are 4 feet or more in height, but they are not ' donkeys '.

Rodents or nibbling animals, i.e. rabbits and hares.

Carnivora is for meat eaters, dogs and cats.   These, though not ' meat animals ', are included to assist in detection of fraudulent substitution.

Whales, though nowadays definitely ' meat animals ', are not included, as the skeletons are not used in the meat industry.

---

* It is unusual to keep domestic pigs after about 4 years old, and at this stage the animal is still growing.   Thus pigs' bones are usually soft, and have the appearance of immature bone (see p. 12).

SKELETONS OF DIFFERENT ANIMALS

The ' **Vertebral Formulae** ' or number of bones in the five regions of the Vertebral Column are, usually, as follows:—

	Cervical	Thoracic	Lumbar	Sacral	Coccygeal
All Ruminants except					
Camel . . .	7	13*	6	5	18-20
Camel	7	12	7	4	15-18
Horse	7	18	6	5	18-20
Ass	7	18	7	5	18-20
Pig	7	14-15-16	6-7	4	14
Dog and Cat . . .	7	13	7	3	18-20
Rabbit	7	12	7	3	7
Hare	7	13	7	3	7

* Many naturalists give the deer as having 14 thoracic vertebrae and 14 pairs of ribs. In my experience this is incorrect. Red deer, fallow, and roebuck, the three species indigenous to the United Kingdom, all have 13 thoracic vertebrae and 13 pairs of ribs.

All mammals have 7 cervical vertebrae; an absolutely invariable rule. In the pig, dog, cat and rabbit the ligamentum nuchae is small and weak. In the horse it forms a single rope, but in the ox and sheep is double.

The thoracic vertebrae frequently vary by one and, more rarely, by two; thus oxen may be found with 12, 14 or 15 thoracic vertebrae. Cats with 12 and rabbits, both wild and domestic, with 13 are not unusual. As the number of ribs corresponds to the number of vertebrae, breeders try to perpetuate strains with extra thoracic vertebrae and ribs as an extra pair of chops is gained thereby. The very long thorax of the horse will, however, always be noticeable in dressed carcases.

Irregularities in the thoracic vertebrae are often compensated for by corresponding variations in the lumbar region. Thus a pig with 15 T.V. may have 6 L.V., while one with 14 T.V. may have 7 L.V.

The sacral vertebrae are usually fairly regular in number, though occasionally one of them fails to fuse with the others or, alternatively, one of the coccygeal vertebrae will fuse to the sacrum. The sacra of the different animals can, however, be distinguished as follows.

In ruminants (Figs. 8 and 9) the first transverse processes which articulate with the ilium are markedly longer than the others, and are directed straight outwards; thus the bone looks like a T. In horses (Fig. 11), the first transverse processes are

2

directed forwards. Thus the bone looks like a Y. In pigs (Fig. 10), the transverse processes are of the same length, and the ends of the first pair, not the upper surfaces, have the facets for articulation with the ilium; thus the whole bone is oblong. In the carnivora and rodents the bone is almost square.

The coccygeal bones vary considerably in different individuals of the same species; and also with age, as the lower ones start to ossify later than the upper. The figures given are therefore only a rough approximation. In most animals

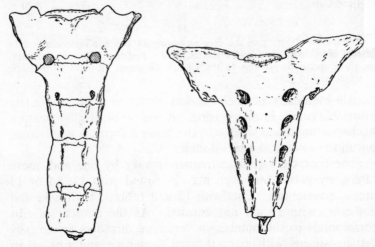

FIG. 10.—Sacrum of pig.   FIG. 11.—Sacrum of horse.

there is no muscle beyond the eighth C.V. and the end of the tail therefore swings loose, but cats have tails that are muscular for their whole length. In distinguishing cat and rabbit carcases (Figs. 28-29), it should be remembered that a cat's tail has fairly thick bones and heavy muscle at the root, while a rabbit's has bones no thicker than a match-stick, with practically no muscle. Goats' carcases can often be distinguished from sheep's by the thin tail of the former, usually erected in rigor mortis (death stiffening), and the fat tail of the latter usually depressed in rigor mortis. The tail of the deer is much thinner than that of the goat.

The Thoracic Cage. *Ruminants* (Figs. 13 and 14). The ribs are broad and blade-like, with comparatively little curvature, so that the section of the thorax is more oval than circular. This is most marked in cattle and the Northern European breeds of goats, but goats of the Mediterranean and tropical breeds, and all sheep and deer, have a somewhat more circular section to the thorax. In all these animals there are normally 13 pairs of ribs, 8 being sternal and 5 asternal, and ribs 2-11 form synovial joints with their cartilages. If a fourteenth pair is present, as is fairly common in sheep, the extra pair are usually ' floating '. The sternum is broad and flat, as these animals usually lie on their chests. The Manubrium, or first section of the sternum, forms a useful guide for ageing beef carcases, for it is purely cartilaginous during the first year, but in the second a red centre of cancellated bone can be seen when the carcase is split. This centre increases gradually in size until it occupies the whole bone at about the fourth year.

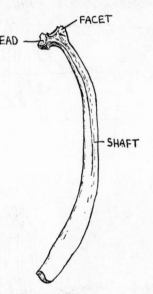

FIG. 12.—Rib of ox.

The camel has 12 pairs of ribs, 8 being sternal and 4 asternal. They are more curved and relatively narrower than those of other ruminants.

Swine have 14 to 16 pairs of ribs, somewhat narrower and distinctly more curved than those of the ruminants, so that the section of the thorax is distinctly circular. 7 pairs are sternal and 7 asternal, and the remainder, when present, are usually floating. The sternum is flat as in ruminants. Ribs 2-5 form synovial joints with their cartilages.

Horses. The ribs (18 pairs) are narrow and circular in section, and strongly curved, giving a circular section to the thorax. Ten pairs are sternal and 8 asternal. In section, the sternum is triangular, thus presenting a sharp edge on which the animal cannot rest, so that horses roll over on their sides when in repose. The manubrium is joined to the second sternebra by a disc of cartilage instead of a synoval joint, and projects in front of the thoracic cage as a vertical disc of cartilage, the ' Cariniform Cartilage', whose outline can be distinctly seen in a thin animal.

In all other animals, dogs, cats, rabbits (and humans), the ribs are narrow and circular in section, as is also the sternum,

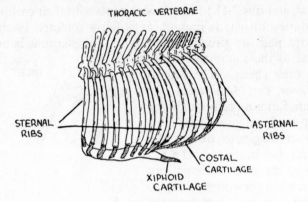

FIG. 13.—Thoracic cage of ox.

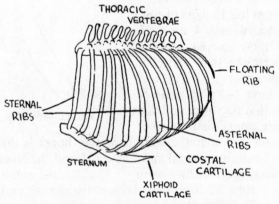

FIG. 14.—Thoracic cage of sheep.

thus providing a means of detecting dogs' carcases in consignments of mutton. In dogs and cats the xiphoid cartilage is narrow and dagger shaped, and very soft and fibrous; in rabbits it is firm and circular, as in the larger animals. In cats, the whole thorax is relatively longer but narrower than in rabbits (Figs. 28 and 29).

Fore Limbs (Figs. 15, 16 and 17). The **Scapula** differs in shape in all animals.

In the *Ruminants* it is strictly triangular with straight sides. The acromion process forms a distinct right angle at the end of the spine. In all these points the scapulae of ox, sheep and goat are similar, but in sheep and goats minor differences in

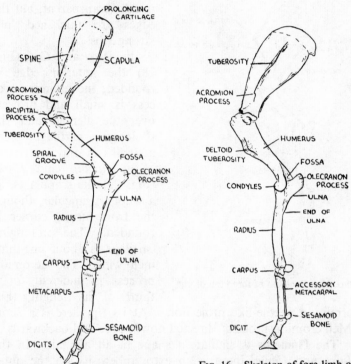

FIG. 15.—Skeleton of fore limb of ox.

FIG. 16.—Skeleton of fore limb of horse.

shape and thickness of the blade occur in different breeds. In deer the upper edge of the scapula is level with the tops of the thoracic spines, thus forming a flat square table over the shoulders. In goats the spines of the thoracic vertebrae form a sharp ridge over the shoulders.

In *Horses* the anterior edge is slightly convex and the posterior edge correspondingly concave. The centre of the spine is bent backwards and roughened to form a small tuberosity to which the trapezius muscle is attached. The acromion process on the spine is very small.*

In *Swine* the anterior edge has an angle in its middle, thus making the bone quadrilateral rather than triangular. The trapezius tuberosity on the spine is large and bent strongly backwards and the acromion process is small. The blade of the bone is very thin and usually transparent, but the edges are thickened into strong ribs.

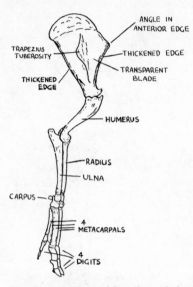

In *Dogs* and *Cats* (Fig. 28) the anterior edge is rounded; the acromion process is small and projects over the glenoid and the prolonging cartilage forms a small rim only.

In *Rabbits* and *Hares* (Fig. 29) the scapula is, as a whole, triangular, though the front upper corner is rounded. The prolonging cartilage is about one-third inch wide. The acromion process is undercut for a third of its length, thus forming a needle-like projection. At its tip there is a short 'Metacromion process' directed downwards and backwards.

FIG. 17.—Skeleton of fore limb of pig.

The Humerus is similar in shape in all animals. In the *Horse* and *Camel* there is an extra tuberosity on the outer side near the top. In the *Pig* the bone is twice as thick at the upper end as at the lower, thus giving it a tapered shape, and the spiral groove is so wide that the whole bone has a ' twisted ' appearance. In other animals, the bone is long and slender.

The Radius and Ulna. In the *Ruminants* the ulna is a long, splint-like bone, sutured to the radius but extending below it to form part of the carpal joint. No movement occurs between the radius and ulna, and by middle age the two bones usually fuse into one. In *Horses* the ulna fuses to the radius before birth and is only half its length. In *Swine* and *Other Animals*

---

* There is a deep notch in the front edge of the glenoid.

the ulna is as wide as, or wider than, the radius, and is some-what larger. The two bones are joined by synovial joints that permit them to rotate when twisting the wrist.

The Carpal bones have no important differences in the different animals.

The Metacarpals. In *Ruminants* the bones equivalent to the two central metacarpals fuse into one bone before birth but retain two distinct medullary cavities. The bone is oval in section and has a flat facet at the upper end for articulation with the carpus, and two condyles at the lower end for articulation with the two digits. One or sometimes two vestigial

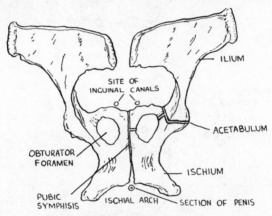

FIG. 18.—Pelvic bones.

metacarpals may be present, as small splinters of bone behind the main bone, but carrying no digits. In *Horses* there is one main metacarpal with one condyle articulated to the digit, and two vestigial bones behind it having no digits. In *Swine* there are two large cylindrical bones in the centre and a pair of smaller ones outside and behind the main bones. All four articulate to digits corresponding to them in size.

The Digits. In *Ruminants* two main digits, with three bones in each, articulate with the condyles of the metacarpal, and two accessory digits with two bones in each are placed behind the metacarpal-digital joints, but these accessory digits do not articulate with the skeleton. *Horses* have only one digit, and *Swine* four complete ones with three bones in each, the two outer ones being shorter than the middle ones. In all these animals the third or last digital bones resemble the hooves of the animal.

In *Cats* (Figs. 28 and 29) the whole forelimb is relatively longer and thicker than in *Rabbits*.

Hind Limbs (Figs. 18 and 19).

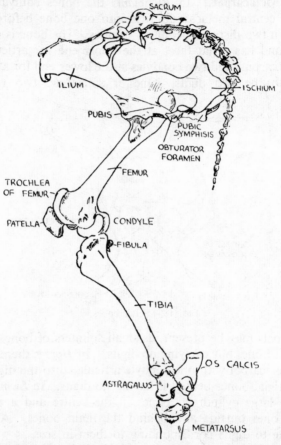

FIG. 19*a*.—Skeleton of hind limb of ox.   Medial view.

The Pelvis.   In *Cattle* (and *Cats*, but not *Rabbits*) the floor of the pelvis slopes downwards and forwards because the posterior end of the ischium is nearly on a level with the internal angle of the ilium, but in all other animals the floor slopes downwards and backwards as the ischium is well below the ilium.   This is most marked in sheep, goats and rabbits. In *Ruminants and Horses*, the wing of the ilium is horizontal and above the sacrum, articulating with a facet on the upper surface of the first sacral transverse process; but in *Swine* and all other animals, the wings of the ilia face inwards and articulate with the ends of the first transverse processes of the sacrum.

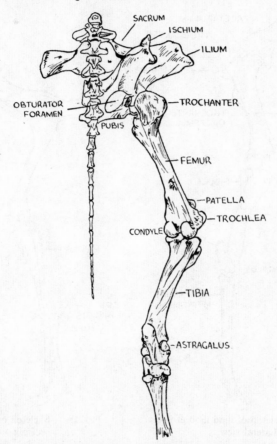

FIG. 19b.—Skeleton of hind limb of ox. Back view.

The Femur is much the same in all mammals. In *Horses* there is an additional or third trochanter on the upper third of the outer surface of the bone corresponding to the extra tuberosity on the humerus. In *Swine* the bone is relatively slender and long.

The Tibia and Fibula. In *Ruminants* the fibula is fused to the tibia, but rarely more than an inch ossifies. It is continued as a slender cartilaginous rod that sometimes reaches as far as the tarsus. In *Horses*, the fibula is a slender splint of bone

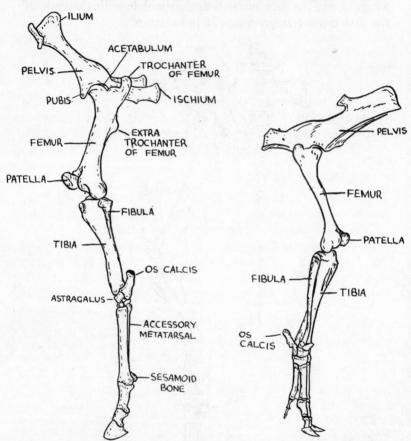

FIG. 19c.—Skeleton of hind limb of horse. Lateral view.

FIG. 19d.—Skeleton of hind limb of pig.

fused to the head of the tibia and again a third of the way down. In *Swine* and other animals (except *Rabbits*), there is a complete though slender fibula joined to the tibia by a synovial joint at the upper end, and reaching the tarsal joint at the lower end. In *Rabbits* (Fig. 29) the fibula is fused to the head of the tibia and the upper third of the shaft as in the horse.

Therefore, if the tarsal-tibial joint of a small animal carcase be opened and two bones be found there, it is the carcase of a cat or dog; if only one, it is a rabbit or hare.

The Tarsus. In most animals there are two flexible joints in the tarsus, one between the tibia and astragalus, moved by the Achilles tendon, and one between the astragalus and lower row of tarsal bones, moved by the flexor and extensor tendons of the foot. Slaughtermen often cut these latter tendons before dressing the carcase to prevent the leg kicking. In *Horses* there is only one flexible joint, the tibio-tarsal joint.

The Metatarsus and digits of the hind limb are similar in all animals to the metacarpus and digits of the fore limb, but are rather longer and rounder in section. Hence the metatarsals of the ox are known as ' round shanks ' and the more oval metacarpals are known as ' flat shanks '.

The Skulls. In *Cattle* (Fig. 20) the cranium can be outlined on the frontal bone as a circle touching a line joining the lower edge of the horns above and a line joining the upper edge of the orbits below. In shooting or pole-axing it is best to hit the centre of this circle, going rather above it than below, as too low a shot will not stun the animal at all, while too high a one will cause partial if not complete unconsciousness. Old bulls and polled cattle of either sex may have frontal bones too thick to penetrate with the ordinary ' killers ', but they can always be stunned with a twelve bore gun fired at less than a foot from the skull; any size shot can be used, as it does not have time to spread at this range. Alternatively, if the animal is quiet, it can be shot or pole-axed from behind the head through the occipital bone, or shot from the side through the base of the ear.

In horned cattle, the frontal bone is extended above the cranium, and forms a round ridge across the top of the head, and at each end of the ridge is a hollow conical process, the Horn Core. The hollows of these cores communicate with the frontal sinus, so that injuries to them are followed by a profuse but seldom serious discharge of blood from the nose. These horn cores start to develop about a week after birth, and if their periosteum is injured then, by burning or by strong caustic chemicals, further growth is checked and the animal remains hornless for life.

In *Sheep, Goats, Camels and Deer* (Fig. 21) the cranium extends relatively further forward than in oxen, and actually lies between the eyes.   Such animals are, however, best stunned by a shot or blow on the highest point of the skull directed straight downwards; or from behind through the occiput.

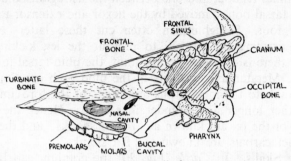

FIG. 20.—Skull of ox.

The horn growth in sheep and goats and antelopes is similar to that of oxen.   In deer only the males have horns, or, more properly, antlers.   These consist of solid compact bony processes growing from the frontal bone but devoid of

FIG. 21.—Skull of sheep.

blood and lymph and periosteum.   They are grown in the spring and, for two or three months, have a covering of skin, the ' Velvet ', which is rubbed off during the summer, leaving the bone exposed.   They break off during the following spring, to be replaced by a new pair and, in many species, an extra branch or ' tine ' is added for each year.   In reindeer, both sexes grow antlers, which are renewed annually.

In *Swine* the shape of the skull varies considerably in different breeds, but all have a large frontal sinus lying in front of, and on top of the cranium, so it is consequently easy to shoot too high and send the bullet above the cranium, leaving the animal fully conscious.   If any form of gun is used, it should be applied just above the line joining the tops of the orbits.   It is not advisable to shoot through the occipital bone, as this is deeply imbedded in fat and its exact position is not easily determined; but a shot through the ears can be used if necessary.

In *Horses* the cranium is well above the line joining the upper rims of the orbits, and its lower pole lies just behind the ' star ' or whorl of hair on the forehead. The best point on which to place the gun is half way between the star and the front end of the mane. The occipital shot can be used, but is usually awkward owing to the height of the head and the thickness of the mane. The ear shot is easier.

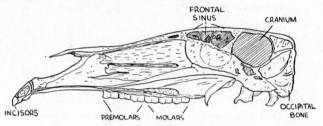

FIG. 22.—Skull of horse.

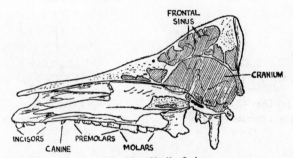

FIG. 23.—Skull of pig.

Teeth (Fig. 24). In *Ruminants* (except camels and some species of deer), the dental formula are T. $\dfrac{0\ 0\ 3}{4\ 0\ 3}$ P. $\dfrac{0\ 0\ 3\ 3}{4\ 0\ 3\ 3}$.

There are no canine teeth at all and no incisors in the upper jaw. But the four pairs in the lower jaw bite against a firm ' dental pad ' or ' gum '. They are ' shovel ' shaped, with broad blades but round shafts or roots and are somewhat loosely attached in their sockets. The molars and pre-molars have the form of square pegs with the grinding surfaces raised into sharp ridges, longest and sharpest on the inside of lower and outside of the upper jaw.　Normally, all the teeth are stained with a black 'tartar'.

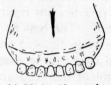

(a) Under 18 months old.

All temporary.

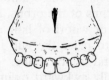

(b) Over 18 months old. Central permanent teeth in use.

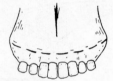

(c) Over 24 months.

Four permanent teeth in use.

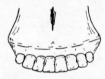

(d) Over 36 months.

Six permanent teeth in use.

(e) Over 42 months.

Eight permanent teeth in use.

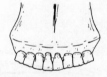

(f) Over 6 years.

Gaps showing between central incisors.

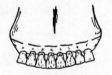

(g) 'Aged'.

Between 7 and 12 years old.

FIG. 24.—Teeth of ox at different ages.

In *Oxen* of quick maturing breeds, the calves are usually born with all temporary teeth cut, but occasionally some may be delayed for two or three weeks after birth.　The dropping of the temporary teeth is followed by the cutting of the permanent ones in the course of a few hours, and they come into wear within a month. These changes occur in the following order:—

6 months		Fourth Cheek Tooth or First Molar
18 months	First Pair or Central Incisors	Fifth Cheek Tooth or Second Molar
24 months	Second Pair or Medial Incisors	First, Second, Sixth Cheek Teeth or First and Second Premolars and Third Molar
36 months	Third Pair or Lateral Incisors ⎱	Third Cheek Tooth or Third
42 months	Fourth Pair or Corner Incisors ⎰	Premolar

Cattle of the slower maturing breeds may be six months or even a year later in showing these changes, and zebu (or humped cattle) and buffalo fully a year later.

In practice, only the incisors are used for ' ageing ' cattle, as the cheek teeth cannot be readily seen in the living animal. There is a wide variation even among closely related animals, and so dentition can only be taken as an indication of age, not a proof. Many dealers avoid mentioning age, and describe cattle as ' two toothed ', ' four toothed', ' six toothed ' or ' full mouthed ', and so do not commit themselves to any exactitude.

At about six years old, the gums of the incisors recede, leaving part of the shafts exposed. By about twelve, the blades are nearly worn out and there is a gap between each pair of teeth, and by fifteen the blades are usually completely worn away, leaving only round ' pegs '. By twenty, these pegs begin to drop out and the animal dies soon after.

In *Sheep* the dental formulae are the same as that for oxen, but the changes occur some six months earlier. A ' broken toothed ' sheep is one with the central incisors chipped or showing signs of wear, and such an animal is in all probability well over four years old. In goats, the changes are about nine months earlier than in cattle.

In *Camels* the dental formulae are T. $\frac{1\ 1\ 3}{3\ 1\ 2}$ P. $\frac{1\ 1\ 3\ 3}{3\ 1\ 2\ 3}$. The canine teeth or tusks appear in both sexes but are larger in males than females, and there are Lateral Incisors in the upper jaw as well as the lower, so only the medial and central incisors are missing from the upper jaw. The central incisors change at $4\frac{1}{2}$ years, the medials at $5\frac{1}{2}$, and the laterals and tusks in both jaws at $6\frac{1}{2}$-7 years.

In *Swine* (Fig. 25) the dental formulae are T. $\dfrac{3\,(1)\ 4}{3\,(1)\ 4}$

P. $\dfrac{3\,(1)\ 4\ 3}{3\,(1)\ 4\ 3}$. There are incisor teeth in both jaws, somewhat widely spaced, and of the same breadth throughout their length, so that they resemble a carpenter's chisels. Females normally

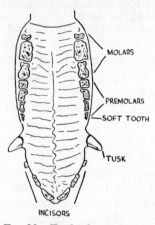

have no tusks, though rudimentary ones are found occasionally, but males, especially entire boars, develop large ones. The lower tusk protrudes from the mouth and develops a sharp edge by friction with the upper tusk, which is behind it and is thus kept short. In most countries it is usual to remove all the tusks as, apart from being dangerous to men, many boars try to savage their sows before or after mating. In some countries, however, only the lower tusks are removed, and then the uppers, not being worn down, grow into nearly complete rings that can be sold as ornaments.

FIG. 25.—Teeth of young boar.

The times of change are approximately:—

6 months		Fifth Cheek Tooth or First Molar
9 months	Tusks and Third or Lateral Incisors	Sixth Cheek Tooth or Second Molar
12 months	First or Central Incisors	Second, Third and Fourth Cheek Teeth or Premolars
16 months	Second or Medial Incisors	
20 months		Seventh Cheek Tooth or Third Molar

The first Temporary Pre-molar remains unshed until old age and when finally dropped is not replaced. This is called the 'soft' tooth.

In *Horses* (Figs. 26*a* and *b*) the dental formulae are
T. $\dfrac{3\,(1)\ \ 3\text{ or }4}{3\,(1)\ \ \ 3}$ P. $\dfrac{3\,(1)\ \ 3\text{ or }4\ \ 3}{3\,(1)\ \ \ 3\ \ \ 3}$. The incisor teeth are oval in section, and in a young horse have a central conical pit or infundibulum filled with black tartar. The centrals change at $2\frac{1}{2}$ years; medial at $3\frac{1}{2}$; laterals at $4\frac{1}{2}$, and tusks at 5. It is very

unusual for mares to have tusks that show through the gums, but often rudimentary ones can be felt below the surface.

In actual practice horses are aged by the shape of the infundibula or pits in the teeth for these change their shape as the teeth wear. Tables showing these changes are given in all books on horsemanship and, by their use, extreme accuracy in ageing can be obtained until the horse is 'beyond mark of mouth'; that is, until all the infundibula are worn out, and the tables of the teeth present plain level surfaces. At this

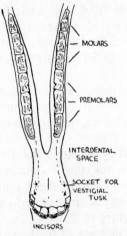
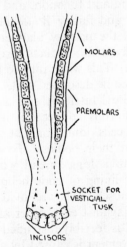

FIG. 26*a*.—Teeth of filly.   FIG. 26*b*.—Teeth of aged mare.

age the animal is over 8 years old; but rough estimates of age can still be made from the fact that the incisor teeth tend to protrude further forward and the gums recede, as age advances, thus giving rise to the expression 'long in the tooth'.

'Bishopping' is fraudulent tampering with the teeth to make the animal appear younger than it really is. By extracting a pair of the permanent teeth, the mouth appears like that of an animal that has just shed the corresponding pair of temporary teeth; but it can easily be detected by the absence of permanent teeth in the sockets. New pits or infundibula are sometimes drilled in old horses' teeth, but the angle and length of the teeth give rise to suspicion in any experienced dealer, and detection is bound to follow a careful examination.

CHAPTER III

MUSCLES AND FAT

White Muscle, Red Muscle, Heart Muscle; Fat; Meat of Different
Animals; the Large Muscular Masses; the Main Fat Deposits.

MOVEMENT of the living body is brought about by the action
of *muscles*, of which there are three kinds: the *Red Muscle* or
' Lean of the Meat' that forms most of the carcase; *Heart
Muscle*, similar in appearance to red muscle, but differing in
structure and function, and only occurring in the walls of the
heart; and finally *White Muscle* that forms the walls of the
bowels, the urinary bladder, the larger blood vessels and, in
fact, any tubes or ducts through which fluids or semifluids are
passed. This white muscle has the simplest structure, and will
therefore be described first.

White Muscle is similar in appearance and structure to
white fibrous connective tissue. It consists of long spindle-
shaped cells, joined only at their extremities, with lymph spaces
between their bodies. To form a tube or duct, these cells
join into a long thread wound spirally round a waterproof
core or lining of endothelium or ' round cells '. During life
these muscle cells are in a constant state of slight tension,
pulling against each other and keeping the duct closed except
when it is forcibly distended by the entry of fluid.

Movement is caused by a sudden increase of the tension of
a cell or group of cells, thus forcibly closing part of the tube
and driving the fluid therein into another, more relaxed, part.
Such movements give rise to ' Pulse ' which causes blood to
travel along the blood vessels, while similar though less violent
movements, called ' Peristalsis ' cause food materials to travel
along the bowels during the process of digestion. The process
of increasing the tension is termed the ' contraction ' of the
muscle, since the ends of each cell are drawn closer together or
contracted, and it is due to an increase in the volume of the
cell contents. A relaxed cell resembles an empty football
bladder, an elongated object with ends far apart, but by
increasing the contents by blowing in air, the bladder becomes
more spherical and the ends are drawn closer together. So,
by increasing the volume of its contents, a muscle cell becomes
thicker and shorter and is said to ' contract '.

50

The increase in volume is caused by a series of chemical changes in the content of the cell, chief of which is the combination of oxygen with a carbohydrate called ' glycogen ' or ' animal starch ' whereby the carbon in the starch joins with the oxygen to form carbon dioxide and the water is set free. A similar process occurs when starch is burnt in air, changing into carbon dioxide and water vapour, but this results in the evolution of considerable heat. In the muscle cells, the heat evolved is less, being only enough to keep the body warm and the process is slower. The glycogen must first be converted into sarco-lactic acid, an acid similar to the lactic acid formed in sour milk, and this acid must then be oxidized further into carbon dioxide and water. After contraction is complete, the carbon dioxide and water are diffused through the lymph surrounding the cell, and the heat is dissipated into it. As the lymph moves continuously past the cells, these waste products are carried away and fresh supplies of glycogen and oxygen are brought in their place.

Each muscle cell is served by a fibril running from a nerve cell and, in some cases the chemical action that causes contraction is brought about by influences from the nerve cell, but this is not always the case with white muscle. If a length of bowel, for instance, is removed from a recently killed animal, it will continue to move although all the nerves leading to it have been cut. In such cases, it is clear that the impulse to contract arises from the cells themselves, and is their response to a previous stretching. Food entering the bowels dilates them and stretches the muscle fibres and, shortly after such stretching they are impelled to contract and cause the peristalsis ' or bowel movements. The nerves to these muscles simply regulate the amount of movement or the violence of the contraction.

In **Red Muscle** (Plate I) the parenchyma or essential tissues are long red fibrils, cells about $\frac{1}{10000}$ inch in diameter (2μ or $\frac{2}{1000}$ millimetre). A red muscle fibril is a tube divided into sections by transverse bands, and each section is served by a nerve fibril and each contains a liquid consisting of *Haemoglobin*, a red material that has the power of holding gases such as oxygen; a protein called Myosin, and a considerable amount of glycogen and fat. As with white muscle, it is normally in a state of slight tension during life, and this tension is increased and the cell contracted by oxidation of the glycogen and other materials, but in red muscle this tension and contraction only occur under nervous impulse. If the nerve is severed or damaged, the muscle loses ' tone ' and becomes soft and flabby and is paralysed or incapable of contraction. The division of the cell into sections enables a sustained contraction to be maintained, as some sections can be contracted while others are ' resting ' and collecting fresh glycogen and oxygen and dissipating the heat and carbon dioxide. The presence of haemoglobin facilitates the exchange of oxygen and carbon dioxide.

Haemoglobin is also found in red marrow and in red blood cells. Its proportion in the muscles varies in the different animals, being greater in the large, dark meat animals, and less in the ' white ' meat animals such as rabbits and poultry. It is also greater in entire males than castrates or females, and greater in old animals than in young.

The fibrils of red muscle are bound together by trabeculae of white areolar connective tissue with numerous capillary blood-vessels and large lymph spaces. This trabecula is called the ' Deep Fascia ', and, in a well nourished animal, globules of fat settle in it to act as an immediate food supply for the fibril cells. Bundles of fibrils just visible to the naked eye form ' muscle fibres ', and these are also bound together by fascia to form ' strands '. Groups of muscle strands are bound into one muscle by a fairly thick ' Superficial Fascia ', also containing fat in a well-nourished animal. Both the deep and the superficial fascia are continued beyond the ends of the muscle fibrils as ropes or sheets that form the ' Tendons ', which merge with periosteum and attach the muscle to the bone. Rope-like tendons are surrounded with ' Tendon Sheaths ', or tubes filled with synovia, the form of lymph already mentioned as being found in the joints that lubricates them and prevents friction.

Since red muscle only works under nervous impulse, the animal is always aware of any movement made by it; but is unaware of the movements of white or heart muscle which take place automatically. The name ' voluntary ' is therefore applied to red muscle and ' involuntary ' to the others, though ' conscious ' and ' unconscious ' would really be better names. Red muscle moves the bones or skeleton of the animal and is

therefore also called 'skeletal' muscle; white and heart
muscle moves the internal organs and is therefore sometimes
called 'visceral' muscle (Viscera = internal organs).
'Banded', 'Striped' or 'Striated' muscle are also recognised
as names for red muscle, though not often used.

Heart or Cardiac Muscle has the same appearance as
Red Muscle, but under the microscope it is seen to consist of
short branched fibrils with no transverse bands. Like white
muscle, it works independently of nervous impulse and the
nerves that serve it simply regulate the speed at which
it works.

When an animal dies slowly, as from a lingering disease,
the glycogen supply in the muscles is gradually diminished as
the circulation becomes weaker and finally ceases. After such
a death the meat remains alkaline in reaction, is flabby and
contains a quantity of liquid protein, much of which will be
wasted on cutting. Such meat is not normally considered fit
for human consumption, although it is not necessarily dangerous. It is, however, lacking in many of the nutritious factors
of normal meat and will putrefy rapidly, as putrefactive
bacteria thrive best in an alkaline medium. If, however, the
animal is killed quickly whilst in good health, the muscle cells
contain ample glycogen and red muscle contains sufficient
oxygen in its haemoglobin to allow this glycogen to be converted into sarco-lactic acid. Beef and horse carcases gradually
increase in acidity for $1\frac{1}{2}$–3 hours after slaughter and by then
there is no glycogen left in the muscle. In the case of sheep
this reaction takes longer, about 7 hours. The process is more
rapid in warm weather. This acidity has an important effect
on keeping quality as it retards the multiplication of any
putrefactive or other bacteria that may be present.

So meat from a recently killed animal is rich in glycogen
but has a low acid reaction and may be alkaline; but, with
the passage of time this glycogen disappears as the acidity of
the meat rises. The sarcolactic acid then converts the collagen,
the protein of white muscle, into gelatine, and white muscle
therefore remains soft and flabby after death; but it coagulates
the liquid myosin of red muscle into a solid and red muscle
therefore stiffens after death. The stiffening is the principal
cause of the 'rigor mortis' or 'setting' of the carcase; the
other cause being the stiffening of the fat on cooling. As the

meat sets, it tends to darken somewhat, due to the absorption of oxygen from the haemoglobin. This change of colour is particularly noticeable in horse meat. If the muscle has been badly nourished owing to starvation or disease, there is little glycogen to form acid and little fat to cool, hence setting is bad and may not occur at all. In the foetus, or unborn calf that has never breathed, there is not enough oxygen even to form sarcolactic acid, and there is practically no fat. Hence such a carcase will not set, and the meat will have a high glycogen content.

The process of ' ripening' the meat, or reduction of the stiffness of rigor mortis is due to the conversion of the collagen in the white areolar tissue into gelatin, by the action of sarcolactic acid. It may take as much as five days to complete.

FATTY ADIPOSE TISSUE

In addition to the fascia or ' marbling' of the meat, adipose tissue or white areolar connective tissue containing fat globules in its lymph spaces, is found in all hollows between muscles, thus rounding off the surfaces, and it also occurs in certain ' Fat Deposits' which will be mentioned later.

The fat of a mammal always contains a certain amount of Stearin a fat which is rare anywhere else in nature either in other animals or in plants. At body temperature (about 100° F.) Stearin is liquid, but it is solid at normal atmospheric temperatures (60° F.) and so the quantity present regulates the firmness of the fat in the carcase. Sheep and goats have a large proportion of stearin so their fat is hard and their carcases are very stiff when cold. Horses and swine have comparatively little stearin so their fat is soft and their carcases limp when cold, though the rigor of muscles is the same in all cases.

Mammalian fat also contains Olein and Palmitin in varying proportions, but these fats also occur in various plants and seeds. Palmitin acts as a solvent for Carotene, a yellow colouring matter abundant in green foods, especially in the spring flush but also found in silage, some roots and some varieties of maize. Animals with a large proportion of palmitin in their fat will accumulate carotene if fed on these foods and so provide ' yellow fat', and this happens with cattle of the ' yellow fat breeds' (Channel Islanders and Zebus) and with horses and to a lesser extent pigs. If, however, such animals are fed entirely on grain, hay or straw, their fat remains fairly white as these foods contain very little carotene to colour the palmitin. Cattle of 'white fat' breeds, all sheep, goats and buffalo have very little palmitin, so they can only assimilate a small quantity of carotene, and their fat remains nearly white no matter how they are fed. If, however, they are badly nourished and lose most of their fat, the little carotene they do absorb is more concentrated and their fat turns yellower.

There are also a number of 'Volatile Oils' in the fat of mammals, and these oils give fat and red muscle their flavour and aroma. Thus well marbled meat smells and tastes better than lean meat; but as volatile oils are practically missing from white muscle and heart muscle, these meats are comparatively tasteless and are usually cooked with strongly flavoured herbs. Volatile oils evaporate readily, hence they will be lacking in meat that has been stored for a long time. Such meat is therefore comparatively tasteless.

COMPARISON OF MEAT OF VARIOUS ANIMALS

Meat	Fat Consistency	Fat Normal Colour
Oxen (Beef Breeds). Red	Fairly firm	White, with slight yellow tint
Oxen (Channel Isles and Humped Breeds). Red	Fairly firm	Yellow
Camel. Red	Fairly firm	Pale yellow
Buffalo and Bison. Dark red	Firm	Pure white
Sheep, Goats, Dogs and Cats Light red	Very firm	Pure white
Deer. Light red	Fairly firm	Yellow
Swine. Light red	Very soft	Grey white
Horses. Dark red	Soft	White or yellow
Whales. Very dark	Liquid (Practically no stearin)	Drained out of the meat as it is cut up
Human. Light red	Soft	Golden yellow

Goat fat is noticeably sticky compared with sheep fat, and it is difficult to skin a goat without leaving a few hairs sticking to the surface. Human flesh is indistinguishable from pork, except for the golden yellow fat which is, however, sometimes found in pigs also. Dog meat and fat are indistinguishable from mutton.

THE MUSCLES

There is no object in memorising all the muscles of the body. In the following list, those that are frequently referred to in the literature of the meat industry have been printed in bold type, and the names and position of these should be learnt by detecting them on a carcase. Others that are rarely referred to are given to assist in the building up of a mental picture of the carcase, but need not be memorised. The smaller muscles, of interest only to surgeons, artists, and others who need an accurate knowledge of their size and position, have been omitted entirely from this work.

THE BACK, NECK AND HEAD

Lumbar and Thoracic Muscles (Plate II).

The Longissimus Dorsi, the ' longest muscle of the back ', and indeed of the whole body, forms the ' eye of the chop '. It starts from the anterior edges of the sacrum and ilium and runs forward to the neck and head, filling the angle between the spinous processes and the transverse processes and, in the thoracic region, covering the upper portion of the ribs as well. The hump of the zebu (humped ox) is formed by the enlargement of the muscle over the first five thoracic vertebrae.

The Longissimus Costarum, the ' longest muscle of the ribs ', runs from the spinous processes of the lumbar vertebrae to the posterior edge of each rib, thus being at first on top of the longissimus dorsi, and later beside it.

The Serratus Dorsalis runs from the spinous processes of the thoracic vertebrae over the longissimus dorsi to the outer surface of each rib. The front half of this muscle pulls the ribs forwards and the back half, aided by the longissimus costarum, pulls them back during heavy breathing.

The Latissimus Dorsi, ' the broadest muscle of the back ', runs from the lumbar spinous processes to the upper arm.

The Multifidus connects each transverse process to the spinous process of the vertebra next but one ahead. The *Intertransversales* connect adjacent transverse processes. In these lie the Intervertebral Lymph Nodes.

The Psoas Muscles (Plate III) lie under the lumbar vertebrae and form the ' tenderloin ' or ' fillet '. They are attached to the transverse processes above and to the muscles of the thigh and inner face of the ilium behind. In front, they are continued on to the diaphragm as the ' Pillars ' or ' Crura '. There are no muscles corresponding to these on the inner side of the thoracic vertebrae.

The Sacrum

The sacrum being inflexible has no muscles corresponding to the foregoing attached to it. In front, its muscular covering is entirely connected with the hind limb and will be dealt with later. Behind, it gives origin to the muscles of the tail.

The Tail

The Levator Caudis or ' lifter of the tail ' corresponds to the longissimus dorsi; the *Lateral Levator* to the longissimus costarum and the *Coccygeus* or *Depressor Caudis* to the psoas. All start from the last two segments of the sacrum and the depressor sends branches to the anus which draw it out for defaecation when the tail is raised. All these muscles terminate at about the eighth coccygeal vertebrae, leaving the remainder of the tail to swing free, as in cattle and sheep; or bound tightly together by strong ligaments as in goats and dogs. Among domestic animals only the cat has muscular control of its tail for the full length.

The Neck (Plates IV and V)

The Longissimus Dorsi continues forwards from the thoracic region and terminates, for the most part, on the spinous processes of the last three cervical vertebrae, but a small, rope-like muscle runs beside the ligamentum nuchae to the head, and this part is sometimes given the name, *Longissimus capitis,* ' the longest muscle of the head '.

The Multifidus and the *Intertransversales* continue for the length of the neck as far as the axis.

The Complexus is a triangular muscular mass filling the area between the ligamentum nuchae and the cervical vertibrae.

The Splenius lies outside the complexus, and is much the same shape.

The Longus Colli lies under the cervical and first four thoracic vertebrae and may be considered as corresponding to the psoas muscles. The trachea or windpipe lies against its lower surface.

The Scalenus or scalene muscle is attached between the anterior border of the first rib and the transverse processes of the last four cervical vertebrae. The two scalene muscles form a fleshy mass that nearly fills the anterior entrance to the thorax, giving passage only to the trachea (or windpipe), the oesophagus and the blood-vessels.

The Brachio-Cephalicus, 'arm to head', runs from the shoulder to the head along the lower half of the side of the neck.

The Sterno Cephalicus, 'breast bone to head' runs from the sternum to the head on the lower surface of the trachea or windpipe. Just before reaching the larynx or voice. box, it divides into two, and runs up each side, so leaving that organ immediately below the skin. Between the sterno-cephalicus and brachio-cephalicus is a deep furrow, called the jugular furrow.

The Jugular Furrow. In this furrow lie the jugular veins and carotid artery that serve the head and the vagus, one of the nerves that serve the heart.

Several small muscles connected with swallowing and with the exact posturing of the head run up the neck to the skull, mandible and hyoid bone.

The Head

The head contains several small muscles, of which only the tongue and the masseters are frequently referred to. The tongue is dealt with among the digestive organs.

The Masseter is the broad sheet of muscle that constitutes the fleshy part of the cheek. Its action is to close the jaw during chewing and to manipulate the food between the teeth.

THE THORACIC WALL (Plate VI)

The anterior end of the thorax is closed by the scalene muscles and pads of fat surrounding the organs that enter it. The posterior end is separated from the abdomen by the diaphragm.

The Diaphragm or midriff (Fig. 31). This consists of a rim of muscle ('the skirt') running from the under surface of the first lumbar vertebra, round the inner surfaces of the asternal ribs to which it is attached, down to the junction of the last bony segment of the sternum with the xiphoid cartilage. Within this ring is a dome-shaped sheet of tendon completely separating the thorax from the abdomen. The apex of the dome enters the thorax as far forward as the fifth rib. Two **Pillars** or **Crura** of muscle, continuous with the Psoas, descend from the dorsal edge towards the centre, the right being somewhat the larger. When these pillars and the muscular rim are contracted, as during inhalation (or breathing in) the tendinous dome is drawn back and flattened so that the cavity of the thorax is enlarged. When they are relaxed and the abdominal muscles drive the abdominal organs forwards, the dome is restored and the cavity of the thorax reduced, thus driving out the air or exhaling. This is the normal method of breathing in a resting animal, but during exercise, the ribs also are moved forwards and backwards by the longissimus costarum and serratus muscles, and this movement draws the ribs apart, so flattening the dome of diaphragm to a greater extent. There is thus a two-fold enlargement of the thorax during heavy respiration, the increase in diameter due to the ribs drawing apart and the extra flattening of the diaphragm.

If the abdominal muscles and the rim of the diaphragm are tensed simultaneously pressure is brought to bear on the abdominal organs and defaecation (passing of dung) is brought about. A similar contraction is used in parturition (or giving birth). Thus the diaphragm is the main muscle of inhalation, defaecation and parturition.

The tendinous sheet is penetrated just to the right of its centre, by the Posterior Vena Cava, the large vein that draws blood from the posterior half of the body. To the left, and slightly above the centre, it is penetrated by the oesophagus or gullet. The top of the left pillar is pierced by the Aorta or main artery of the body, and beside this is the Chyle Cistern, or main collecting centre for lymph. At the junction of the muscular rim with the sternum in a pad of fat on the thoracic side lies the Xiphoid Lymph Node.

The side walls of the thorax may be considered in three layers: an inner layer of muscle and bone; a medial layer of muscles that move the ribs backward and forward; and an outer layer of muscle and bone that forms the attachment of the fore limb and is usually referred to as the Shoulder Girdle.

The inner layer consists of the thoracic vertebrae, the ribs, the costal cartilages and the sternum. The spaces between the ribs are filled by the **Intercostal Muscles,** in two layers; the inner layer with its fibrils pointing downwards and forwards and the outer layer with its fibrils pointing downwards and backwards. In between these two layers between the costal cartilages of the sternal ribs lie the Sternal Lymph Nodes. In addition, the *Transverse Thoracic Muscle* covers the inner faces of the sternal costal cartilages and the upper face of the sternum, so that its contraction will draw the ends of the ribs together, bending the cartilages and thus narrowing the chest.

The main motor muscles of the ribs, forming the medial layer of the wall, are the longissimus costarum, the serratus dorsalis and the serratus ventralis. The first two have been referred to with the muscles of the back, of which they form a part. The *serratus ventralis* joins the ribs and the last three cervical vertebrae to the inner face of the scapula.

The Shoulder Girdle or outer layer of the thoracic wall, consists of the scapula and, joining it to the thoracic spinous processes, the **Rhomboid Muscle** attached to the inner face of the prolonging cartilage, and the **Trapezius** attached to the spine of the scapula, and lying above the rhomboid. These two muscles form the bulk of the meat of the ' middle ribs '. The lower end of the scapula and upper end of the humerus are joined to the sternum by the **Pectorals**, which form the bulk of the brisket.

THE FORE LIMB

The Latissimus Dorsi that draws the shoulder back and the Brachio-cephalicus that draws it forward have been mentioned with the muscles of the back and neck, of which they form a part.

On the outer surface of the scapula, between the spine and the anterior edge is the *Supraspinatus*, and between the spine and the posterior edge the *Infraspinatus*, while the inner surface is covered by the *Subscapularis*. The large fleshy mass filling the angle between the posterior edge of the scapula and the humerus consists principally of the *Triceps* attached to the head of the Ulna. Inside it lies the *Teres* and outside it the *Deltoid* running to the upper part of the humerus only. From the bicipital tuberosity in front of the glenoid, the *Biceps* run to the head of the radius and the *Coracoid* to the middle of the inner front edge of the humerus. The *Flexors* and *Extensors* of the metacarpus and digits lie round the radius and ulna, and form the meat of the ' Shin '.

THE ABDOMINAL WALL (Plate VII)

The side walls of the abdomen or ' Flanks ' somewhat resemble those of the thorax, in that they consist of two muscular sheets, the **External Abdominal Oblique** muscle, whose fibres point downwards and backwards, as do those of the external intercostal muscle, and the **Internal Abdominal Oblique** muscle, whose fibres point downwards and forwards as do those of the internal intercostal muscle. Each of these muscles is extended across the floor of the abdomen by a sheet of tendon that joints it to its fellow. On the outer tendinous sheet may be seen a thin line of ligament running from the sternum to the pubis. This is the *Linea Alba* or white line and, at its centre, the **Umbilicus** or Navel, the scar left over the orifice through which passed the umbilical blood-vessels that served the foetus during its development in the uterus. In the male, the penis is lightly attached to the linea alba behind the umbilicus, and in the female the mammary glands or udder are firmly attached to it and the tissue on either side. Between the two tendinous sheets lies a thick pad of fat, the **Abdominal Fat.**

The Rectus Abdominis stretches as a broad muscular sheet from the pubes to the sternum inside the tendinous sheet of the internal oblique muscles. It is not, however, a continuous muscle, but consists of alternate bands of muscle and tendon that give it a mottled appearance.

The Transverse Abdominal muscle forms a ' V ' in the front half of the abdomen. It lies on the rectus, with the point of the V just touching the sternum and the sides running down the edges of the abdominal wall.

As explained previously, these muscles, when contracted, thrust the abdominal organs against the diaphragm, so pushing its tendinous dome forwards and causing exhalation. When contracted simultaneously with the rim of the diaphragm, they cause defaecation or parturition.

Lying on the outer side of the abdominal wall is the

Panniculus or 'Bark'. This muscle attaches the skin to the underlying structures and twitches it when irritated. It is irregular in its distribution, and is missing altogether over most parts of the body. In cattle, sheep and goats, a strong fold of panniculus runs down to the patella forming the **'Knee Fold'** or **'Skin Fold'**, and on its inner surface immediately below the junction of the sacrum and lumbar region lies the Prefemoral or Precrural Lymph Node. This muscle cannot be extended to any great length, and so prevents these animals kicking straight out behind like horses. Holding this muscle tightly with the hand or a crook or loop of rope round the body prevents the animal stepping backwards and makes it easy to control.

In sheep and goats, the panniculus covers the sides of the thorax as well as the belly, and in deer it covers the lumbar region of the back as well. In horses and swine, there is no skin-fold to the patella, but only an easily extensible tendinous sheet.

The anterior end of the abdominal cavity is closed by the diaphragm. The posterior end is continuous with the pelvic cavity, but the anterior muscles of the thigh, which arise from the inner face of the wing of the ilium and from the psoas muscles, mark the division between the two cavities. The oblique abdominal muscular sheets join with these anterior thigh muscles, and their tendinous sheets join with the anterior edges of the pubic bones. In the female, this junction is complete, but in the male, a small gap is left on each side of the central line forming the Inguinal Canals.

The Inguinal Canals. Through these canals blood-vessels and ducts pass to the testicles, together with a few fibrils of the internal oblique muscle. This is called the Cremaster Muscle, and it raises the testicle in cold weather or during excitement. The Superficial and Deep Inguinal Lymph Nodes lie on the posterior sides of the canals, the former at the external and the latter at the internal end. The penis passes right through the scrotum from the back to the front between the canals. In castrates, the blood-vessels, ducts and muscle wither away, and the canals tend to close somewhat, while fatty tissue spreads through them, thus completely occluding them. 'Inguinal Hernia' is the condition in which portions of the intestines also pass through an inguinal canal into the scrotum.

THE HIND LIMB

The *Iliacus* runs over the inner face of the ilium to the trochanters of the femur, and is partly covered by a portion of the psoas muscle that takes much the same course. The internal and external iliac arteries and veins run over the abdominal surfaces of the iliacus and the iliac lymph nodes are found close to the blood-vessels immediately below the sacro-lumbar junction.

The Outer Side of the Thigh (Plate VIII) (the ' Silverside ') is covered by the *Tensor Fascia Lata*, which runs from the outer angle of the ilium to the patella, and the **Gluteus** muscles which run from the spinous processes of the sacrum, over the top of the ilium, to the outer side of the femur.

The Posterior Part of the Thigh (Plate IX) is covered by the **Biceps Femoris** on the outer (or silverside) edge. In oxen, this runs from the outer end of the ischium to the back of the tibia; but in other animals it runs from the upper surfaces of the ilium, over the ischium, thus forming a rounded buttock instead of the prominent ' Pin Bones ' of the ox. In humans, this muscle ends as a strong tendon that can be felt below the knee on the outer side. The inner (or ' topside ') edge of the back of the thigh is covered by the **Semimembranosus,** a broad mass of muscle, and the **Semitendinosus,** a thinner, rope-like muscle, both of which start below the ischium and combine lower down to join the back of the tibia beside the biceps. In humans, these two muscles end in a pair of twisted tendons that can be felt behind the knee on the inner side. Underneath the semitendinosus, close to the junction of the semimembranosus and biceps lies the Popliteal Lymph Node.

The Inner Side of the Thigh (Plate VII) (the ' Topside ') is composed of a mass of muscles starting from below the ischium and pubis, and joining the inner surfaces of the femur. These muscles are usually referred to collectively as the **Adductors** (addition = drawing together), since they draw the thighs together. They form the greater part of the ' topside '. Separately they are known as the *Obturator*, that closes the obturator foramen of the pelvic bones and runs to the top of the femur; the *Main Adductor*, just above this, and the **Gracilis** nearest the skin. The Gracilis joins its fellow just below the pubic bones, and the two must be cut apart when splitting the carcase. Then, in the female, a bean-shaped area of red muscle is exposed, while in the male it is triangular in shape, with the channel of the penis and possibly the penis itself running round the outer edge. Outside the penis or its channel may be seen the Retractor Penis muscle and the ' Root of the Penis ', a red muscular mass; but both these are small in castrates.

The Anterior Side of the Thigh is covered by a large muscular mass, the **Quadriceps,** which passes from the top end of the femur to the patella and thence to the head of the tibia. By contraction, it pulls up the patella which in turn pulls up the tibia and swings the leg forward. The muscle is only attached to the femur at its upper end and, if this is severed, it falls free of that bone. The four portions of which it is composed are known as the *Lateral Vast, Medial Vast* and *Inner Vast* muscles next to the bone, and the *Rectus* in front of the medial vast. *The Sartorius* in most animals is a small, rope-like muscle that fits between the rectus and inner vast muscle. In man it is of considerable importance, and so is always mentioned in anatomical books.

The Leg. Behind the tibia lies the **Gastrocnemius,** a double muscle whose tendon forms the **Achilles Tendon** that pulls on the os calcis to straighten the leg. Below the gastrocnemius lie the extensors and flexors of the foot.

Many small muscles connected with the exact posturing of the limb have been omitted.

THE LARGE FAT DEPOSITS

As stated above, all living cells contain a small quantity of fat, the Intra-Cellular fat, but its total quantity is not great. Fat is accumulated in greater quantities in the deep fascia between muscle fibres, and in the superficial fascia covering the individual muscles. There are also large deposits of fat in certain regions of areolar tissue known as the Large Fat Deposits or Depots. They should be detected on carcases.

The Subcutaneous Fat. Except in the comparatively small areas occupied by the Panniculus muscle, the skin is attached to the underlying structures by a loose areolar tissue, which, in a well-nourished animal, becomes heavily impregnated with fat, the Subcutaneous Fat. It is usually thickest over the posterior, two-thirds of the thorax, the lumbar and sacral regions, where it forms the 'Back Fat' which gives the back its rounded and level contours. In a starved animal it is absorbed and the outline of the spinous processes of the vertebrae becomes visible and the animal is said to be 'Razorbacked'. The Periorbital *Fat or Eye Pad* is a pad of subcutaneous fat on which the eyeball rests. It is the first to be absorbed if the animal is starved or ill. Hence the early appearance of 'Sunken Eyes' in an unthrifty animal. In virgin females, the subcutaneous fat practically fills the udders, forming the *Mammary Fat* or 'Dug Fat', leaving only a small region of lactating (milk-forming) tissue at the base of the teats; but when they come into milk, this lactating tissue increases and invades and replaces the mammary fat to some extent. This replacement recurs to a greater and greater extent with each lactation, so that, in an old cow the dug fat is small and may be missing altogether. In males, the penis runs through a zone of loose areolar tissue round the junction of the two gracilis muscles and then along the linear alba, and this areolar tissue allows for the expansion of the organ; but in castrates the penis does not expand and so the areolar tissue in this region becomes filled with fat. The **Pelvic Fat** or 'Rump Fat' is continuous with the subcutaneous fat of the buttocks and fills all parts of the pelvis not occupied with other organs. In males, the pelvis contains only the rectum or end of the bowels and the urinary bladder, and so there is ample room for a large accumulation of rump fat; but in females, the body of the uterus is also situated in the pelvis and there is therefore less rump fat. The remains of the broad ligament of the uterus can be seen running transversely across this fat. If the female has borne young, the rump fat is negligible in quantity, as it has given way to allow for the enlargement of the uterus.

The Abdominal Fat is the thick pad of fat lying between the tendinous sheets of the Abdominal Oblique Muscles.

The Sub-Peritoneal Fat. The inner surface of the abdominal wall is lined with a thin layer of fat covered with a serous membrane, the Peritoneal Membrane, which provides a smooth surface against which the abdominal organs can move without detectable friction. Usually this fat is so thin that the underlying muscles can be clearly seen, even when cold and set, but under the Psoas muscles in the lumbar region

3

this membrane forms a pair of pouches, each of which is occupied by a kidney and the Renal Fat or Kidney Knob. A loop of the membrane supports the bowels and is called the Mesentery and this loop also contains a quantity of fat, the Mesenteric Fat or 'Skirt Fat'. A similar loop called the Omentum supports the stomach and contains the omental fat or 'Caul Fat'.

The Sub-Pleural Fat lines the inner surface of the thoracic wall in a manner similar to the peritoneal fat, and, like it, is covered with a similar membrane, the Pleura. As a whole, this fat is scanty, but over the sternum it becomes thicker and then is sometimes referred to as 'Heart Fat'. The anterior end of the thoracic cavity is blocked with a thick pad of sub-pleural fat, the 'Throat Fat' through which runs the trachea or wind-pipe, the oesophagus or gullet and some blood-vessels. A loop of membrane hanging in the Mediastinum or space between the two lungs contains the *Mediastinal Fat*.

THE DIFFERENT ANIMALS

Oxen. There are two additional deposits that are found only in ruminants.

Brisket Fat. Between the pectoral muscles and the sternum there is a thick layer of fibrous tissue heavily impregnated with fat. This forms the *Brisket Fat*. It is usually thicker in stall-fed than in pasture-fed animals. In very fat animals of some breeds there is a large pendulous accumulation of subcutaneous fat below the front end of the sternum. This is sometimes also called 'Brisket Fat', but 'Dewlap Fat' would be a better term.

Scrotal or Cod Fat. When calves are castrated, the scrotum fills with lobulated fat, called 'Cod Fat'. This consists of an outer layer continuous with the subcutaneous fat, a medial layer continuous with the abdominal fat, and a central core formed by the sub-peritoneal fat but usually separated from it by the closure of the inguinal canals. Cod fat is lobulated and so can be distinguished from mammary fat which is in flat layers or 'laminated'; but both fats can be modelled with a warm iron to simulate each other. Occasionally an entire bull will accumulate a small quantity of cod fat, but this is developed entirely from the subcutaneous fat and is therefore laminated, not lobular, as is the cod fat of a steer.

Note that the hump of the zebu (humped ox) is entirely muscular, not fatty, as is that of the camel.

Sheep. The Panniculus muscle is fairly extensive and covers the sides of the thorax and part of the back, so there is less subcutaneous fat in these areas. Brisket and cod fat form as in oxen, but to a proportionally lesser extent. Otherwise, meat breeds have proportionally larger fat deposits than oxen, but in wool breeds such as Merinos, the fat may be so scanty that the carcase is practically unmarketable. In the Mediterranean zones ' Fat Tailed ' sheep are kept for milking and their lambs provide the Astrakhan furs. These sheep develop a large bag round the first eight coccygeal vertebrae, and when grazing is good during the winter rains, this fills with fat and swells to such a size that the ewes cannot be mated; but during the arid summer months it is reduced and all breeding occurs then. The rest of the carcase has but little fat, and so is of small value. Amputation of the tail is sometimes practised in hopes of driving the fat into the rest of the carcase, but it results in very little improvement.

In *Goats* of Northern Europe there is but little fat even in the fat deposits, but these goats are all of milch strains. Reasonably fat goats are produced in Southern Europe, and some tropical countries. In these the renal fat or kidney knob tends to assume a pear shape as against the almost spherical shape in the sheep; a fact that may help in differentiating the carcases if necessary.

In *Camels* the hump or humps consist of strong fibrous tissue heavily impregnated with fat in well-nourished animals. When starved, the fat is absorbed, but the fibrous tissue is strong enough to maintain the shape of the hump, though it tends to sag somewhat towards the top. In the dromedary or Arabian camel one such hump is formed over the thoracic vertebrae. In the Bactrian or Chinese camel, a second hump forms above the sacrum.

In *Horses* there is a fairly extensive panniculus muscle and the subcutaneous fat is correspondingly less, even in unworked animals. No cod fat is formed on castration.

In *Swine* (Plate XII), even wild swine, there is a great tendency to lay down fat in all the deposits. The peritoneal fat or ' Flair ' may be more than an inch thick and may submerge the kidney knob. The abdominal fat is also thick. In domestic breeds there is no panniculus muscle but its place is taken by an extra layer of subcutaneous fat which is so thick that it gives the impression of a bulk too large for the muscles to move or the bones to support. Actually, however, this is a false idea, for a healthy pig will show considerable activity however fat it is. On good feeding, extra fat continues to accumulate in the sub-cutis throughout the first four or five years of life; hence the farmers say 'a pig never stops growing'. The dermis or true skin also contains a considerable quantity of fat which makes it more nutritious than the skins of other animals.

There is no cod fat formed by the male. In the female, the mammary fat extends along the length of the abdomen and thorax as far forward as the forelimbs.

The pleural and pelvic fat are similar to those of other animals.

In *Cats* there is usually a considerable amount of fat in the peritoneal and abdominal deposits, even when the animal appears to be starved. The renal fat is always present in large quantities, though it does not completely cover the kidneys or form a ' knob '.

In *Rabbits* and *Hares*, wild specimens usually have very little fat in any of the deposits, even when apparently plump, but the quantity of fat varies greatly in the different strains, especially in domestic breeds. There is, however, never very much renal fat, and the kidneys are therefore fully exposed on evisceration.

The division of the carcase into butcher's joints is a matter rather outside the scope of this work, and is fully dealt with in various books on meat technology, but the following table may assist in fixing the location of the various muscles. The cuts given are those of the London and Home Counties, and I am indebted to Mr. Frank Gerrard for their description.

HINDQUARTER

Thin Flank
> Ends of last three ribs. Rectus, transverse and oblique abdominal muscles. Part of the diaphragm.

Rump
> Sacrum and wing of ilium. Psoas and gluteus muscles. The iliac blood vessels. The iliac lymph nodes at front edge and sciatic lymph node at

back edge under the sacro-sciatic ligament. These nodes may be cut when separating the joint.

Loin and Wing End

Lumbar vertebrae. Thoracic vertebrae XI, XII and XIII and half of X. Upper ends of ribs XI, XII and XIII. Longissimus costarum. Longissimus dorsi. Psoas. Oblique abdominals. Intercostals and part of diaphragm. The intervertebral lymph nodes lie against the bodies of the vertebrae between the transverse processes.

Thick Flank

Patella. Vastus or quadriceps femoris. Knee fold of panniculus, rectus and transversus abdominis and tendinous sheets of oblique abdominals with the abdominal fat between. The prefemoral or precrural lymph node lies on the inner face of the panniculus.

Leg of Beef

Tibia and cartilage of fibula, os calcis, astragalus. Gastrocnemius and achilles tendon and flexors and extensors of the foot. The ends of the thigh muscles except the vastus.

Aitchbone

Pubis and the trochanters and half the head of the femur. The upper ends of the gluteus adductors semimembranosus and semitendinosus, biceps femoris, vastus or quadriceps. The sciatic lymph node lies on the front edge against the rump, under the sacro-sciatic ligament.

Topside

The adductors of the thigh, part of the vastus or quadriceps.

Silverside

Femur. Semitendinosus and semimembranosus biceps femoris, and part of the vastus or quadriceps. The popliteal lymph node lies at the lower end under the semitendinosus and may be exposed in cutting off the leg of beef joint.

FOREQUARTER

Shin of Beef

Radius, ulna and top row of carpal bones. Biceps, triceps and flexors and extensors of the digits.

Flank

Lower ends and cartilages of ribs X, XI, XII and XIII. Oblique and transverse abdominal and rectus and the abdominal fat between the tendinous sheets. Part of the diaphragm.

Brisket

Sternum. Lower ends and costal cartilages of ribs I-VI. Pectorals, serratus, scalene and the intercostal and transverse thoracic muscle and part of diaphragm. The ' heart fat ' or sternal portion of sub-pleural fat, in which lies the xiphoid lymph node. Suprasternal lymph nodes lie between the costal cartilages, and presternal on the first sternal segment.

Clod

Humerus. Sterno cephalicus, brachio cephalicus, pectorals, biceps, triceps and deltoid.

Forerib

Thoracic vertebrae VII, VIII, IX and X and upper end of ribs. Cartilage of scapula. Longissimus dorsi, latissimus dorsi, intercostals. Intervertebral lymph nodes lie between the transverse processes.

Back Ribs

Thoracic vertebrae III, IV, V, VI and heads of ribs only. Part of scapula. Part of trapezius, rhomboid, latissimus dorsi, longissimus dorsi and intercostals. Intervertebral lymph nodes.

Top Ribs

Upper end of ribs III, IV, V, VI, but not vertebrae, and part of scapula. Intercostals, deltoid, rhomboid, part of pectorals, and serratus, latissimus dorsi.

Leg of Mutton Cut

Upper end of ribs I and II, but not vertebrae. Intercostals, rhomboid.

Chuck

Dorsal vertebrae I and II and heads of ribs. Longissimus dorsi, trapezius and rhomboid.

Blade Bone

Scapula, part of. Supra spinatus, infra spinatus, trapezius rhomboid, deltoid, triceps. The axillary lymph node lies between the scapula and ribs and the pre-scapula lymph node between the point of the shoulder and the first rib.

The vertebrae referred to above consist of half the bone, as in splitting the carcase the spinal column is divided.

CHAPTER IV

SKIN AND MEMBRANES

Skin, Hair and Horn; Mucous Membrane; Meninges and Serous
Membranes.

The Skin consists of thick, closely woven fibrous tissue
covered on its outer side with thin membranes of round cell
tissue (Fig. 27).

The fibrous tissue, the *Dermis*, *Cutis* or '*True Skin*'
averages about $\frac{1}{4}$-inch thick in cattle, but its actual thickness
varies in different parts of the body. Yellow elastic fibrils
which are insoluble and indigestible predominate in its structure
but a few white fibrils, readily digestible, are present as well as
some fat globules in the labyrinth of lymph spaces that runs between the fibrils. The inner surface, against the body, is
covered with a meshwork of capillary blood-vessels, and these
penetrate the dermis at intervals of an inch or so, and protrude
on the outer side as 'Papillae'. The dermis is attached to
the body in most places by a loose areolar tissue of white fibrils
that is easily torn; and, in a well-nourished animal, the spaces
in this tissue fill with fat, forming the 'Subcutaneous fat'.
Elsewhere it is attached by red muscle fibres, forming the
Panniculus muscle or Bark which twitches the skin; and in
such areas a knife is necessary when flaying the carcase.

The round cell covering, the *Epidermis*, *Cuticle* or '*Scarf
Skin*' is about $\frac{1}{50}$-inch in thickness. It consists of several
layers of Epithelium, a tissue that resembles endothelium in
being made of round cells packed so closely that waterproof
membranes are formed. The epidermis thus prevents lymph
from leaving the body and prevents water or air from entering
it through the skin. The innermost layer of epithelium,
lying next to the dermis, is the 'Germinative' or 'Malpighian'
layer. The cells are quite simple in structure, and their only
peculiarity is that in coloured skin they contain granules of
pigment called 'Melanin'; numerous in black skins, scantier
in brown, and missing altogether in blonde skins. The amount
of melanin may be increased slightly by exposing the living

skin to sunlight, but the greatest portion is born with the animal, and does not vary.   Animals with no melanin in the skin are called 'Albinos', and tend to pass on the fault to their offspring.

There are no blood-vessels or lymph spaces in the epidermis, so the germinative epithelium feeds on the lymph in the adjacent dermis;   and the cells, having fed full, divide, the outer half

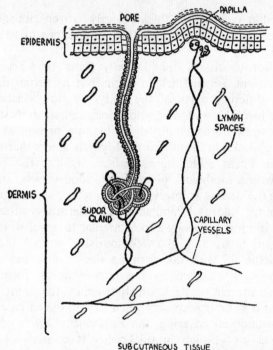

FIG. 27a.—Micro-structure of skin.

being pushed out away from the dermis.   These half cells re-form in complete cells, looking rather like a floor of bricks laid on end.   They form the Columnar Epithelium.   As new columnar epithelium is formed, the old one is pushed out further, and, being deprived of lymph and nourishment, the cells shrink into cuboid forms, forming the 'Cuboidal Epith-elium'.   In the next stage, the cells shrivel into flat, horny discs completely devoid of liquid cytoplasm, and forming the 'Squamous Epithelium'.   The outermost layer consists of dry horn like cells forming the 'Cornea' or horny covering. It is continually flaking off forming 'scurf'. The cornea alone is capable of absorbing a certain amount of water during life and can be softened and partly removed by prolonged soaking.

This, however, is the only part of the living epidermis that will absorb water; but dead epidermis is no longer waterproof. As soon as the cells of the cuboidal columnar and germinative layer die, water can penetrate to the lymph spaces in the

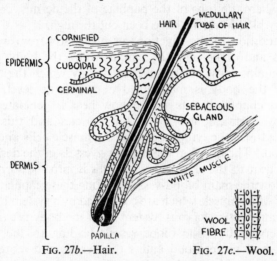

FIG. 27b.—Hair.   FIG. 27c.—Wool.

dermis, and with it the putrefactive bacteria. Hence the importance of hanging the carcase as soon as possible after slaughter, as the abattoir floor is bound to be wet and fouled with innumerable putrefactive organisms.

It is important to realise that the whole epidermis grows from the germinative epithelium, which is formed round the animal very early in foetal life. It does not grow, as one would think, from the dermis. If an area of epidermis, including the germinative layer, is destroyed, it can only be repaired by growth in from the sides. The cells of the uninjured germinative layer can multiply sidewards, as well as outwards, but the new germinative layer so produced will have no melanin, no sweat glands, and no hair; so a colourless, dry and bare 'scar' results that lasts for life. Such scars are formed when animals are branded.

If the epidermis be scratched lightly, so that only the outer epithelium is marked, the scratch will disappear in a few hours as new growth of cells are formed. If the scratch be deep enough to penetrate the germinal epithelium and reach the dermis, a clear yellow lymph will exude and clot over the scratch forming a light brown scab that will drop off in a day or so as new epidermis forms beneath. If a wide area of epidermis be scraped off (as sometimes happens' when shaving) bleeding starts from several points an inch or so apart, where the tops of the papillae of the dermis, containing capillary blood-vessels, have been cut through.

In addition to the functions of protection from water and bacteria and of keeping the lymph within the body, the skin also contains most of the mechanisms by which the temperature of the body is maintained at a definite level. In the previous chapter it was shown how heat is generated in the body by chemical activity in the muscles and this heat is dissipated into the lymph between the muscle cells and so into the blood. The blood in the capillary vessels in the dermis pass on this heat to the skin which radiates it into the surrounding air. Now the main blood-vessels feeding these capillaries have walls of white muscle which are controlled by a system of nerves, the ' Sympathetic Nervous System '. If the body becomes hot, these nerves allow the blood-vessels leading to the skin to expand, and more blood enters the dermis and more heat is lost. Skin reddens when hot. Similarly, if the body is becoming cold, less blood reaches the skin and less heat is lost. Skin pales when cold, and it also shrinks somewhat as the capillary vessels empty; and when so shrunken, the papillae of the dermis show through the epidermis as ' Goose Flesh '. The same mechanism controlling the amount of blood in the dermis causes certain parts of the skin to ' blush ' under excitement, especially sexual excitement.

Sudor, the watery part of sweat, is produced from small holes or ' pores ' in the skin. Each pore is the opening of a tube or duct of the epidermis, entering the dermis and ending in a convoluted portion, the sudor gland. The sudor itself consists of excess water in the blood, some salts, principally sodium chloride, and urea, a compound of ammonia formed by the breaking down of proteins, together with the surface cells flaking off from the inner side of the duct; it is, in fact, a dilute form of urine. A capillary blood-vessel is entwined with the convoluted gland and supplies the material from which the sudor is formed, and this, being under the same control as the other blood-vessels of the dermis, expands when warm, so supplying more sudor, which cools the surface, and contracts when cold, thus reducing, or even stopping, the supply. Human beings and horses have sudor glands all over the body, but other animals only have them in the bare skin at the end of the nose.* Sheep, goats, camels and cats have none at all.

Hair and Sebum. A hair is produced in a ' follicle ' or invagination of the epidermis entering deeply into the dermis and ending in a papilla. The corneal layer cannot flake off, and so is pushed out as a minute tube of horny material, forming the hair or bristle. Around the follicle is a cluster of cells forming the ' Sebaceous Gland ' which produces an oily substance, the ' Sebum ', which flows along the hair keeping it pliant and shiny and rendering it waterproof. (In human beings and horses the sebum mixes with the sudor and renders the sweat oily.) Sebum contains many volatile oils that give the animal its specific scent; and also its individual scent, by which keen scenting animals like dogs can recognise one individual from another. The skin round the anus is particularly rich in sebaceous glands. At the root of each hair is a small white muscle by which the hair can be erected; and this is under the same control as the blood supply, so that in warm weather the muscle relaxes and allows the hair to lie flat and in cold weather it contracts and erects the hair to make a thicker coat. In dogs and cats the hair erects under terror or rage to make the animal look larger and more dangerous.

Horn is formed in the same way as hair. A specially thickened ring of skin is formed, with follicles almost touching each other, and from each follicle a tube of horn emerges and fuses with its neighbour. The sebum is replaced by Periople, a substance resembling varnish and secreted by a ring of glands on the skin round the outer edge of the horn, forming the ' Periople Ring '. A *Hoof* consists of a wall of horn with a pad of very thick ($\frac{1}{2}$-inch or so) epidermis in the centre. The inner surface of the wall has numerous ridges or ' horny laminae ' about $\frac{1}{100}$ inch in height, which dovetail with

---

* To be strictly accurate oxen also have minute sudar glands opening into the hair follicles, but the amount of water excreted by them is too small to affect the temperature of the body.

similar ' sensitive laminae ' on the epidermis beneath, and making a firm attachment. There are no laminae in the horns of the head, which are therefore easily knocked off. Claws and finger nails have essentially the same structure as the wall of a hoof.

Leather. If a skin has all the fat removed and is then dried completely, it will resist putrefaction for years, as will dehydrated meat or other tissues; and this is the method used by primitive tribes for treating skins. Such skins, however, are liable to attack from beetles and other insects, and, if they become wet, will absorb moisture and putrefy rapidly. To make leather, the hair and epidermis are scraped off, the lymph washed out of the lymph spaces, and a weak acid, such as tannic or chromic acid, applied which dehydrates the fibrils and converts them into a horn-like substance that will not putrefy readily. Various oils are then worked into the lymph spaces to make the fibrils pliable and render the whole hide waterproof. Finally, wax or varnish is applied to one or both surfaces. The hide from a properly bled carcase will obviously contain less lymph than that of an animal that has died of natural causes, or one that has been killed when hot and tired after a hunt. ' Dead ' and ' heated ' hides are therefore more difficult to tan and are of little value.

Hair and Wool. To spin and weave fibres, it is essential that they should be rough. Most animals have hair composed of smooth fibres that would slip out of the yarn and unravel, but the wool-bearing animals, sheep, camel, llama and some breeds of goat and rabbit, have hair composed of rough fibres due to the epithelial cells that form them overlapping to some extent, and such hairs can form ' wools '. All these can be spun and woven; but, in addition, the best wools have the central or medullary tubes of the fibres filled with a cellular material that prevents them from absorbing water. Most ordinary hair is used for stuffing and felting; felt being made of hair and glue mixed together and rolled out into a mat. The stiff bristles of swine are used for ordinary bristle-brushes and the long hairs from the inside of the ears of oxen are used for the artists' brushes known as ' camel's hair brushes '. Lanolin, the basis of most cosmetic ointments, is made from sebum removed from hair and wool before processing.

Horn and Hoof. These are usually made into buttons, the residue being ground down as fertiliser. Recently, however, there has been some demand for horn for chemical fire extinguishers for use in petrol or electrical fires when water is inadvisable. 'Staghorn' made from the antlers of deer, is really compact bone, as there is no horny covering to the antlers. While the antlers are growing, the bone is covered with epidermis only, but this is rubbed off during the summer, leaving the bare bone exposed.

There is a widespread belief that horn and hoof is the basic material of glue. This is quite incorrect. Glue is made entirely from white fibrous tissue or white muscle.

The Different Animals

The hides of **Oxen** are known as 'cow hides', and supply the greater part of shoe leather. As the skin varies in thickness in different parts of the body, it is split into five

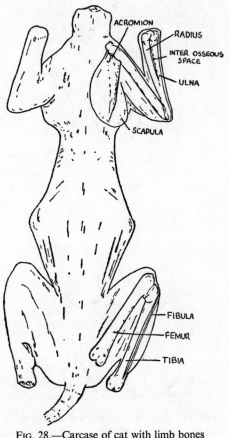

FIG. 28.—Carcase of cat with limb bones exposed.

or six thin layers, and these are placed together in such a manner that a uniform thickness is obtained. A good waterproof leather is made rather stiff in this manner but sufficiently flexible for most purposes.

Sheep skins are split into two layers, the outer layer forming 'Skiver', used for lining shoes, bags, etc. The inner layer is used for suede and 'chamois' leather and various other purposes, one of which is the manufacture of parchment. 'Kid leather' is usually made from goat skins.

Both sheep and goats have large collections of sebaceous glands between the hoofs, that emit a strong scent, which probably help the animals to follow each other in thick bush country. Deer have similar collections of sebaceous glands just under the eyes, but their purpose is not evident.

Horse hides provide a soft, pliable leather, superior to cow hide for many purposes; this pliability being due to the relatively large lymph spaces in the dermis that enable it to absorb large quantities of oil. The area of skin over the rump, known as the 'Shield', is, however, composed of a very coarse dermis with comparatively scanty lymph spaces, and this must be removed for special treatment in tanning. It is used, after treatment, for machine belts and the like. 'Horse hair' from the manes and tails has many uses, as stuffing for cushions and as a 'stiffener' for cloth, and a 'binder' for mortar.

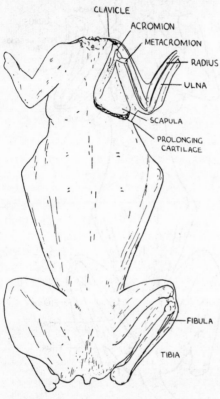

CLAVICLE
ACROMION
METACROMION
RADIUS
ULNA
SCAPULA
PROLONGING CARTILAGE
FIBULA
TIBIA

FIG. 29.—Carcase of rabbit with limb bones exposed.

The 'Chestnuts' on the inner surface of the limbs are thickened portions of epidermis similar to the 'sole' or portion inside the wall of the hoof. Their function is not known, but they occur on all four limbs of the horse and on the fore limbs only of the ass. The 'Ergots', behind the ends of the metacarpal and metatarsal bones (the 'Fetlock Joints') are true horn and represent vestigial hoofs.

Camel hides have no peculiarity and tan very similarly to cow hides. The Pedestal or horn-like growth below the sternum and the Callouses over the carpal joints are thickened epidermis similar to the 'chestnut'.

Pig's skin differs considerably from that of other animals. As stated above, there is no panniculus muscle in the domestic pig; but its place is taken by an extra layer of subcutaneous fat. In the skin itself there is a far greater proportion of white fibre to yellow, and white fibre is digestible; and in domestic pigs a considerable quantity of fat accumulates in the lymph spaces, two facts which render the pig skin more nutritious than other skins. The fat must, however, be removed before tanning, and the white fibre rendered insoluble, both processes that make pigskin expensive. The subcutaneous fat is soft and greasy and needs some protection, so the skin is usually left on the carcase. In the pig, the hair follicles are large and arranged in groups of three, and they penetrate the dermis, so the treated skin is penetrated with holes, about $\frac{1}{100}$ inch diameter, but this can be easily imitated.

The boar develops a large circular patch of thickened epidermis over each shoulder. This can be softened by lengthy boiling and thereafter cut up into brawn. Male pigs have a few long bristles with very large sebaceous glands on the inner side of the carpal joints, the 'Devil's Mark'.

[Human skin has the hair follicles ungrouped and evenly spaced and, except on the scalp, they are less than $\frac{1}{300}$ inch in diameter. Its outer surface is pitted with sudor pores (sweat glands). It contains very little white fibre and so is comparatively elastic.]

Mucous Membranes. The digestive or 'alimentary' tract (mouth and bowels), the respiratory tract (nose and windpipe), and bladder and uterus are lined with a special form of skin called 'Mucous Membrane'. In structure, it resembles the epidermis, having germinal columnar and cuboidal epithelial layers, but there is no corneal layer and (usually) no melanin granules. It is thus pink in colour, since the sub-mucous layer, corresponding to the dermis, can easily be seen through it. The outer layer of cells, cuboidal in shape, continually secrete a slimy material, the *Mucus*,* which keeps the surface moist and slippery and washes away dead cells on the surface before they have time to dry into cornea. To increase the quantity of mucus, there are frequently numerous glands, some being simple bags formed in the membrane, some being branched tubes, and some being convoluted tubes like sweat glands. Some mucous membranes can absorb liquids, and these have either large papillae or smaller projections called villi on them. Fuller descriptions of each mucous membrane will be given with the different organs.

The sub-mucous layer, corresponding to the dermis, is rarely more than $\frac{1}{20}$ inch in thickness. Beneath it lies white muscle, red muscle or cartilage, according to the organ it is found in. As with the skin, the sub-mucous layer only nourishes the germinative epithelium but plays no part in creating it. The germinative epithelium of mucous membrane is formed early in foetal life, and any subsequent injuries to it must be repaired by sideways growth of adjacent healthy mucous membranes.

The Meninges. These are three membranes lining the cranial cavity and vertebral canal and covering the brain and spinal cord within. They are developed from the same source as the epidermis of the skin, but early in foetal life become buried within the body. Each membrane maintains, throughout life, a thickness of only one cell, and so they resemble endothelium rather than epithelium. The membrane lying next to the bones and acting as periosteum to them is called the Dura Mater (Hard Mould); that lying next to the brain and spinal cord and acting as capsules to them is the Pia Mater (Soft Mould), and between them is a mesh of thin fibres, the Arachnoid (spider's web). Through the spaces of the arachnoid flows a form of lymph, the cerebro-spinal fluid. The membranes and fluid act as a water-bed for the brain and spinal cord and protect them from injury due to shock, while in the spinal column they prevent friction between the bone and the cord when the backbone is bent.

The Serous Membranes. These are membranes of endo-thelium, one cell in thickness, derived from connective tissue

* Note that the noun ' Mu*cus* ' refers to the slimy material given out by the top layer of cells. The adjective ' Mu*cous* ' must qualify a noun; e.g. ' mucous membrane ' or ' mucous fluid '.

and they line the body cavities and support the internal organs. Each forms an enclosed bladder or ' Sac ' filled with lymph that allows the internal organs to move without friction. Two serous membranes have already been mentioned: the *Peritoneal Membrane* in the abdomen (Fig. 43), enclosing the peritoneal sac or *Peritoneum*, in which lie the digestive organs and the Pleura in the thorax (Fig. 50), enclosing the Pleural cavity, in which lie the lungs. The third is the *Pericardium*, also in the thorax (Fig. 50), enclosing the Pericardial sac containing the heart. The serous membranes are supported by red muscle, bone, or connective tissue.

To obtain a clear idea of these serous sacs, imagine first that a body cavity, say the abdomen, contains no organs, but is wholly occupied by a bladder adhering to the muscular walls and filled with lymph. The organs, intestines, stomach, etc., develop at intervals between the muscular walls and the membrane forming the bladder. As these organs increase in size, the bladder envelops them and adheres to them, but still remains adherent to the muscular wall between them. Finally, the organs practically fill the abdomen, but the wall of each organ as well as the abdominal wall are covered with the membrane or the bladder, so that the inner surfaces of the bladder rub together during bowel movement. The lymph has now been squeezed out into a thin film that lubricates all these inner surfaces and minimises friction.

Many students experience difficulty in distinguishing between Mucous Membrane and Serous Membrane.

Mucous membrane lines tubes that lead to the surface. It is comparatively thick, $\frac{1}{50}$ inch or more, and is covered with Mucus, the slimy material found in the nose.

Serous membrane is in sheets lining the abdomen and thorax. It has no communication with the surface of the body. It is microscopically thin and is covered with lymph, the clear yellow fluid similar to synovia or joint oil.

Synovial Membranes. These have already been described as lining the synovial joints between bones (page 13) and forming the sheaths of tendons and the bursae. They, and the sacs they form, have the same formation as the serous membranes.

CHAPTER V

THE NERVOUS SYSTEMS

Brain; the Central Nervous System; the Sympathetic Nervous System; Slaughter, without and with Stunning.

The Brain (Plate XIV) may be considered as consisting of three main parts, the *Cerebrum* in front, the *Cerebellum* behind, and the *Medulla Oblongata* below. The first two are contained entirely within the cranial cavity, while the third is partly within it, and partly in the spinal canal of the first four cervical vertebrae. All three are surrounded by the meninges and bathed in cerebro-spinal fluid, as described in Chapter IV (page 80) on Skin and Membranes.

The **Cerebrum** consists of two *Cerebral Hemispheres*, really half ovals in shape, with their long axes lying fore and aft. Each has a grey white colour and appears to have been made of a highly convoluted cord. On section, it will be seen that below the grey matter is some glistening white material and in the centre of each hemisphere is a hollow space, the *Cerebral Ventricle*, filled with cerebro-spinal fluid. At the anterior pole of each hemisphere is a small ' Olfactory Bulb ' in which the sense of smell is received.

The **Cerebellum** lies behind the cerebrum and, in domestic animals, is about half its size; in humans it is about one-tenth its size. It looks like a finer cord more intricately convoluted than the cerebrum, but also consists of grey matter outside and white matter inside, with a small ventricle in the centre.

The **Medulla Olbongata** is cord-like in shape and connects the brain to the spinal cord, and is, in fact, often considered as part of the spinal cord. It differs from the cerebrum and cerebellum in having white matter outside and grey matter inside, this grey matter being in the form of an ' H '.

Other parts of interest in the brain are: the *Pons* or ' bridge ' lying below the organ and apparently connecting together the two cerebral hemispheres, the cerebrum and the medulla : the *Pituitary Body*, about the size of a hazel nut on a small stalk lying in front of the pons and dealing with sexual activities ; and the *Pineal Body*, a very small body, lying between the cerebrum and cerebellum on the upper side, whose function is not yet known.

The grey material in the brain consists of nerve cells, polygonal in shape, each with one long fibril, the axon and one or more very short fibrils, the dendrites. The dendrites meet dendrites from other nerve cells and enable them to communicate together and pass on impulses and sensations. The axons run down into the white matter, which is composed of millions of these axons, and there run to other parts of the brain and spinal cord. There are two quite different kinds of nerve cells present in the brain and elsewhere in the body, identical in appearance, and only distinguishable by experiments: the Sensory or Receptor nerves that receive sensations of touch, taste, smell, sound and sight, and the Motor nerves that convey impulses to the muscles, causing red ones to contract and regulating the contraction of white and heart muscle. In the cerebrum there are probably also special nerve cells that deal with the phenomenon of ' Thought ', ' Reasoning ', and ' Memory '.

It is common knowledge that if the brain is injured or drugged the animal becomes unconscious, that is to say, is unaware of its surroundings, and of what is happening to it, and is incapable of performing any voluntary movements. Actually, however, this applies only to the cerebrum, which is responsible for keeping the animal informed of its surroundings and for enabling it to determine what movements to make. This determination is then passed on to the cerebellum and the medulla that transmit it, in the form of impulses, to the muscles concerned. The cerebrum is therefore responsible for consciousness and the rest of the brain for movement.

If the cerebrum alone is injured, as by a pole-axe, the animal becomes unconscious and falls and lies still, because the cerebrum is incapable of determining further movement. Further movements can, however, occur, and will do so if the animal is bled to death or dies from any cause other than injury of the cerebellum or medulla. Just before bleeding is complete, i.e. at the point of death, regular trotting or galloping movements start under impulses received from the cerebellum, but originated without thought or determination. These

'Reflex Movements' may continue for 10 or 20 minutes after the heart has ceased to beat, but can be stopped or entirely prevented by 'Pithing' or driving a wire into the cerebellum, or a knife into the medulla between the atlas and the skull. They are quite distinct from the struggles of a conscious animal, for struggling movements are due to thought and determination and therefore include attempts to rise and escape. Reflex movements show no attempt to rise.

The cerebrum can also be inactivated by lowering the blood pressure in the head, as happens in nature when an animal faints. If the blood-vessels in the neck are cut so that the blood pressure in the head falls, the animal is practically unconscious in less than 9 seconds. Unconsciousness may also occur by raising the blood pressure in the head until some of the capillary blood-vessels are ruptured. This produces *Apoplexy.*

Sleep is a partial unconsciousness, of varying depth, caused by lowering of the blood pressure in the cerebrum, but as far as is known, the ordinary meat animals never reach the depth of unconsciousness that men do; a half-conscious doze being the deepest sleep they need.

The cerebellum and medulla are not, as a rule, inactivated as easily as the cerebrum and, for practical purposes, it may be taken that nothing short of direct injury will inactivate them. It is not easy to injure the cerebellum without also injuring the cerebrum; but the medulla may be cut by passing a knife between the skull and the atlas or, less easily, between the atlas and axis. The animal falls and remains motionless, but is still conscious, though unable to move, because the thought developed in the cerebrum cannot be transmitted as impulses to the muscles by the cerebellum or medulla. This condition is called 'the Nightmare State'.

The last portion of the medulla, within the third and fourth cervical vertebrae, contains the 'Respiratory Centre', which sends the impulses to the diaphragm and rib muscles that cause breathing. If it is injured, as it probably is in beheading (a method of slaughter used by some Indian tribes), respiration stops immediately, and the heart therefore dies before all the blood has been pumped out of the body. The respiratory centre can also be inactivated by severe pain and also by electric shocks; both of these causing 'Death by Shock', which is the usual term for death by stoppage of breathing. It is sometimes produced in pigs when the ' Electrical Stunning Apparatus ' has been applied too far back on the neck. The respiratory centre works without stimulus from the cerebrum, but is regulated by the amount of carbon dioxide in the blood. As this increases, the centre becomes more active and the animal, unconsciously, breathes faster and so gets rid of the excess.

THE CENTRAL NERVOUS SYSTEM

The Spinal Cord may be considered as starting in the fourth cervical vertebrae immediately after the medulla, or may be taken to include the medulla. It has the same appearance as the medulla, a white glistening rope, with a grey H in the centre composed of nerve cells. It stretches as far as the centre of the sacrum, and is covered by the three meninges, of which the pia mater ends with the cord but the dura mater and arachnoid continue into the first coccygeal bone.

Nerve fibrils leave the grey matter at both ends of the uprights of the H and collect together to leave the cord as ' nerves '. These nerves, or bundles of fibrils, arise from the cord between two vertebrae, the two above being receptor or sensory and the two below being motor. The sensory nerve joins the motor nerve on the same side in a small mass of grey nervous matter called a ' Ganglion ' situated on the side of the spinal canal just above the intervertebral cartilaginous disc. From this ganglion a ' Mixed Nerve ', containing both sensory and motor fibrils, passes out and branches or ' ramifies ' through the adjacent areas of the body. Some of the smaller branches become either sensory or motor according to whether they lead to the skin only or a muscle only; but they remain as mixed nerves as long as they lead to both. The posterior end of the body is ennervated by a bundle of nerves leaving the end of the spinal cord, giving it the appearance of a horse's tail. This is called the ' Cauda Equina ' (Lat. = mare's tail), and these are the nerves which are drugged in ' Spinal Anaesthesia ' given to prevent pain in difficult parturition.

Injuries to the spinal cord cause numbness or paralysis or both in the adjacent areas of the body and all behind the injury, but do not affect parts in front of it.

The cells of the H in the spinal cord are responsible for the numerous ' Reflex Actions ' or involuntary actions carried out in response to sensations without the animal willing them and, often, without it being aware of them. For instance, if a fly settles on the skin, a sensation is conveyed by the sensory fibrils to the cells in H of the spinal cord. These pass on the information to appropriate motor nerve cells, and a stimulus is sent to the panniculus muscle, causing the skin to twitch; possibly also the muscles of the tail are stimulated to swing it round; but the cerebrum will only be informed if the sensation is severe or unusual. There are innumerable reflex actions constantly being performed throughout life, both waking and sleeping, of which the movement of the ears to catch sounds, the reduction of the pupil of the eye in bright light, the ' start ' at a sudden noise or unexpected sight or smell are examples.

THE SYMPATHETIC NERVOUS SYSTEM

The Sympathetic Nerves are the nerves that regulate the activity of white and heart muscle and the glands, and convey sensations from the internal organs to the cerebrum.

This system is based on a pair of nerves that run down, one on each side of the vertebral column, *outside* the spinal canal, beneath the transverse processes and adjacent to the vertebral bodies. At each intervertebral disc there is a ganglion from which one nerve runs to the white muscle in the vicinity and one to the ganglion of the central nervous system, thus keeping the two systems in contact and co-operation. The white muscle is found in the walls of the larger blood-vessels, in the walls of the gut, and at the roots of each hair, and elsewhere. Cold stimulates the sympathetic nerves and they cause white muscle to contract; while heat has the opposite effect. Now, when a red muscle contracts, it generates heat, and this extra heat relaxes the white muscle in the walls of the blood-vessels that nourish it. Hence the vessel expands and the muscle gets more blood and extra nourishment, and the generated heat is dissipated more rapidly. It has already been shown how the skin responds similarly and so extra heat generated in the muscles is finally dissipated into the air. Thus, no matter what work is being performed or what the temperature of the surrounding atmosphere, the warm blooded animals maintain their bodies at the same temperature as long as they are in good health.

Actually, human beings have this system most highly developed, and when healthy never vary their temperature more than a degree from 98·4° F. Horses vary between 98° and 100° F., the smaller ponies having higher temperatures than larger horses; cattle and pigs may go from 98-103° F., according to the weather and the muscular work they are doing. Sheep and goats may reach 106° F. without any sign of fever. There are, however, many other signs of fever besides the temperature that are taken into consideration in making a diagnosis.

The cold blooded animals, fish, frogs, etc., in fact, every animal except mammals and birds, have no sympathetic system, and vary their temperature according to their surroundings. An active fish in cold water is a few degrees warmer than that water but, if the water be warmed, the temperature of the fish will rise by an exactly equivalent amount. The same is true of new-born mammals and newly hatched birds, and they must therefore be kept warm until their sympathetic nerves are working well. The mother is equipped by nature to provide this warmth.

The Sympathetic System can be stimulated throughout the whole system by excitement, especially fear. This causes contraction of the blood-vessels leading to the skin, hence paleness and a sensation of cold causing shivering; erection of the hair in most animals, and violent movement of the bowels and bladder with possible evacuation of both. Simultaneously branches of the sympathetic nerves that lead to the heart cause an increased rate of heart beat. If the fear is intense and prolonged this may cause rupture of some of the capillary blood-vessels and extrusion of blood into the lymph spaces, causing ' Blood Splash '. Hence the importance of quiet handling of the animals before and during slaughter.

In many organs, the activity of the sympathetic system is regulated by opposing nerves, the ' Para-sympathetic Nerves '. We are only concerned with one pair, the Vagus Nerves. These leave the skull by two small foramina just beyond the wings of the atlas, and run down the neck to the heart, where they regulate the stimulating affect of the sympathetic nerve.

Normally these two nerves work in co-operation, the sympathetic nerves increasing and the vagus reducing the rate of the heart beat, and the two together keeping the rate correct for the needs of the animal.

If the throat is cut by a transverse cut, as in the Jewish or Mohammedan method of slaughter, both vagus nerves are cut, but the sympathetics are not affected, and so stimulate the heart and cause very rapid bleeding. If an electric stunner is placed on the front of the neck, instead of the head, an easy mistake to make with pigs, both vagus nerves may be stunned and so the sympathetic nerves will cause the heart to race, and as the throat has not been cut, this may cause a rapid rise in blood pressure, with blood splash in the muscles, and a possibility of death from apoplexy before the animal can be properly ' stuck '. The stunner should never be applied behind the ears.*

The nervous systems of the different animals do not differ sufficiently to warrant separate descriptions.

* Blood splash may also occur in the carcase of an animal which has been stunned by a shot in the cerebrum, if there has been a long delay between shooting and opening an artery. The cause of this is not yet known.

CHAPTER VI

THE VASCULAR SYSTEM

Circulation of the Blood; the Heart; Arteries; Capillaries and Blood Sinuses; Veins; the Main Arteries and Veins; the Thymus Gland; Bleeding for Slaughter; the Composition of Blood; Clotting; Serum; Lymph; Lymph Nodes; Spleen and Haemolymph Nodes.

BLOOD carries the materials needed for maintaining the life and activity of the individual cells, and removes from these cells the used up or ' burnt ' material resulting from their activities. It flows through a series of tubes or *Blood Vessels*, being kept moving by the pumping action of the *Heart*, which forces blood along the *Arteries*, the blood-vessels leading from the heart to the organs, and draws blood out of the *Veins*, the blood-vessels leading from the organs back to the heart. The extremities of the arteries are joined to the veins by *Capillary Blood Vessels* running through the capsules and trabeculae of the organs. The whole process is called the ' *Circulation of the Blood* '.

The course of the circulation is, briefly, as follows. Blood is driven by the *right* side of the heart into the lungs, where it picks up fresh oxygen from the air and gets rid of the excess carbon dioxide accumulated as a result of muscular activity. It is drawn out of the lungs by the suction exerted by the *left* side of the heart, and driven out to the rest of the body, part going to the bowels to pick up digested food, part to the kidneys to excrete or get rid of urea, which is the product of decomposed protein or cell material, part to the muscles and other organs to bring them nourishment and remove their waste products, and part to the skin to get rid of excessive heat. These parts will all mix again in the veins which lead back to the right side of the heart, and this side will therefore contain a mixture of blood rich in food material, blood free of urea, blood rich in carbon dioxide, and cool blood from the skin. This will be driven to the lungs as before.

It will be noticed that the left and right sides of the heart have no communication with each other. The right side of the heart contains blood rich in everything except oxygen, and the left side, blood rich in oxygen but freed of excess carbon dioxide.

The Heart is manifestly the centre of the circulatory system. It consists of a hollow muscular organ, conical in shape lying on the centre line of the thorax with its apex about level with the fifth rib and its base raised rather higher and level with the second rib. It is composed of the special Cardiac Muscle or Myo-cardium, found nowhere else in the body. The fibrils are red, but short and branched, and have no bands or striations, and they are capable of continuing to contract or ' beat ' without nervous impulse. They are arranged to form a four-chambered bag; two anterior chambers, the left and right *Auricles*, and two posterior chambers, the left and right *Ventricles* (Fig. 30).

The auricles have thin walls and lie towards the outer edge of the base of the heart. When dead and in rigor, they are empty and fully contracted and rather like small ears (auricle = small ear). The outer portion of each is a blind sac, but the central portion is entered by veins and communicates with the ventricle on the same side. The ventricles have thick walls and appear to constitute most of the dead heart, but in life, when the auricles dilate with blood the difference in size is not so apparent. The left ventricle has a thicker wall than the right (as it has to pump the blood further), and constitutes two-thirds of the heart, including the apex. The right ventricle has the same sized cavity as the left but a thinner wall which does not reach the apex or point of the heart. On the outer aspect the two ventricles appear to form one organ, but on opening the heart, it is seen that they are separated by a thick wall of muscle, the *Septum*. An artery leaves each ventricle at its front or base and passes forwards between the two auricles, the *Pulmonary Artery* from the right ventricle going to the lungs and the *Aorta* from the left ventricle going to all the rest of the body.

The cavities of the auricles and ventricles are lined with a thin coat of fibrous tissue covered with endothelium which renders them watertight. This forms the Endocardium. Folds of endocardium separate each auricle from its ventricles. There is an orifice in each of these folds, allowing blood to pass from the auricle to the ventricle. On the right, the rim of the orifice has three cusps that hang down into the ventricle in such a manner as to form a valve that allows blood to pass from the auricle to the ventricle, but, when the ventricle

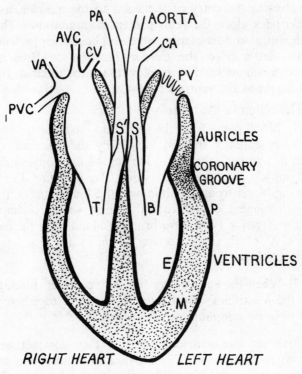

FIG. 30.—Diagram of heart.

AVC	= Anterior vena cava	PA	= Pulmonary artery
CV	= Coronary vein	CA	= Coronary artery
VA	= Vena azygos	S'S	= Semilunar valves
PVC	= Posterior vena cava	B	= Bicuspid or mitral valve
T	= Tricuspid valve	E	= Endocardium
PV	= Pulmonary veins	M	= Myocardium
P	= Pericardium		

The *tendinous cords* have been omitted for the sake of clarity

contracts, they are forced back over the orifice and prevent the return of blood. This forms the *Tricuspid Valve*.* A similar valve, the *Mitral Valve*,* with two cusps only, allows

* As an aid to memory Mitral and Left both contain L. 'Mitral' comes from the same root as 'Mitre', the double crown of a bishop,

blood to pass from the left auricle to the left ventricle. Similar valves, the *Semilunar Valves*, occur at the origin of the aorta and pulmonary arteries, allowing blood to pass into the arteries but preventing its return to the ventricles. There are no valves at the entry of the veins to the auricles, as valves further back along the veins prevent regurgitation. The cusps of the mitral and tri-cuspid valves are held open by tendons of yellow elastic fibre, the *Cordae Tendinae* or *Heart Strings*, which stretch sufficiently to allow the cusps to close, but open them again as the ventricles relax.

The action of the heart is as follows:

(1) Blood pours from the veins into the auricles; that from the lungs entering the left auricle by the Pulmonary Veins, seven in number; that from the rest of the body entering the right auricle by three main veins, the *Posterior Vena Cava*, bringing blood from the abdomen and hindquarters, the *Vena Azygos* bringing blood from the chest wall and diaphragm, and the *Anterior Vena Cava* bringing blood from the head and arms. A fourth small *Coronary Vein* brings blood from the heart muscle itself.

(2) When the auricles are full they contract, forcing blood into the Ventricles. Both auricles contract together, though they have no communication with each other.

(3) When the ventricles are full, they contract while the auricles relax and rest. This closes the mitral and tricuspid valves with an audible thump that is the first sound in the heart beat, and the blood is forced into the arteries.

(4) The ventricles relax and rest, and the semilunar valves close, making the second sound of the heart beat.

(5) After a pause during which the heart muscle rests, the whole operation is repeated.

This cycle of events, the 'Heart Beat', is controlled by the Vago-sympathetic nervous system. Stimulation of the sympathetic nerves by work, excitement or certain drugs results in shortening the resting phase, and so quickening of the rate. Stimulation of the vagus brings about a longer rest period and slower beat. If all the nerves are cut, the beat continues but is irregular in rate. A heart carefully removed from the body and placed in a warm nutrient medium will continue to beat for several hours, although its nerves have been severed.

The rate of heart beat varies inversely with the size of the animal. Thus resting horses in a cool atmosphere have a rate of 35-40 beats per minute; oxen 40-60; swine 55-75; sheep and goats 60-80; but very slight alterations in atmosphere, strain on the muscles, or emotions may make very big differences in rate. Even handling for examination will produce some disturbance, so heart rate alone is no guide to the animal's state of health, though it may be a help in making a diagnosis from other symptoms.

Most of the blood driven into the aorta by the left ventricle leaves the thorax and goes to the head, limbs and abdomen, so the pressure within the thorax is considerably less than that of the atmosphere, and a constant suction is maintained on the veins leading into it and back to the heart. This suction causes blood to flow along them, and also tends to stretch out or expand the chambers of the heart as soon as the phase of contraction is finished. It has also a considerable bearing on the function of respiration, as will be shown later. The state of ' partial vacuum ' or suction in the thorax can be perceived in a recently slaughtered animal by listening as the liver is removed and the diaphragm pierced, when the inrush of air into the thorax can be distinctly heard. If tubes are inserted into veins in this region, no blood will come out, but air will be drawn in and mix with the blood, sometimes with fatal results, but if the free end of the tube be inserted in liquid, that liquid will be drawn into the blood stream and may be used for carrying in medicinal agents. The operation is called Intravenous Injection.

On the outer surface of the heart is a deep groove separating the auricles from the ventricles, the Coronary Groove. In this groove lie the Coronary Artery and veins that serve the heart muscle. Two or three visible branches of these vessels run down the outer surface of the ventricles towards the apex of the heart. In most animals, the coronary grooves are filled with fat which hide the blood-vessels, but in swine they are clearly visible.

The heart itself is contained in a sac of fibrous tissue, the *Pericardium* (Fig. 50) or ' *Heart Bag* ', attached to the sternum from the second to the fifth rib and to the costal cartilages of the same ribs on the left side.   On the right side a lobe of the right lung lies between the cartilages and the pericardium, hence heart sounds are most clearly heard on the left side. The apex of the pericardium touches the diaphragm and is just opposite the reticulum or second stomach of the ruminant. Hence pieces of wire swallowed by cattle tend to pierce the

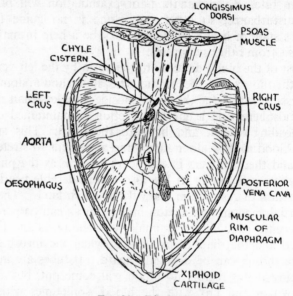

FIG. 31.—Diaphragm.
(After Schmaltz. Anat. de Pferdes.)

reticulum, the diaphragm and finally the pericardium, producing the condition known as ' Pin in the Heart '.   The inside of the pericardium is lined with a serous membrane which is reflected on to the surface of the heart, covering it and the coronary vessels and forming a completely enclosed sac, the *Pericardial Sac*.   The cells of this membrane secrete lymph which lubricates the surfaces and allows the movements of the heart to occur without detectable friction, as do the synovial sacs in joints of bones.   This lymph is continually drawn away by the suction of the veins and is as continually renewed by the cells of the membrane.

The hearts of the different animals can most readily be recognised by the fat in the coronary groove, but the following differences may be noted.

In ruminants there are three visible branches to the coronary vessels, one running down each side and one at approximately the junction of the two ventricles. The aortic semilunar valve is supported by two pieces of cartilage, the OSSA CORDIS, or 'Heart Bones', which can easily be felt if a finger is inserted into the aorta as far as the valve. In oxen over 5 years old these may harden into actual bones, but in young beasts and in sheep and goats of any age, they are cartilaginous. In deer, they are very soft, forming flexible fibrous plates only.

In horses there are only two visible branches to the coronary vessels, one on each side of the ventricles. There are two moderator muscles in the left ventricle as well as the one in the right. There are no heart bones. The whole organ is more conical than that of the ox.

In swine there is very little fat on the heart. There may be two or three visible branches to the coronary vessels, but the central one, if visible, is very small and short. The heart is more spherical than that of the ox. There are no heart bones.

Dogs, cats and rabbits have almost spherical hearts, but the hare has a conical heart. None of these animals have heart bones.

The Arteries (Fig. 32a) all have the following structure:—

(a) An inner tube of endothelium continuous with the endocardium.

(b) A tube of yellow elastic very closely packed fibrous tissue.

(c) A tube of white muscle fibrils arranged as a spiral around the lumen so that, on contraction, the lumen of the tube is reduced.

(d) Another tube of yellow elastic connective tissue similar to (b).

(e) A coat of loose areolar tissue.

The outer coat of areolar tissue is easily torn, and enables the artery to be drawn out of the surrounding tissues with very little effort. The coats of yellow elastic and white muscle fibrils are intimately connected and cannot be easily separated.

In the large arteries near the heart the elastic tissue is thick and strong and will keep the artery open even when empty, while the muscular layer is comparatively thin and weak, but in the smaller arteries the muscular layer predominates and the elastic layers get thinner and finally are extinguished. Such small arteries collapse when empty. In extreme old age, all three layers tend to become cartilaginous, producing a pulseless ' hardened artery '.

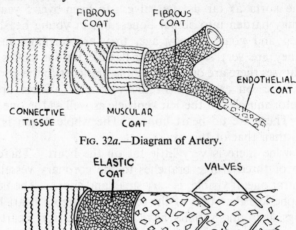

FIG. 32a.—Diagram of Artery.

FIG. 32b.—Vein.
(After Turner's Anatomy.)

On the contraction of the ventricles, blood is forced into the arteries, distending them at their origin. This distension stimulates the white muscle to contract and, as it does so, the blood is forced further along the tube, distending it as it flows. Thus a wave of distension, followed by a wave of contraction, travels along the whole length of the artery, starting immediately after the second heart sound, and causing the ' Pulse '. The pulse is weak in the larger arteries but becomes comparatively stronger as they get smaller and their muscular tissue increases. Most arteries are deeply buried in other tissue, so in the living animal the pulse can only be felt at certain points where they are near the surface. In animals, the most convenient points are under the tail near its root, and under the

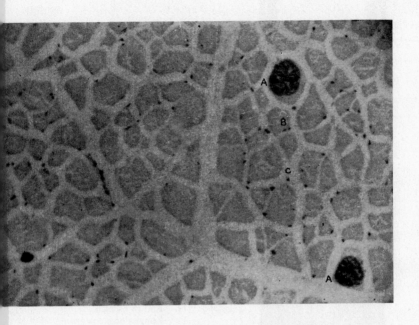

PLATE I.—PHOTOMICROGRAPH OF RED MUSCLE.

Cross-section showing trabeculae of white connective tissue and parenchyma of red muscle cells. The venules are filled with blood, but the arterioles and capillaries are empty, and therefore cannot be seen.

AA.   Venules containing blood cells
B.   Nuclei of red muscle cells
C.   Nuclei of connective tissue

[Facing page 96.

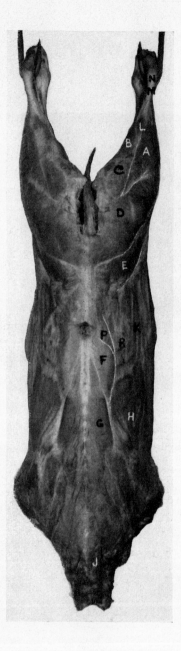

PLATE II.—SUPERFICIAL MUSCLES OF BACK.

(*Veal carcase, female.*)

A. Biceps femoris
B. Semimembranosus
C. Semitendinosus
D. Gluteus
E. Tensor fascia lata
F. Longissimus dorsi
G. Trapezius
H. Latissimus dorsi
J. Splenius
K. External oblique abdominal
L. Gastrocnemius
M. Achilles tendon
N. End of oscalcis
P. Longissimus costarum
R. Serratus dorsalis

PLATE III.—VENTRAL MUSCLES.

(Veal, carcase, female.)

A. Quadriceps or vastus
B. Gracilis
C. Cut surface of gracilis, indicating sex. Note absence of channel and muscles of penis
D. Tendinous sheet extending external oblique muscle
E. Rectus abdominis
F. Transverse abdominal muscle
G. Muscular rim of diaphragm
H. Renal fat, with portions of right kidney visible
I. Renal fat, with portions of left kidney visible, moved to position assumed during life
K. Pectoral muscles, cut
L. Pectoral muscles, tendons
M. Triceps
N. Aorta with psoas muscles on each side
O. Internal intercostal muscles, covered with pleural membrane
P. Patella
R. Olecranon process of ulna
S. Sternum, split

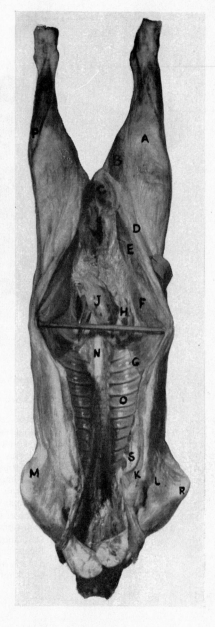

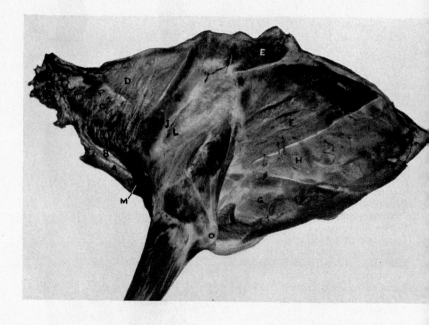

PLATE IV.—SUPERFICIAL MUSCLES OF FOREQUARTER.

(Forequarter of cow carcase.)

A. Sterno-cephalicus
B. Jugular vein in jugular furrow
C. Brachio-cephalicus
D. Splenius
E. Trapezius
F. Latissimus dorsi
G. Pectorals
H. External intercostals
J. Spine of scapula
K. Supraspinatus
L. Infra spinatus
M. Biceps brachii
N. Triceps brachii
O. Olecranon process of ulna

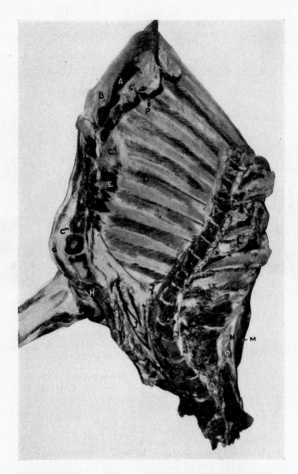

PLATE V.—MEDIAL MUSCLES OF FOREQUARTER.

(*Forequarter of cow carcase.*)

A. Transverse abdominal cut
B. Tendinous sheets extending oblique abdominal muscles, with abdominal fat between
C'. Peritoneal membrane covering sub-peritoneal fat
C''. Pleural membrane covering sub-pleural fat
C'''. Brisket fat
D. Internal intercostal muscles covered with pleural membrane

E. Transverse thoracic muscles covered with pleural membrane
F. Sternum, split
G. Pectorals cut
H. Sterno-cephalic muscle
J. Scalene muscle
L. Multifidus muscle
M. Rhomboid muscle
N. Ligamentum nuchae
O. Complexus
P. Muscular rim of diaphragm

PLATE VI.—FOREQUARTER. DIAPHRAGMATIC END.

(Forequarter of cow carcase.)

- A. Longissimus dorsi muscle
- B. Intertransversalis muscle
- C. Multifidus
- D. Latissimus dorsi muscle
- E. External intercostal muscle
- F. Internal intercostal muscle
- G. Muscular rim of diaphragm
- H. Internal abdominal oblique muscle ⎫ Abdominal fat
- J. External abdominal oblique muscle ⎬ between these
- K. Rectus abdominis
- L. Transverse abdominal muscle
- M. Aorta
- N. Body of vertebra

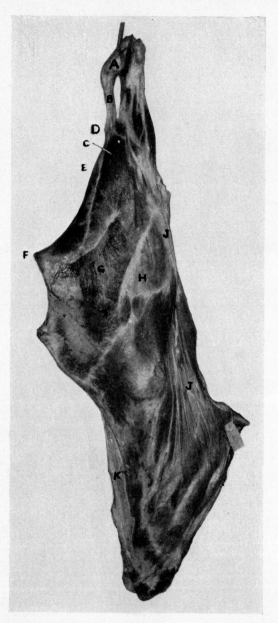

PLATE VIII.—OUTER SIDE OR
SUPERFICIAL MUSCLES OF
HINDQUARTER.

(*Hindquarter of cow carcase. Ve*
aged. Note poor rigor mortis.)

A. Os calcis
B. Achilles tendon
C. Biceps femoris
D. Gastrocnemius
E. Semitendinosus
F. Ischium
G. Gluteus
H. Tensor fascia lata
J. Panniculus
K. Londissimus dorsi

[*Facing page 9*

lower jaw bone. Pulse is entirely automatic and continues in time with the heart beat even when all nerves have been killed, but the sympathetic nerves regulate the extent of the contraction and so control the amount of blood driven through any particular artery.

If a living artery be completely severed the elastic fibrils tend to draw it up into the surrounding tissues, thus reducing the blood flow. On the death of the animal, the arteries empty themselves into the capillary blood-vessels and veins.

The arteries branch throughout the system, becoming smaller as they do so, and gradually losing their elastic coats. When the elastic coats have completely disappeared they are called 'Arterioles'. Arterioles are of microscopic size, but still retain some white muscle fibrils which pulse, and the strength of this pulse is also controlled by the sympathetic nerves; thus regulating the amount of blood passed through them to the needs of the organ they serve. Arterioles discharge into *Capillary Blood Vessels* or *Blood Sinuses*.

Capillary Blood Vessels consist of one layer only of endothelial tissue. Unlike all other blood-vessels, they branch and rejoin each other; whereas arteries and arterioles branch, getting smaller in doing so, but do not rejoin, and veins join together, growing larger in doing so, but do not branch. Thus capillary blood-vessels form networks which run through the capsules and trabeculae of all organs and so nourish the parenchymatous cells and oxygenate them. The endothelial cells of which they are formed are very elastic and capable of considerable distension to allow extra blood to permeate the organ in times of activity. It is believed that the entire blood of the body could be contained in the capillary blood-vessels only if they were all equally distended at once. The walls of the capillary blood-vessels are slightly porous, and a small quantity of the liquid part of the blood, the *Plasma*, can permeate through them into the lymph spaces between the parenchyma cells; but by far the greater part of the plasma continues its course to the *Veins*.

Blood Sinuses are large, clearly visible hollows filled with blood from arterioles. They may be considered as very large capillaries, and the tissues in which they are found are called ' *Cavernous Tissues* '. Cavernous tissue has the appearance of

4

cancellated bone tissue, and occurs in the pads of the feet inside of the hoof (the part corresponding to the ' ball of the finger ' in humans), round the salivary glands, in the udder and elsewhere. *Erectile Cavernous Tissue* is found in the genital organs. In this tissue, the outflow of blood can be stopped by the contraction of a red muscle, so that the blood sinuses become engorged with blood and enlarged. All cavernous tissue eventually empties into veins.

Veins (Fig. 32(*b*)) have the same structure as arteries, except that the muscular coat is missing and the elastic coats are much thinner; thus they have no pulse. They start as vessels of microscopic size, sometimes called *Venules*, and join each other, increasing in size after each junction, to end as veins with a diameter of about 2 inches, the Venae Cavae which empty into the heart. In small veins, the endothelial lining is drawn across the lumen at intervals of 4 to 6 inches, forming valves similar to those of the heart; but as the veins increase in size, the valves are more widely spaced, and the largest veins, the Venae Cavae and the Jugulars, have no valves at all. Generally speaking, the veins follow the same courses as the arteries, but are usually placed nearer the skin and, as the current in them is slower than in the arteries, they have wider diameters.

The pressure of blood in the capillaries is not high, and would not be sufficient to produce an appreciable current in the veins. Smaller veins are emptied by compression caused by alteration in the tension of the muscles around them and, as the valves prevent return flow, they refill from the capillaries. Hence the importance of muscular exercise to maintain a good circulation and good health. Larger veins are emptied by the suction from the heart. The whole circulation, from left ventricle to arteries, from arteries to capillaries, from capillaries to veins, from veins to right auricle, from right auricle to right ventricle, from right ventricle to pulmonary artery, from pulmonary artery to capillaries in the lungs, from lungs to pulmonary veins, from pulmonary veins to left auricle, and from left auricle to left ventricle occupies (in the ox) about 17 seconds.

The main arteries of the body are as follows:—

The Pulmonary Artery rises from the right ventricle and runs forward between the two auricles for an inch or two, then turns upward and divides into two. The two arteries so formed run backwards between the lungs and enter them near the diaphragm beside the bronchial tubes or air passages.

The Aorta, main artery of the body, rises from the left ventricle and passes forward between the auricles, giving off the *Coronary* artery just beside them. The coronary artery runs round the coronary groove and feeds the heart muscle

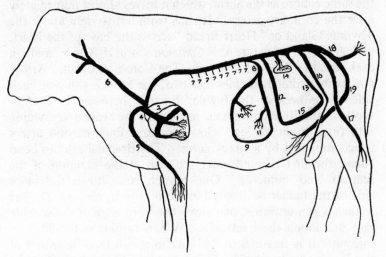

FIG. 33.—Diagram of main arteries.

1. Coronary artery
2. Aorta
3. Ventricle
4. Brachio-cephalic trunk
5. Brachial artery
6. Carotid artery
7. Intercostal arteries
8. Coeliac axis
9. Gastric arch
10. Splenic artery
11. Hepatic artery
12. Anterior mesenteric artery
13. Posterior mesenteric artery
14. Renal artery
15. Mesenteric arch
16. Spermatic artery
17. External iliac artery
18. Internal iliac artery
19. Circumflex iliac artery

by branches visible and invisible. It is peculiar in that it has no muscular coat and so no pulse of its own, the contraction of the heart muscle on which it lies providing sufficient impulse for the blood stream in it. The Aorta then passes forward beside the main pulmonary artery, to which it is attached by a ligament, and passing between its division, turns upward to the vertebral column which it reaches about the second thoracic vertebra. It then runs backward, attached to the lower side of the vertebrae, through the top of the diaphragm, to end at the last lumbar vertebra. At each intervertebral joint, a pair of small branches are given off to feed the skin and muscles in the vicinity. In addition, the following main branches are given off.

The Brachio-Cephalic (Arm-Head) Trunk. This has nearly the same calibre as the aorta, which it leaves almost immediately after the coronary artery. It runs from left to right above the Thymus Gland or ' Heart Bread ' across the base of the heart, giving off, at its centre the *Common Carotid Artery*, and on each side the *Brachial Arteries*. The Common Carotid Artery almost immediately divides into two, one branch going up each side of the neck in the Jugular Furrow, between the Sterno-cephalic and Brachio-cephalic muscles to the head, and dividing into three branches just below the ear. Each carotid artery is accompanied by a vagus nerve. The Brachial arteries bend round the first rib and enter the arm at the junction of the scapula and humerus. One branch runs down the inner side of the humerus, deeply buried in muscle, and two smaller branches run upwards, one along the front edge of the scapula and one along the back edge. When brining a forelimb by injection, it is essential to find and inject all three branches of the Brachial artery. The blood pressure in the Left Brachial Artery is somewhat higher than that in the right, owing to it being nearer the aorta, hence the greater liability of the left shoulder region to develop ' Blood Splash ' from rupture of the capillary vessels if the heart beat be suddenly accelerated.

The Coeliac Artery or **Coeliac Axis** leaves the aorta just behind the diaphragm and sends a branch—the Hepatic Artery—to the liver, and other branches to the stomach (or stomachs of the ruminant) and the spleen. Many of these branches join each other, forming what are called ' Arterial Arches ', so that, should the movements of the stomach compress one branch, blood can still flow round by other routes.

The Anterior Mesenteric and Posterior Mesenteric Arteries leave the aorta in the lumbar region and supply the intestines. They meet each other at the intestines forming an arterial arch.

The Pair of Renal Arteries leave the aorta between the two mesenteric arteries, and flow to the kidneys, right and left.

Each is as big as the arteries of the hind limb, showing that as much blood flows through a kidney as flows through an entire limb.

The Pair of Ovarian Arteries in females and the **Spermatic Arteries** in entire males leave the aorta just behind the Posterior Mesenteric artery. They flow down the lower face of the ilium to the ovaries, or through the inguinal canal to the testicles. In castrates, these arteries atrophy (shrink) and often disappear.

The aorta ends in two pairs of large arteries, the two External and two Internal Iliac arteries.

The External Iliac Artery flows over the lower face of the ilium, passing in front of the pubis and entering the inner side of the thigh. It continues as the *Femoral Artery* down the thigh deeply buried in the adductor muscles, turning round the back of the Femoro-tibial joint (Stifle), and is finally distributed amongst the muscles of the tibia.

The Internal Iliac Artery continues backward on the inner surface of the ilium and ischium and turns round the ischial arch to pass forward as the *circumflex iliac artery* to the penis or udder. Branches of this artery feed the root of the penis or vagina, the anus and the tail, as well as many of the muscles of the hind quarter.

The main veins of the body are as follows (Fig. 34):—

The Pulmonary Veins are seven in number. They are filled by capillary blood-vessels in the lungs and open by separate orifices into the left auricle. In the ox it discharges into the vena azygos.

The Coronary Vein draws blood from the heart muscle. It accompanies the coronary artery and discharges by its own orifice into the right auricle.

The body behind the diaphragm is drained by the **Posterior Vena Cava.** This large vein starts at the last lumbar vertebra and runs forward beside the aorta as far as the diaphragm. It then leaves the backbone and runs down beside the liver, in which it is partly embedded, as far as the centre of the diaphragm. This it penetrates to run forward between the mediastinal and diaphragmatic lobes of the right lung to enter the right auricle just in front of the coronary vein. It is filled by the *Iliac Veins*, the *Ovarian* or *Spermatic Veins*, and the *Renal Veins*, all of which accompany the corresponding arteries.

The Portal System

The Mesenteric Veins from the intestines do not, however, enter the posterior vena cava direct but join each other to form one large *Portal Vein*. This enters the liver and immediately divides up into capillaries which join the capillaries formed by the hepatic artery. Thus the liver has two blood supplies ; oxygenated blood from the hepatic artery, and blood rich in food materials but poor in oxygen from the mesenteric

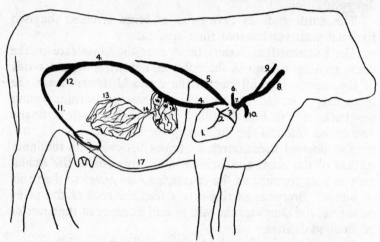

FIG. 34.—Diagram of main veins.

1. Ventricle
2. Coronary veins
3. Auricle
4. Posterior vena cava
5. Vena azygos
6. Thoracic lymph duct
7. Anterior vena cava
8 and 9. Jugular veins
10. Brachial vein
11. Internal iliac vein
12. External iliac vein
13. Mesenteric and splenic veins
14. Portal vein
15. Hepatic capillaries
16. Hepatic veins
17. Milch vein (dairy cows only)

and portal veins.* The liver is drained by several small *Hepatic Veins* which run into the posterior vena cava where it lies partly embedded in that organ.

The diaphragm itself and the walls of the thorax drain into the comparatively small *Vena Azygos*, which runs below the thoracic vertebrae, parallel to the aorta, and discharges into the right auricle slightly below the posterior vena cava.

* In the ox it is common to find a small vein connecting the portal vein with the vena cava, so that not all of the mesenteric blood passes through the liver.

The head, neck and forelimbs are drained by the *Anterior Vena Cava*, a short but capacious vein starting near the junction of the first or second sternebrae, behind and above the thymus gland ('heart bread') and passing below the brachio-cephalic trunk to empty into the right auricle near its lower edge. It has no valves. It is formed by the junction of four jugular veins. The *Brachial Veins*, accompanying the brachial arteries, discharge into it near its origin, their orifices being guarded by valves.

The two **Deep Jugular Veins** run down each side of the neck in the jugular furrow just above the carotid arteries with the vagus nerves running between them and the arteries. They are comparatively small, and missing altogether in the horse.

The two **Superficial Jugular Veins** run below or outside the carotid arteries. They are large and valveless and therefore show a slight 'Jugular Pulse' or throb as the auricle contracts and the blood flow in them and the Vena Cava is checked. If the head is extended, so that the brachio- and sterno-cephalic muscles are relaxed, the flow in the superficial jugular can be stopped by pressure of the thumb in the furrow. The vein will then become engorged and swollen and blood can be drawn from it by lancing it or inserting a hollow needle, a process that causes no pain or discomfort and is the usual method of obtaining blood for examination or experiments. On removing the pressure, the flow is resumed and all bleeding stops.

If a hollow needle be inserted in the superficial jugular, without engorging it, air will be sucked in and will mix with the blood. There is a widespread belief that this is immediately fatal, and that animals can be slaughtered by this method, but actually, though it is an extremely dangerous process in men, most animals can absorb a vast amount of air in this way without ill effects. If the free end of the needle be attached to a tube inserted in a cup of liquid, the liquid will be sucked into the vein and will mix with the blood, and this is the normal method of administering 'intravenous injections' to animals.

The Mammary Gland or Udder in cows, ewes and mares has, at its base, a venous arch which is drained by a branch of the internal iliac vein corresponding to the internal iliac artery. In addition, a small vein, the *Anterior Mammary Vein*, runs under the skin of the abdomen forward to the xiphoid cartilage where it joins a tributary of the Vena Azygos. In milch cows of good dairy breed this vein becomes greatly enlarged and is known as the 'Milk Vein'. The milking capabilities of a cow can be assessed to some extent by its size.

The Thymus Gland or **Sweetbread.** This is a pale yellow lobulated mass, lying on the sternum between the anterior entrance to the thorax and the heart ; while in young, rapidly growing animals it is continued up the jugular furrows, medial to the superficial jugulars, as far as the upper third of the neck. As the animal approaches maturity, the portion in the neck, the 'Throat Bread', disappears. Later the portion in the thorax, the 'Heart Bread', also disappears, being replaced with a fatty deposit, but in oxen the heart bread persists throughout life. The Thymus produces a hormone that regulates the growth of young animals and checks the development of their sex organs until puberty is attained.

The following points can now be considered. If an animal is slaughtered by a transverse cut across the neck, as in the Jewish and Mohammedan methods, both carotid arteries and all four jugulars will be severed. Although the vessels will shrink back into their surrounding tissues, the pressure of blood is so high in the carotids that fairly rapid bleeding will occur and the carcase be well 'bled out'. The blood in the veins will, however, have been contaminated with bacteria, though probably only a few, and some of these will be drawn to the heart and distributed through the meat before bleeding is complete. It is possible therefore that meat from such a carcase may be somewhat earlier in decomposing.

If the animal is slaughtered by a longitudinal cut along the jugular furrow deep enough to split the carotid, bleeding again is complete and rapid, but the same objection applies, that bacteria may enter the system via the opened superficial jugular vein.

If the animal is slaughtered by cutting the skin at the entrance to the thorax, lifting aside the heart bread, and cutting the junction of the carotids, bleeding is very thorough and rapid, and no veins being open, there is no risk of bacteria being swept through the whole carcase. If, however, the knife be driven in too far or too much to one side, blood will be sucked into the thoracic cavity staining the meat on the ribs. This is called 'oversticking', 'back bleeding', or 'rib splash'.

If the animal is hung by the hind legs before being stuck, bleeding is perhaps better in most of the carcase, but the weight of the bowels may obstruct the flow of blood through the mesenteric and portal veins, resulting in the intestines being badly bled. The statement that the posterior vena cava is closed by the weight of the abdominal organs and results in bad bleeding of the whole hind quarter is incorrect, as the vena cava where it crosses the diaphragm is embedded in the liver which will prevent it closing.

If the animal is pithed and the cerebellum or medulla oblongata destroyed before bleeding is complete, the post-mortem movements do not occur, and the small veins in the muscles are not well emptied. If the body is allowed to 'kick itself out' before pithing, the contraction and swelling of the muscles will empty all the veins thoroughly.

Some writers argue that the skull should not be pierced by the stunning instrument, as this also results in veins being opened. It is, however, difficult to ensure complete unconsciousness without piercing the skull, and humane considerations usually outweigh this objection.

The Blood itself is an opaque, dark purple liquid, rather darker if taken from the veins than if taken from the arteries, where it contains more oxygen, but the difference is not great. If kept in a stoppered bottle it retains its colour, but if exposed to air it rapidly becomes bright scarlet, the 'blood-red colour', as it absorbs oxygen. If mixed with fresh water it becomes transparent and looks like red wine. It has a salty taste and a characteristic smell. Soon after leaving the body it 'clots', being converted into a red jelly from which a clear yellow fluid, the *serum*, exudes.

Under the microscope, blood is seen to consist of numerous cells floating in a clear fluid, the *Plasma*. Most of the cells are red, but about one in a thousand is transparent or 'white'. 'Blood counting' is the process of ascertaining the percentages of the red cells and the different kinds of white cells to assist in diagnosing diseases.

Red Blood Cells or Erythrocytes (the latter word is rarely used), constitute about one-third of the volume of the blood, there being about 5 million in a cubic millimetre. They are circular biconcave discs (except in the camel, in which animal they are elliptical, and biconvex), and they have no nuclei. They are produced by the red marrow cells in the bones, but appear to be no longer living when they reach the blood, as they no longer divide or have independent movement or activity. They are swept round by the blood stream, assimilating oxygen where it is abundant, as in the lungs, and giving it up where it is scarce, as in the tissues. This process is purely automatic and does not need living cells to perform it. Note that red cells do not carry carbon dioxide and this gas is dissolved in the plasma.

The cells themselves consist of thin walls enclosing a red liquid protein, *Haemoglobin*, and a fair amount of common salt (sodium chloride), and some water. Haemoglobin has the power of absorbing and yielding certain gases very easily, turning red when full of oxygen and purple when lacking it, but if exposed to carbon monoxide, the poisonous compound in coal gas and motor car exhaust fumes, it absorbs it and will not yield it again so becoming useless as an oxygen carrier.

If fresh water be added to blood, the salt in the red cells draws it in, so causing them to swell up and burst, thereby releasing their haemoglobin and causing the ' port wine ' effect. This is called ' laking the blood '. If strong salt solution be added to blood, water is drawn out of the red blood cells, and they shrivel up but do not release their haemoglobin. Water containing 0·85 per cent. salt has the same proportion as that in the red blood cells and will not alter them at all or affect the blood. Actually solutions between 0·75 per cent. and 1 per cent. have no harmful effect, and are therefore called ' Normal Saline '. Salt water can be rendered drinkable by diluting it with fresh water till ' normal ' percentage is reached. Animals can be kept for short periods in good health on sea water (3 per cent. salt) diluted with twice its quantity of fresh water, a useful matter in those abattoirs and quarantine stations in which fresh water is scarce. Long periods on normal saline may, however, affect digestion.

' **White Cells** ' **or Leucocytes** average about 5,000 per cubic millimetre of blood. They are living cells with nuclei and definite powers of movement of their own and, though normally swept round with the blood stream they can, on occasion, leave the blood-vessels by creeping between the cells that form the vessel walls. They have a flowing or ' amoebic ' method of movement and, if they meet any foreign matter such as invading bacteria or other disease organism, they flow round it and engulf it and finally digest it. Thus they are the police force of the community of cells that form the body ; and are its main protection against invasion and disease. There are five different kinds of leucocytes, but as their functions are all similar, these differences need not concern us.

If the foreign material is too large for the leucocytes to engulf, they will burst themselves in their endeavours to do so. When they burst, they release a substance called ' *Thrombo-plastin* ' and this causes blood and lymph to clot. If blood is drawn from the body, the leucocytes will burst themselves on the side of the vessel in which it is caught as they try to engulf it, or, if it is spilled on the ground, they will burst in endeavouring to engulf the soil and dust. In a bandaged wound, they burst on the fibres of cloth. Dusting a wound with powder will also hasten clotting, as will the application of a strong solution of salt which will shrivel up the cells and draw out of them the thrombo-plastin. In most abattoirs, the blood is stirred round with a switch, which bursts the cells and rapidly causes the clot to collect on the twigs, then the clot can be lifted out, allowed to drain dry, and be dealt with separately from the liquid serum remaining.

It must be realised that thrombo-plastin is the causal agent of the clotting, not the material of the clot itself. Thrombo-plastin is principally supplied by the leucocytes, which form only $\frac{1}{3000}$ of the volume of the blood, whereas the clot is nearly half the volume. Other tissue cells also supply thrombo-plastin, as is shown by the fact that blood from a jagged wound surrounded by quantities of damaged tissue will clot more quickly than blood from a clean cut, but even allowing for this, it is clear that the greater part of the clot must be formed from material dissolved in the blood, and precipitated or drawn out by the action of the thrombo-plastin.

Blood Platelets. These are circular, disc-like cells, about one-third the size of the red blood corpuscles, and numbering about 1 to 200,000 per cubic millimetre. They appear to be developed from the endothelium of the capillaries of the bone marrow and lungs, and when blood is shed they are ruptured like leucocytes and, like them, liberate thrombo-plastin to form the clot.

The liquid part of the blood is called 'Plasma', a clear, slightly yellow liquid identical with lymph, the liquid found round all living cells in the tissues and in the synovial cavities, the serous membranes and the meninges. 'Plasma', in fact, is the name given to lymph when it is in the blood-vessels. Plasma and lymph consists of four substances; 'Serum', a constant liquid similar to plasma in appearance; 'Fibrinogen', 'Prothrombin' and Calcium Compounds. These last three are in solution in the serum and, like most dissolved substances, are invisible in the liquid. If thrombo-plastin be added to this mixture, it causes the calcium to combine with the pro-thrombin forming 'Thrombin', and thrombin, when combined with fibrinogen, forms 'Fibrin', the actual material of a clot. Fibrin is insoluble in serum and so precipitates out in the form of a tangled mass of fine threads in which the red cells are caught up to form the familiar red jelly like mass of clotted blood. The process may be summarised thus:—

Serum + Fibrinogen + Prothrombin + Calcium == Plasma.

Under the influence of Thrombo-plastin from damaged cells

Prothrombin + Calcium = Thrombin,

and Thrombin + Fibrinogen == Fibrin, the actual clot.

[Some authorities hold that there is an additional factor in the plasma, Anti-prothrombin, which prevents the Prothrombin from combining with Calcium, and that the action of thrombo-plastin from the damaged cells is to neutralise the anti-pro-thrombin and allow the prothrombin to combine with calcium. The equations above would then be altered as follows:—

Serum + Fibrinogen + Prothrombin + *Antiprothrombin* +
Calcium == Plasma.

Then thrombo-plastin from damaged cells removes or neutral-ises antiprothrombin, and

Prothrombin + Calcium == Thrombin.

Thrombin + Fibrinogen = Fibrin, the actual clot.

This theory, though widely held, is not universally accepted.]

Various substances are used medicinally for delaying the clotting of blood, but it is unusual to employ them in abattoir practice in this country. In some countries, however, 'anti-coagulates' are added to keep the blood liquid, and so facilitate handling. All these are usually various salts of citric acid, which precipitate calcium and so prevent the formation of thrombin and therefore of fibrin. The practice is to be deprecated, as calcium is an extremely important nutritious element in the blood, and its removal therefore spoils the food value.

The condition known as 'Haemophilia' is an inability to clot the blood, due to a lack of thrombo-plastin in the cells. It is rare in animals but has been recorded in swine, dogs and rabbits.

Serum, the constant, non-clotting part of the plasma and lymph, is the liquid remaining after the clotting materials have settled out. It is about 90 per cent. water, 1 per cent. glucose (a form of sugar), 1 per cent. fat, and 0·88 per cent. sodium chloride (common salt), sodium bicarbonate and other salts. The remainder consists of protein material, which can be roughly divided into albumens which coagulate on heating (as does 'white' of egg), and globulins which remain liquid. Serum taken from the veins or the lymph contains about 47 per cent. carbon dioxide in solution, this solution being assisted by the presence of sodium bicarbonate, in much the same way as this gas will dissolve in 'soda water' forming an effervescent solution. When the blood passes through the lungs, some of this carbon dioxide passes out into the air, so leaving only 44 per cent. in the arterial blood. Thus the serum conveys the carbon dioxide manufactured in the muscles away from them to the lungs. Serum also feeds the muscle cells with glucose and fat, which they convert into glycogen or animal starch. It replaces this glucose from the liver where it is stored, and the fat from the fatty deposits around the body. It also dissolves the used or burnt up protein material from the cells and carries it to the liver, where it is converted into Urea, which is passed out in the urine and sweat.

Serum has another important function, namely the carriage of 'Antibodies', the second line of defence against invading organisms. When a quantity of foreign protein enters the body, the serum both in the plasma and lymph gradually acquires an antibody or substance that will destroy that protein. If, therefore, disease organisms enter the body and are not destroyed by the leucocytes, an antibody that will destroy them is gradually built up in the serum. The process is slow and may take a week or ten days to develop its full strength, but if the animal survives long enough, the invaders will be destroyed and the animal recover. Furthermore, it will retain this antibody and be ' immune ' or incapable of developing that disease again for some time, in some cases for life. ' Vaccines ' are cultures of weak or dead organisms that are injected into a man or animal to cause him to build up antibodies and to become immune. ' Protective serum ' is serum obtained from a recovered animal and injected into men or other animals so that the antibodies therein will protect them immediately if they have already been invaded or are likely to be in the near future. Vaccines take several days to develop the antibodies, but their effect lasts a long time; protective sera give immediate but short-lived protection.

Immune sera are also used to detect substituted meat and to recognise blood stains in criminal cases. Laboratory animals, usually rabbits, are injected with solutions of horse protein, dog protein, human protein or protein from other animals, and they build up antibodies against these proteins. Then, if a pie is suspected to contain, say, dog meat, a small portion is treated with serum obtained from a rabbit immunised against dog proteins and if dog meat be present it will be destroyed by the serum, while if no dog meat is present, the material will be unaffected. Similarly, if a stain on a cloth be suspected of being human blood, it is treated with serum obtained from a rabbit immunised against human proteins; and if the blood be human, the stain will be destroyed, but otherwise will remain unaltered. These tests are of great value, not only in criminal cases, but in many other branches of research.

Human serum shows a phenomenon known as ' Blood Groups '. The serum of people in one group contains an antibody against the red blood cells of people in another group and will destroy them if the two are mixed. It is believed that similar groups occur in horses and probably other animals, but it is not known for certain as yet.

Lymph is the fluid found outside the blood-vessels in all tissues, and it has much the same constitution as plasma, from which it is formed. The endothelial lining of the walls of large blood-vessels and the endothelial walls of capillary blood-vessels are not completely watertight but allow a small quantity of plasma to seep out into the surrounding tissues. This seepage forms the lymph, which permeates all living tissue except the teeth and the epidermis of the skin, and so surrounds the cells with a nutrient fluid. It wanders through the labyrinth formed by the spaces between the cells, and finally finds its way to *Lymph Ducts*. These lymph ducts are thin walled vessels of very fine calibre, but with valves similar to the valves in veins though much more closely spaced. The lymph ducts join each other as do veins, and finally run into one large

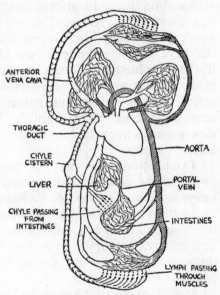

FIG. 35.—Diagram of blood and lymph circulation.

duct (about the thickness of a pencil in the ox), the Thoracic Duct.

The Thoracic Duct runs under the thoracic vertebrae parallel with the aorta from the diaphragm to the second rib. The posterior end of this duct lies in the upper edge of the rim of the diaphragm, and is somewhat enlarged to form the *Chyle Cistern*, which collects all the lymph from the abdomen and hind limbs. The anterior end discharges into the anterior vena cava, whose suction tends to keep it empty, and thus the lymph returns to the blood again and becomes Plasma. Ducts from the chest wall, the lungs, the head and neck, and the forelimbs join the thoracic duct in its course through the chest (Fig. 35).

Lymph circulation is slow compared with blood circulation. A ' subcutaneous injection ' into the lymph spaces beneath the skin, or an ' intra-muscular injection ' into the lymph spaces between muscle cells takes three or four minutes to reach the heart. The actual pressure in the lymph spaces is negligible, and they depend principally on muscular movements in the surrounding tissues to squeeze them out and empty them. If that muscular movement does not occur, the part becomes swollen and ' puffy ' or ' oedematous ', and flesh cut from it will have a pale, wet appearance and lymph will drip out of it when it is hung up. If the heart action is faulty, the suction in the vena cava and thoracic duct will be weak and the whole carcase will be oedematous, particularly the abdomen, which develops ' ascites ' or ' pot-belly '. Fat tends to deposit from slow moving lymph, and to infiltrate the organs, making them soft and greasy.

Lymph from most parts of the body is slow in clotting, owing to the absence of leucocytes; in fact it will not clot unless mixed with blood or damaged tissues, but on its way to the thoracic duct it picks up leucocytes and carries them to the blood stream, thus keeping up the supply in the blood. The organs that supply leucocytes are called Lymph Nodes, formerly Lymph Glands, though they are not in any sense ' glands '.

Lymph Nodes or ' **Kernels** ' (Fig. 36) are organs varying from 1 inch to 4 inches in size (usually), oval or spherical in shape, and pale yellow in colour, with frequently irregular cores of black material stained with melanin. In the pig they are more pink or orange in colour. Each node lies in a thick outer bed of loose fatty tissue, and is surrounded by a capsule of close fibrous tissue from which trabeculae, devoid of capillary blood-vessels, run into the centre. The parenchyma consists of ' islands ' or patches of irregular polygonal cells that can be recognised as young leucocytes. These are mostly joined to the trabecula cells, but occasionally break free. Lymph enters the node by one or two ducts, flows between the islands and leaves it by a single duct, having picked up a few leucocytes in passage. Should any foreign material, such as disease organisms, have entered the lymph stream elsewhere, the young leucocytes will seize it and endeavour to devour it. Thus, the lymph node has two functions: the supply of fresh leucocytes and the filtration of the lymph. The painful swelling in the axilla that follows a 'poisoned' (i.e. infected) wound in the hand, or in the groin following a poisoned foot, is due to the 'inflammation' of the lymph nodes or the fight between the leucocytes and the invaders.

Meat inspectors examine certain of these lymph nodes to enable an estimate to be formed as to how far an infection has spread through a carcase. The positions of some of these have been given with the muscles and the remainder will therefore be given hereafter in describing the organs they guard, and a full list is given in the appendix. It must be emphasised, however, that nothing short of actual detection on a carcase will ever impress their position on the memory or give a true picture of the area each one serves.

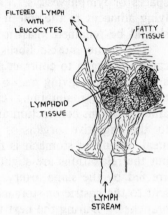

FILTERED LYMPH WITH LEUCOCYTES

FATTY TISSUE

LYMPHOID TISSUE

LYMPH STREAM

Fig. 36.—Microscopic structure of lymph node.

Chyle is the name given to lymph found in the ducts leading from the intestines. It differs from other lymph in being very rich in fat absorbed from the digested material. These ducts lead to the chyle cistern, where the chyle mixes with ordinary lymph from the hind quarters.

Synovia, Pericardial Fluid, and **Cerebro Spinal Fluid** have been dealt with elsewhere. They may all be considered as forms of lymph, and the cavities wherein they are found may be considered as very large lymph spaces.

Lymphoid Tissue. Collections of young leucocytes such as are found in the interstices of the trabeculae of lymph nodes, are termed 'lymphoid tissue'. They are strongly vegetative and, as they mature, they divide and send one half away to join the stream. Lymphoid tissue is not confined to the lymph nodes but is found in other organs, chief of which are the Spleen, the Haemolymph Nodes, and 'Peyers Patches' in the intestine.

The Spleen or Melt (Fig. 41) lies against the stomach, but has no actual connection with it or any of the abdominal organs. It is purple in colour and consists of a firm fibrous capsule from which trabeculae of white fibres and white muscle cells arise. The parenchyma consists of lymphoid tissue, visible as white pin points on cut surfaces, with a labyrinth of cavernous blood spaces between, the two forming a grumous mass commonly called ' Spleen Pulp '. The organ has no lymph spaces or lymph vessels. (The ' gastro-splenic ' lymph nodes lying adjacent to the spleen have no connection with it, and should be renamed ' gastric lymph nodes '.)

The white muscle fibrils in the trabeculae of the spleen cause the organ to contract and relax rhythmically about once a minute, thus giving rise to the ' Splenic Pulse ' which assists the heart in maintaining circulation; and by varying the amount of this contraction and relaxation, the supply of blood to the digestive organs is regulated. Immediately after a meal, when the stomach is full, the contractions are vigorous but the relaxations are slight; and as the stomach and spleen are fed by the same artery, the Coeliac Axis, more blood is sent to the gastric or stomach branches and less to the splenic branches. During the next three or four hours, the intestines fill with food and become congested with blood, and this blood passes by the Portal Vein to the liver. The spleen also discharges its blood into the portal vein, but when this is engorged with blood from the intestines, the splenic blood is dammed back and so the organ enlarges. Thus the spleen is small immediately after a meal, gradually enlarges during the next three or four hours, and then slowly reduces again to its normal size.

The spleen has two other functions. First, it supplies leucocytes to the blood, as the cells in the parenchyma mature, break free and float away in the portal vein. Secondly, it has the power of destroying old worn out red cells and, in doing so, it liberates their haemoglobin into the plasma. Most of this haemoglobin is removed by the liver, but a small trace passes through into the general circulation and this gives the plasma its yellow tint.

The spleens of the different animals can easily be distinguished.

In the ox (Fig. 37) it is oblong with rounded ends. It lies across the front end of the upper surface of the rumen, with its long axis transverse to the length of the body.

In the sheep and goat (Fig. 38) it is more or less circular or 'oyster' shaped. It also lies on the front end of the rumen.

In swine (Fig. 39) it is long and thin like a dog's tongue. It lies on the outer or left side of the stomach towards the posterior edge and may touch the intestines.

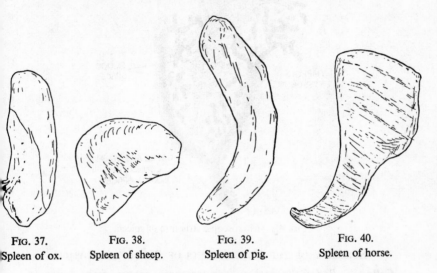

FIG. 37.
Spleen of ox.

FIG. 38.
Spleen of sheep.

FIG. 39.
Spleen of pig.

FIG. 40.
Spleen of horse.

In the horse (Fig. 40), it is curved and broad above, but pointed below, like a broad-bladed scythe. It lies on the outer or left side of the stomach over the back edge, and touches the small intestine.

Haemolymph Nodes are numerous only in ruminants. They are small bodies, each the size of a pea, consisting of an outer capsule, with trabeculae, and cavernous blood spaces and lymphoid tissue as in the spleen. A small arteriole feeds each node and breaks up into capillaries which fill the cavernous blood spaces that communicate with each other and finally empty into a small vein. They have no lymph ducts or lymph spaces. Haemolymph nodes are found chiefly in the back fat and along the aorta, but may occur elsewhere in the body, and are believed to act as accessory spleens. They are entirely absent in humans, horses and pigs, but a few are found in dogs.

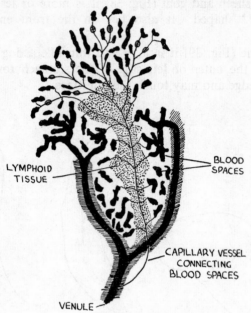

FIG. 41.—Microscopic structure of spleen.

SUMMARY OF THE CONSTITUENTS OF BLOOD AND LYMPH

Cells.   *Red Cells* or *Erythrocytes* carry oxygen from lungs to tissues.

White Cells or *Leucocytes* destroy invaders and when injured give out Thromboplastin, which causes clotting.

Platelets when injured also give out Thromboplastin, which causes clotting.

Plasma.   *Fibrinogen* combines with Thrombin to form Fibrin, the solid portion of a clot.

Prothrombin combines with calcium under the influence of Thromboplastin to form Thrombin.

Calcium Compounds combine with Prothrombin under the influence of Thromboplastin to form Thrombin.

(Anti-prothrombin [doubtful] prevents calcium combining with Prothrombin until neutralised by Thromboplastin.)

Serum carries CO_2 from the tissues.

Contains Water, 89 per cent. approx.

Glucose, 1 per cent. approx., to feed cells.

Fat, 1 per cent. approx., to feed cells.

Destroyed protein material to be made into Urea.

Sodium Chloride 0·85 per cent. to prevent blood cells from 'laking' or bursting.

Sodium Bicarbonate 0·15 per cent. to dissolve CO_2.

Albumen⎱
Globulin⎰ 8 per cent.

Antibodies to destroy invaders.

Plasma with cells as found within the blood-vessels = Blood.

Plasma without cells as found outside the blood-vessels in the tissues = Lymph.

Plasma without cells and without clotting materials = Serum.

CHAPTER VII

THE DIGESTIVE SYSTEM

The Alimentary Canal; the Digestive Processes; the Different Animals.

A. THE ALIMENTARY CANAL

The Digestive Tract or **Alimentary Canal** is a continuous tube running from the mouth to the anus. Certain glands open into this tube, pouring in *Digestive Juices* that modify the composition of the nutritious material in the food and dissolve it so that it can pass through the walls of the intestine and enter the blood and lymph streams. The alimentary canal can be considered as consisting of the following parts (Fig. 42, *a*, *b*, and *c*).

The Mouth is a cavity lined with mucous membrane, which covers the red muscles of the lips, cheeks and tongue. The tongue itself is a mass of red muscle fibres running in all directions so that it can be twisted and pulled to all parts of the mouth to knead the food and clean the cavity. The mucus secreted by the membrane renders the food slippery to enable it to slide down the oesophagus or gullet.

Saliva, the first of the digestive juices, is provided by three pairs of *Salivary Glands*. The *Sublingual Glands* lie under the tongue between the two jaw bones and discharge by 20 or 30 minute openings on the under side of the tongue. The *Sub-maxillary Glands* lie inside each angle of the jaw and discharge into large ducts which open as a pair of orifices on the floor of the mouth beneath the tip of the tongue. The *Parotid Glands* lie behind the jaw beneath the ears and discharge by long ducts opening in the cheeks opposite the third cheek teeth. The salivary tissue has a yellow hue; it is supported by trabeculae dividing it into hemispherical glands about $\frac{1}{2}$ inch in diameter. There are numerous capillary blood-vessels in the trabeculae and some cavernous blood tissue and the whole gland is well impregnated with fat.

The Submaxillary Lymph Node lies against the lower jaw bone close to the angle of the jaw and the *Parotid Lymph Node*

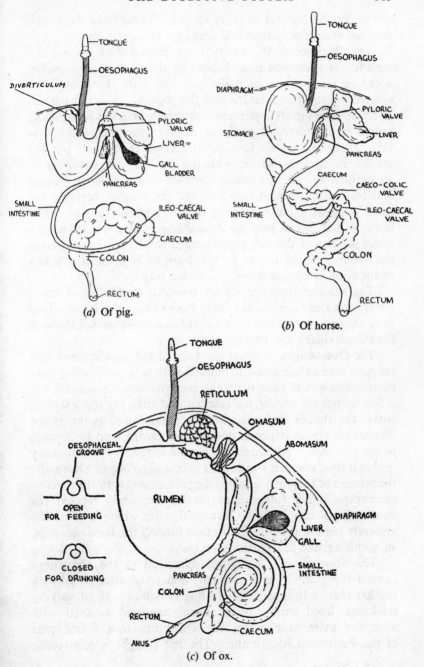

(a) Of pig.

(b) Of horse.

(c) Of ox.

FIG. 42.—Diagram of alimentary canal.

lies under the Parotid Salivary Gland.   These filter the lymph received from the tongue and cheeks.

The Pharynx is the cavity lying immediately behind the mouth.   It is entered from behind by the trachea or windpipe with the oesophagus or gullet just above it.   In front, it is entered by the nasal cavity and the mouth.   A small curtain of red muscle covered with mucous membrane, the *Soft Palate*, separates the pharynx partly or wholly from the mouth, but this can be drawn up to close the nasal cavity and put the mouth in communication with the trachea and oesophagus. In swallowing, the soft palate is drawn up and the oesophagus and trachea are pulled forward, and the tongue, carrying the food, is drawn back, so closing the entry of the trachea.   The food is then forced into the oesophagus.   In some animals, a small process of the soft palate, called the *Uvula*, hangs across the opening of the larynx or windpipe, to give warning if any of the food is ' going down the wrong way '.

The sides of the pharynx are bounded by the hyoid bone. On it rests the *Pharyngeal Lymph Nodes* that filter lymph from the nose and also refilter lymph that has already passed through the submaxillary and parotid nodes.

The Oesophagus or gullet is a tube of red muscle lined with mucous membrane and surrounded with a loose areolar connective tissue.   It runs from the pharynx down the neck, for a few inches on top of the trachea and then on the left side, enters the thorax and passes between the lungs as far as the diaphragm which it penetrates near its centre, and terminates in the stomach.   Although the muscle is red, it is involuntary in that if food enters it swallowing is bound to occur.   Normally the tension of this muscle keeps the tube closed with the mucous membrane lining folded into pleats, but when relaxed for swallowing it can easily be distended, after which it constricts violently behind the distension, thus forcing the food onwards. In vomiting, the movement is reversed.

The Stomach is a U-shaped dilatation of the alimentary canal lying behind the diaphragm under the asternal ribs on the left side.   It consists of a white muscular wall of varying thickness, lined with mucous membrane and covered with a serous membrane called the Omentum that forms part of the Peritoneal Membrane.   The left upright is referred to as the Cardia and into this the oesophagus opens; the central or lowest part of the U is the Fundus, and the right upright, usually shorter than the left, the Pylorus. The cardia is usually wide and the pylorus narrow, so giving the organ a pear-shaped appearance when straightened out. The pylorus is surrounded by a strong ring of muscle called a Sphincter that restricts the passage of material from the stomach to the intestine to a small but regular trickle. In most animals the sphincter protrudes into the intestine forming a ' non-return valve', the *Pyloric Valve*, so that material cannot normally pass backward from the intestine to the stomach. The main duty of the stomach is to store food so that meals can be large and infrequent but the intestine still receives a regular supply; but while the food is so stored, it is kneaded up with the saliva by the movement of the muscular wall and so salivary digestion occurs here. Further digestion, due to Gastric Juice secreted by the mucous membrane, also occurs in the stomach.

The mucous membrane lining shows four different zones.

(1) A zone of pink or white plain mucous membrane continuous with that of the oesophagus.

(2) A zone of grey coloured membrane containing numerous glands that, however, secrete only a slimy fluid similar to saliva but having no effect other than that of moistening the food. This zone is found in the cardia.

(3) A zone of brown coloured membrane containing numerous glands that secrete the active gastric juice. This occupies most of the Fundus.

(4) A zone of grey coloured membrane secreting both mucus and active gastric juice, but the latter in very small quantities. This occupies the pylorus.

It is customary to call zones (2) and (3) the ' Glandular Stomach ' and (1) and (4) the ' Muscular Stomach ', meaning ' muscle only ' part. The food, after leaving the stomach, is referred to as ' Chyme '.

The Small Intestine joins the stomach at its Duodenal end or Duodenum, and the large intestine at its *Ileac* end or *Ileum*, the part between being the *Jejunum* or ' empty ' part since after death it is always empty. These names are for reference only, as there is no clear division between the parts. The whole intestine consists of a tube of white muscle of uniform calibre, covered on its outer side with serous membrane and lined within with mucous membrane. During life it undergoes an almost continual contractile movement, starting from the duodenum and sweeping along to the ileum like the movement of an earthworm. This is the 'Peristaltic Movement'. Peristalsis is caused by the muscle fibres themselves, though its speed and strength is regulated by sympathetic nerves; but if these nerves are cut and the intestine removed from a living or recently killed body, peristalsis will continue for several minutes. Hence, after death, all the chyme is found swept down to the ileum, leaving the jejunum empty.

The mucous membrane lining the intestine has the feel of a thick pile carpet, due to the presence of numerous ' Villi ' or small projections into the lumen of the tube. Each villus contains a capillary blood-vessel and a minute lymph duct called a 'Lacteal'. The lacteals absorb fat from the chyme, thus converting their lymph into chyle. After leaving the villi, they combine to form larger chyle ducts which pass through the adjacent Mesenteric Lymph Nodes and thence to the chyle cistern, but a few lacteals from the duodenum flow into the liver without passing lymph nodes. The capillary blood-vessels are filled from the Mesenteric Arterial Arch and absorb nutrient material other than fat from the chyme. After leaving the villi, they combine to form the Mesenteric Veins, which again combine with the vein from the spleen to form the Portal Vein flowing to the liver (not the posterior vena cava). Thus most of the nutrient material in food is absorbed by the small intestine.

Between the villi are small pits or ' crypts ' in the mucous membrane and some deeper glands, both of which give out the Succus Entericus, the third of the digestive juices. At irregular intervals on the surface of the membrane are oval or circular patches of rough material, free of villi and crypts, called ' Peyer's Patches '. These are masses of minute lymph nodes, whose purpose is not known with certainty. They are commonest in the ileum.

The ileum protrudes through the wall at the side of the large intestine, and is closed with a sphincter, forming the Ileo-caecal Valve, operating in the same manner as the pyloric valve.

The Large Intestine has a structure basically similar to that of the small intestine, namely a white muscular tube covered with serous membrane and lined with mucous membrane, but this mucous membrane is smooth and devoid of villi and crypts though containing a few deep glands and some Peyer's patches. The muscular wall is so thin as to be transparent and show the dark green or brown colour of the intestinal contents, but some thicker ribbons of white muscle run spirally along the whole length, and, by their contractions, wrinkle the whole intestine into bulbous sacculations. The content of the large intestine is called *Faecal Material,* and consists of the undigested material in the food, unused digestive juices, mucous, water and a rich growth of certain ' bile-tolerant ' bacteria that probably play some part in digestion. Peristaltic movements cause this mass to move along the intestine and, during its course, most of the water is absorbed by mucous membrane, leaving a moist but firm matter, the *Faeces* or dung.

The large intestine is divided into two parts, one part in the form of a blind ended tube, the *Caecum* or *Blind Gut,* and the other in the form of a tube opening into the rectum and called the *Colon.* There is no clear line of division between the caecum and the colon but it is usually considered as being on a level with the ileo-caecal valve. Material entering the caecum must be returned to the colon by the same route and its function is therefore not clear. In the human subject, a small gland is found at the blind end, the Vermiform Appendix of the Caecum, colloquially called ' the Appendix ', but this does not occur in any domestic animal (except the rabbit, in which it is very large). Its function is not known with certainty.

The Rectum is a simple tube of white muscle lined with mucous membrane but having a serous coat on its anterior end only. It terminates in a sphincter, the *Anus* or *Bung.* The rectum stores the faeces until a convenient time for de-faecating, but in farm animals it is very short, so that passage of dung cannot be long delayed, and is comparatively frequent. Only in dogs and cats is the rectum long enough for them to become ' house-clean '.

Both the intestines and the anterior end of the rectum are suspended in folds of fibrous tissue heavily impregnated with fat and covered with serous membrane (part of the peritoneal membrane). This is the *Mesentery* (Fig. 43) or *Skirt Fat* or *Crown Fat*. In it lie the *Mesenteric Lymph Nodes*, close to the intestines, and the mesenteric veins, filled by capillaries from the villi and discharging into the portal vein.

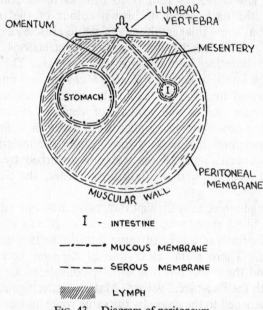

I - INTESTINE

—·—·—· MUCOUS MEMBRANE

— — — SEROUS MEMBRANE

▨▨▨ LYMPH

FIG. 43.—Diagram of peritoneum.

The Peritoneum (Fig. 43) is the cavity covered by the serous membrane lining the internal surfaces of the abdominal muscles, the surfaces of the omentum and mesentery and the surfaces of the stomach, intestines, and parts of the rectum and bladder. It is continuous throughout, and in the male forms a completely closed sac containing lymph that surrounds each separate organ. A reference to the diagram will make its formation clear. In the female, there are two small ducts, the Oviducts or Fallopian Tubes, that open into the peritoneal sac, as will be described in Chapter IX (on the Uro-genital Organs).

The Liver, the largest gland in the body, lies against the right side of the diaphragm and the abdominal floor, stretching nearly as far back as the umbilicus or navel. Buried in its left edge is part of the Posterior Vena Cava. Its abdominal surface is concave, and shows in its centre the large orifice that gives entry to the portal vein, and the smaller hepatic artery close by. A ring of fat round these contains the two or three *Hepatic and Pancreatic Lymph Nodes*. The diaphragmatic surface is convex and attached to the diaphragm by three ligaments. Thus, unlike other abdominal organs, it does not hang free in a peritoneal fold.

The outer surface shows a glistening capsule of fibrous tissue, containing trabeculae that divides the organ into square lobules, with sides of about $\frac{1}{30}$th inch. Numerous capillary blood-vessels run through the trabeculae, fed by both the hepatic artery and portal vein, and discharging into six or seven very short hepatic veins which open direct into the Posterior Vena Cava. The parenchyma consists of square shaped cells, brown in colour, that fill the lobules. From the centre of each lobule arises a minute ' *Bile Duct* ', and these join together to make larger, visible, bile ducts, finally forming three or four large ducts which discharge into the *Gall Bladder*. This is a blind sac of white muscle, lined with mucous membrane, its orifice communicating with both the large bile ducts and the *Hepatic Duct* which discharges into the duodenum close to the pyloric valve.

Bile or **Gall** is dark green in colour, and is responsible for the colour of the faeces. It is used in commerce for making paints and dyes. It is manufactured by the liver parenchyma cells that use amongst other things haemoglobin obtained from the plasma, and so prevents this accumulating when the old red blood cells are destroyed in the spleen. Interference with the functioning of the liver by disease or poisons is often shown by ' Jaundice ' or the development of a yellow tint throughout the whole carcase due to the deepening of the colour of the plasma and lymph as the haemoglobin accumulates in them.

Besides its digestive action, which will be dealt with later, bile is an efficient disinfectant, and kills or checks the growth of most bacteria, all, in fact, except the ' Bile Tolerant ' bacteria that thrive in the large intestine. Hence it is used for detecting if food has been contaminated with faeces. Specimens of the food are placed in test tubes with a suitable medium containing bile or bile salts. If no faeces are present, the medium remains unaltered, but if any faecal contamination has occurred, the bile-tolerant bacteria always present in faeces multiply, and in the course of one or two days render the medium cloudy. This simple test is probably the most useful hygienic safeguard in application to-day.

The liver has many other functions, besides the production of bile, and these will be described later.

The Pancreas, 'Oak Leaf Gland' or **Gut Bread** is an irregularly shaped gland, of creamy yellow colour and somewhat resembling a salivary gland. It lies between the stomach and the duodenum being attached to the latter, and discharges pancreatic juice by one or two ducts which enter the duodenum close to the hepatic duct. This is the last of the digestive juices. Pancreas is sometimes sold as ' Sweetbread ', and sometimes used in sausages, but this latter use is unwise, as the pancreatic juices tend to dissolve the casings and cause them to burst.

B. THE DIGESTIVE PROCESS

Digestion is the process of converting the nutritious material in food into a form which is soluble in blood or lymph, so that it can be conveyed to the different parts of the body for assimilation by the cells. This conversion is carried out by certain agents called *Enzymes* and their action is called *Zymotic Action* or *Zymosis*.

The zymotic process is somewhat obscure. Similar changes can be brought about by chemical action, by adding strong acids or alkalis or by applying heat or electrical currents, but all such chemical actions are accompanied by a distinct alteration in temperature. Zymotic action takes place without any appreciable change in temperature. Further, chemical actions will take place in any temperature, but Zymotic action only occurs in the region of body temperature (90°-105° F.), it is checked temporarily by cold and permanently stopped by heat. The enzymes that cause zymotic action remain unchanged thereby and, though they are dissolved in the digestive juices, they are not absorbed by the wall of the intestines, which selects only the watery part of the digestive juices and the nutritious material dissolved therein. The enzymes are not specific, but if taken from one animal, will act equally well in the gut of another, or in test tubes in laboratories.

The full study of enzymes and zymotic action belongs to the science of Biochemistry. Only a few of the most important are dealt with here.

Digestion of Carbohydrates. *Carbohydrate* is the name given by chemists to compounds which include the *Starches* and *Sugars*, both of which have molecules consisting of approximately equal parts of carbon and oxygen with twice the quantity of hydrogen, but starches have molecules consisting of 80,000 to 100,000 atoms, and are nearly insoluble, while sugars have molecules consisting of twenty to forty atoms only and are very soluble. In the animal body are found Glycogen, or animal starch, and Glucose or animal sugar, the glycogen being the main food required by muscle cells to enable them to move. Most of the food taken by herbivorous animals, ruminants, horses and swine, as well as our own food, is starch in some form or other. It is commonest in grain seeds and tubers such as potatoes, but also occurs in grass, hay or straw. Most of the conversion of starch into sugar occurs in the small intestine, but in human beings and pigs the saliva contains an enzyme called Ptyalin, that is capable of doing so under alkaline conditions. Its effect, however, is small, for the bulk of the food does not remain long enough in the mouth, and when swallowed it is soon acidified by the stomach juices. Probably the main use of ptyalin is to dissolve any particles of starch adhering to the teeth, and the main use of saliva is to moisten and lubricate the food. In cattle and cats, saliva is produced in excess, this excess being utilised for cleaning the coat, by licking.

Sugars are rare in natural foods; in fact they are only found liberally in fruits. They can, to a certain extent, be used to replace starches, but their use is limited by the fact that the digestive juices other than saliva are not produced until the stomach and intestinal walls are distended with solid food. As sugars dissolve almost immediately in saliva they will not produce this distension.

When the starches have been converted into sugars, they dissolve in the chyme and are drunk in or absorbed by the cells forming the walls of the villi in the small intestine. These cells hand them on to the capillary blood-vessels which all flow finally into the liver. In the liver, the sugars are converted back into glycogen or animal starch, and thus form a store of carbohydrate that ensures a constant supply between meals. The glycogen in the liver is converted into glucose or animal sugar at such a rate that the blood always has about 1 per cent. glucose dissolved in it. The muscle cells absorb the glucose from the blood and convert it again into glycogen which is their main source of energy, and the connective tissue cells, especially areolar tissue cells, absorb sugar to convert into fat as a store against possible periods of starvation.

The change of glucose into fat is brought about by removal of oxygen. Glucose, as has been said, consists of equal parts of carbon and oxygen combined with twice the quantity of hydrogen. Fats consist of carbon combined with approximately twice the quantity of hydrogen but only a trace of oxygen. The process of fattening an animal consists, therefore, of feeding it ample starch to make glucose, and restricting its muscular activity so that the muscle cells do not absorb it, so that it can be laid down as fat.

The reverse process of converting fats into glucose and glycogen during periods of starvation is not so simple, and can only be performed by the liver. During starvation, therefore, fat is released from the areolar tissues to the lymph stream, and conveyed to the liver, where it is converted into glycogen. In a badly nourished animal the liver is found to be heavily impregnated with fat awaiting conversion, while the other tissues are free of it. The carnivorous animals that do not eat much starchy food make most of their glycogen by first converting protein into fat, and then sending this fat gradually to the liver for conversion to glycogen.

Digestion of Proteins. Proteins are the substances that actually build up the cells, forming cell walls, nucleus and cytoplasm. An animal's body consists of some thirty or forty different proteins intimately mixed, but in different proportions in the different animals. Plants are also built up of mixtures of various proteins, usually somewhat different from animal proteins. The protein molecules are extremely complex, but consist, for the most part, of carbon, oxygen and hydrogen, to which are joined one or more minerals such as sulphur, phosphorus, calcium and others, the whole molecule being linked together by a group consisting of one part of nitrogen combined with two of hydrogen. This is called the '*Amide*

Group', or more commonly the 'Nitrogen Group', and it is the essential part of the molecule. The value of the protein as food depends on the amount of the nitrogen groups available for digestion. When the nitrogen group is broken off the whole molecule disintegrates and the various components pass into solution and enter the blood stream, to be circulated round the body and seized by any cells that need renewal. Nitrogen groups are rebuilt into new proteins. Surplus carbon and hydrogen are built up into fats, surplus minerals are passed out in the urine, and unused nitrogen groups turn into Uric Acid and similar compounds, as also do the nitrogen groups from worn out protein in exhausted cells. Uric acid and similar compounds pass back to the liver, where they are converted into Urea, which passes out in the urine and sweat.

The value of meat as a food lies in the fact that it consists principally of proteins which fill the system with nitrogen groups and ensure rapid renewal of worn out tissue. Furthermore, the minerals required to complete the protein molecules are much the same in all animals. Herbivorous animals get all their nitrogen requirements from the plants, but frequently their mineral requirements are different from those of the plants, and when this occurs they will suffer from ' Mineral Deficiency'. Wild animals find places where the soil contains the missing minerals and they will visit them periodically to eat large quantities of it. Such places are called ' salt licks ', and are well known to all big game hunters. Modern farmers have their soil and fodder analysed, and provide their stock with blocks of salt containing the necessary elements.

Sodium chloride or common salt is not a mineral that is ever lacking in pasture. Ample for all the needs of the body is present in all herbage, and the craving that livestock show for it is simply a matter of flavour. It is, in fact, only a condiment, improving the taste of the food and so stimulating the flow of saliva.

The actual disintegration of the protein molecule is brought about by several enzymes: Pepsin in the gastric juice, Trypsin in the pancreatic juice, and the remainder in the succus entericus. In sucklings, there is an additional enzyme, Rennin, in the gastric juice that coagulates the protein of milk so that it will distend the intestine and cause the other juices to flow.

5

' *Rennet* ' is an extract from the stomachs of young calves containing rennin and used to make curds for cheese and other purposes.   The other enzymes are not used commercially in food, as they have a bitter taste, but trypsin is used in the preparation of some leathers to dissolve the weaker proteins out of the skins.   The juices of some tropical fruits have the same effect as pepsin but are sweet to taste, and these are sometimes used as ' Tenderizers ' to partially digest tough meat and make it more palatable.

Digestion of Fats.   Most fats are repulsive to the digestive mucous membrane and, if eaten in large quantities with nothing else, cause vomiting and diarrhoea, but when mixed with other foods, a considerable amount can be tolerated.   Hence the practice of taking butter with bread, and lard or suet with flour in the form of pastry.   When so mixed, the fats repel the watery digestive juices and delay the processes of digestion. To a certain extent this is beneficial, as it prevents too early a return of the hunger pangs and gives a sensation of satisfaction after each meal, but if excessive fat be eaten, even when mixed with other food, digestion is delayed too long and absorption cannot be completed.   In addition to this duty of delaying digestion, fat is the solvent or vehicle by which vitamin A in the food is dissolved and carried round the body.   Thus, though fat can be built up in the mammalian body from excess carbohydrate and protein, most mammals require some fat, though not too much, in their diet, and it must be well mixed with other foods.

The repulsion of water by fat is overcome by bile, which breaks up the fat into an *Emulsion* or milky liquid consisting of minute droplets of fat which will mix readily with water.. This property of bile is made use of in some abattoirs, where it is the practice to empty a gall bladder into a bucket of water and use the mixture for cleaning the grease off knives and hands. After emulsification, the digestive juices can mix with the fat and *Lipase*, an enzyme in the pancreatic juice, converts it into soap, which dissolves and is absorbed by the villi.   In the villi, the soapy material is reconverted into fats suitable for the animal and passed to the Lacteals for inclusion in the Chyle, which carries it to the Lymph stream.   After the Lipase has acted, digestion of the carbohydrate and protein can proceed unhampered

Digested fat will produce 2½ times the energy of carbohydrates, and so is a valuable factor in food limited only by one's capability of digesting it. Natural fats are, however, scanty in most vegetable foods, and herbivorous animals therefore build up most of their own fat from carbohydrates. We, in effect, use them as machines to manufacture and accumulate fat for us to eat and, in this respect, the pig is the most efficient of all.

Volatile Fats. These give aroma and flavour to the food, but they evaporate readily and, unlike most fats, will usually dissolve easily in water. Hence food that has been overcooked or stored for a long period tends to lose its flavour. Owing to the readiness with which volatile fats dissolve, they are rapidly assimilated and distributed round the body, so animals that have eaten aromatic food will have their meat, milk and breath tainted for some hours after the meal. The unpopularity of the prolific and hardy goat is largely due to its preference for strongly tainted herbage and the cunning it shows in obtaining it, and hence the frequency with which its meat or milk is tainted.

Diets and Rationing. Of recent years considerable scientific research has been carried out in the economic dietary of men and animals. While the subject is rather outside the scope of this work, an explanation of the following terms may be useful.

A Balanced Diet is one in which the protein, fat and carbohydrate are mixed in the proportions found most suitable for a particular species of animal.

A Maintenance Ration is one that will keep an animal alive without loss or gain of weight, when it is not working, giving milk or pregnant.

The Nitrogenous Ratio, sometimes called the *Albuminoid Ratio*, is the proportion of the proteins to the sum of the carbohydrates, the fats multiplied by 2·5, and the indigestible matter or roughage. The multiplication of the fats by 2·5 is to allow for the fact that they provide 2½ times the energy that carbohydrates do. The N.R. should lie between 1 : 4 and 1 : 8, according to the species, age and use of the animal. It is really the factor by which the body building power of the diet is judged.

The Calorific Value is the value obtained when a sample of the food is burnt in oxygen. The heat given off is measured in units called *Calories*, and the result provides an estimate of the energy value of the diet or its power of producing muscular work.

The Carbohydrate Equivalent. The protein content is multiplied by 1·9 and the fats by 2·5 and the carbohydrates are added to the sum. The result provides an estimate of the fattening power of the food.

For accurate dieting, a number of corrective factors must be applied in each case. The science of *Dietetics* is concerned with the discovery of these factors and their application to different foodstuffs.

Accessory Food Factors. In some animals (not cattle or horses) symptoms of deficiency diseases appear when well-balanced diets of protein fat and carbohydrate alone are fed. It has been found that for these animals certain additional factors must also be present. They are called *Vitamins* or vital bodies from a mistaken idea that the food must contain some living material to be fully nutritious. It is now known, however, that these factors are not living, and in fact the chemical composition of many of them is known. Most of them are manufactured by plants, and, if the diet contains sufficient vegetables, no vitamin shortage occurs, but humans, birds and rats kept without vegetable food for a long period show symptoms of deficiency.

The most important vitamins are these:—

Vitamin A. Necessary for growth in young animals for building up antibodies for resisting disease and for preventing ' brittle bone ' (osteomalacia) in adults. Lack of it also produces eye trouble. Abundant in green vegetables and red coloured ones (carrots and tomatoes), also in meat and milk. Can only be absorbed if dissolved in fat.

Vitamin B. Lack of this causes a nervous condition called *Beri-beri* (Polyneuritis). Abundant in the germ and bran of grains and in meat and also green vegetables.

Vitamin C. Necessary for cell division. As the epithelial cells of the skin and mucous membranes must be constantly dividing, lack of vitamin results in death of the epidermis and raw exposed areas of dermis or submucosa. This condition is called *Scurvy*. The vitamin is present in all green vegetables and is abundant in citrus fruits, oranges, lemons and grape fruit. There is none in meat.

Vitamin D. Necessary for good bone growth, and its absence causes *Rickets* in young animals. This vitamin is abundant in cod-liver, halibut-liver and salmon-liver oils, but there is good evidence that it can be produced in the mammalian body by the action of sunlight on the skin.

Many other vitamins, of less importance, are believed to exist.

Indigestible Matter or Roughage. It is essential for food to contain a certain amount of indigestible matter to keep the intestines distended to maintain their activity. This material must be absorbent, so as to take up the used digestive juices and remove them from the system, and must provide a good bed for the growth of bacteria in the large intestine. If it is lacking, constipation and serious disturbance of the system occurs. In herbivora, the roughage consists principally of minute fibrils of wood, present in all green vegetables. In carnivora, it consists principally of the indigestible yellow fibrous tissue in the meat.

Water. The demands of the body for water are considerable, as each breath exhaled carries a considerable amount of water vapour, the kidneys and the sweat glands are continually excreting water, and the enzymes of digestion are all dissolved in water. Most of the watery parts of the digestive juices are, however, re-absorbed, the food eaten usually contains a considerable amount of moisture, and finally the decomposition of carbohydrate in the muscles results in carbon dioxide and water. The amount extra required for drinking is therefore very slight, but it is an absolute essential to life, let alone health. It is, of course, impossible to lay down any rule as to the amount of drinking water required by any animal, as need varies with the state of the atmosphere, the nature of the food, and the amount of work being done, so the best rule is to ensure free access to water at all times. If rationing of water must be resorted to, horses and cattle are taken to require 6 gallons a day per head. Females in milk require 4 gallons extra water for each gallon of milk produced. Sheep and swine should be allowed at least 2 gallons per head. Hard water containing calcium salts in solution has a better flavour than soft or ' acid ' water and is considered better for livestock, but it is doubtful if any water really contains sufficient minerals to make any appreciable difference to the animal that drinks it. The only real essential is an ample supply.

All water drunk flows directly to the colon from which it is absorbed into the blood stream.

The Hormones of Digestion. It has been shown that the digestive juices will not flow until the intestine has been distended, and this holds true for the juices of the pancreas and liver, two organs that have no visible connection with the intestinal contents. When, however, the intestine is distended these two organs are stimulated to act by means of *Hormones*.

A Hormone (= ' messenger ') is a substance in the blood stream that stimulates the action of organs other than that in which it is produced. On being distended, the walls of the small intestine not only produce the succus entericus to digest the food, but also produce a hormone, *Secretin*, which enters the blood stream. Secretin travels round the circulation having no effect anywhere except on the pancreas, which it stimulates. Blood taken from a recently fed animal and injected into the veins of a fasting animal, not necessarily of the same species, will stimulate the pancreas in the same way, due to the secretin in the injected blood.

When the pancreas is stimulated by secretin, but not before, it produces another hormone, *Insulin*, which circulates in the blood in the same way as secretin, but has no effect anywhere except on the liver. When the liver is stimulated by insulin, but not before, it converts sugar into glycogen or, if sugar be lacking in the meal, it converts fat. Thus, to ensure that the liver is kept well stored with glycogen, insulin must be provided by the pancreas, and insulin is only provided when the pancreas is stimulated by secretin, and for secretin to be supplied the food must be capable of distending the small intestine.

It has been mentioned previously that a starving animal accumulates fat in its liver. This fat cannot be converted into glycogen, as the intestines are not distended and so no secretin is produced, hence the pancreas does not produce insulin, and the liver cannot use the fat provided to it. Thus a very fat liver is evidence of starvation. In the disease Diabetes Mellitus, the pancreas is unable to produce insulin, even when secretin is present, and the patient is therefore unable to store sugar in the liver, and so passes it out in his urine. This can be remedied, to some extent, by giving injections of insulin made from ox pancreas obtained in the abattoirs.

There are many other hormones in the body, some of which will be mentioned later. Secretin and insulin are the only two connected with digestion.

SUMMARIES

I. THE DIGESTIVE PROCESSES

The Mouth supplies *Saliva* which, in pigs, contains the enzyme Ptyalin.

Ptyalin converts starch into sugar.

The Stomach supplies *Gastric Juice*, which contains the enzymes Rennin and Pepsin.

Rennin (in sucklings only) coagulates milk.

Pepsin starts the digestion of proteins.

The Liver supplies *Bile*, which emulsifies fat and kills unwanted bacteria.

The Pancreas supplies *Pancreatic Juice*, which contains the enzymes Lipase and Trypsin.

Lipase converts emulsified fats into soaps.

Trypsin continues the digestion of proteins.

The Small Intestine supplies *Succus Entericus*, which contains several enzymes that complete the digestion of protein, setting free the nitrogen groups and the minerals.

The Small Intestine also provides the hormone *Secretin*, which causes the pancreas to provide the hormone *Insulin*, which causes the liver to convert and store sugars (and fats if sugar is lacking) as glycogen,

II. Assimilation and Excretion

The Carbohydrate Cycle.   Sugars are absorbed by the Villi of the small intestine and enter their capillary blood-vessels which lead to the Mesenteric Veins, which lead to the Portal Vein, which enters the Liver.   In the liver they are converted into Glycogen (animal starch).   The glycogen is converted into glucose (blood sugar) at such a rate that the quantity in the blood is always maintained at the same level.   Glucose is drawn from the blood by the muscles and converted by them into glycogen which they use as fuel.   Glycogen, when oxidised, yields water and carbon dioxide, which is excreted by the lungs.   Glucose is also drawn from the blood by areolar tissue which converts it into fat.

Protein Cycle.   The nitrogen groups and minerals are circulated in the blood and seized by cells in need of repair or extra material, and are built up by them into new proteins. As these proteins wear out, they yield uric acid and similar compounds of nitrogen.   These return to the liver, where they are converted into Urea, which is excreted by the kidneys.

Fat Cycle.   The soaps are absorbed by the Lacteals, or minute lymph ducts in the villi, being reconverted into fats in the process.   These fats are conveyed by the lymph stream to the large fat deposits and other areolar connective tissue, where they are stored till needed.   Additional fats are provided by unused glucose and unused atoms of carbon and hydrogen in the protein molecules.   When carbohydrates are lacking in the diet, fat is removed from the deposits to the liver, and is there converted into glycogen.   Excess fat in the food cannot be digested and is passed out with the faeces.

Water.   Water in the intestines, whether it enters with the digestive juices, or is produced during the processes of digestion, or is taken in by drinking, is absorbed by the Colon.   Only sufficient remains with the faecal material to keep it soft.

III. The Liver

The numerous functions of the liver have been dealt with separately above, but it will be as well to summarise them here. The liver

(i) Removes haemoglobin from the plasma.

(ii) Manufactures bile (of which haemoglobin is a constituent).

(iii) Stores carbohydrate in the form of glycogen.

(iv) Converts fat into glycogen when other supplies of carbohydrate are short.

(v) Converts uric acid and similar compounds into urea.

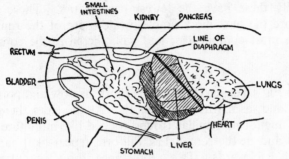

FIG. 44a.—Right aspect of pig.

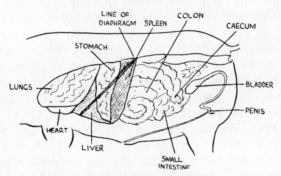

FIG. 44b.—Left aspect of pig.

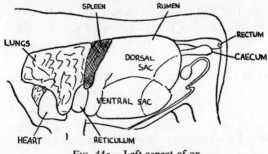

FIG. 44c.—Left aspect of ox.

It is easy to see, therefore, its importance in the maintenance of health.   The ancients, who considered the liver as the centre of one's being, were probably nearer the truth than the moderns who give the heart this place.

DIGESTION IN DIFFERENT ANIMALS

It is convenient to consider first the organs of the pig, as generally these have the fewest peculiarities.   Those of the horse are the next most simple, while those of the ruminants are the most complicated, and will, therefore, be considered last.

TONGUES

The Pig's Tongue (Fig. 45a) is short, narrow and pointed at the tip and, as a whole, is smooth.   At the sides there are a few 'Fungiform' papillae (round topped like miniature mushrooms) and at the root a few Piliform (spear-like) papillae * pointed backwards.   Two, sometimes three, circular, flat-topped papillae occur just in front of the piliform ones, these are the 'Vallate' or 'Circumvallate' papillae (walled round papillae) or Taste Buds by which strong flavours are appreciated.   Delicate flavours are recognised by the aromas which impinge on the mucous membrane at the back of the nose.

The Horse's Tongue (Fig. 45b) is long and round ended or 'spatulate'.   It is smooth and devoid of papillae except for two vallate papillae near the root.

The Ox's Tongue (Fig. 45c) is short, broad and pointed. Its upper or dorsal surface is covered with short piliform papillae directed backward that give the surface a rough feel. The edges have very large piliform papillae, 1 to 2 inches in length, that interlock with similar papillae inside the cheek. The back part of the upper or dorsal surface is raised to form a large 'Prominence of the Dorsum of the Tongue', usually called the 'Dorsum' only.   Its surface shows some thirty odd vallate papillae.

Sheep and Goat's Tongues are similar to that of the ox, but the piliform papillae near the tip are short and blunt, giving a

---

* Pilum = a spear.   These papillae are often erroneously described as 'Filiform' which means 'thread-like' or long thin and very flexible and is manifestly absurd when applied to short thick and strong objects with pointed tips.

smoother feel. The prominence of the dorsum is relatively smaller.

Deer have comparatively smooth tongues, with very short papillae and very small dorsal prominences.

STOMACHS

The Pig's Stomach is large, and occupies most of the region under the left asternal ribs and from there stretches right across the floor of the abdomen. The oesophagus enters near the middle of the organ, and at the left extremity is a small *Diverticulum* or blind sac (the ' cat's bladder '). A small area round

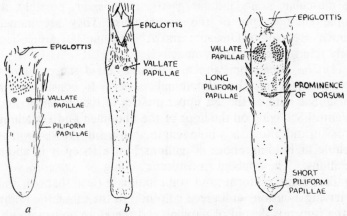

FIG. 45.—Tongues of (*a*) pig; (*b*) horse ; (*c*) ox.

the oesophageal orifice is purely muscular and is lined with plain mucous membrane, and this is marked off by a clear line from the rest of the organ, which is all glandular. In this glandular portion the three zones are quite distinct: the left half, or cardiac region, has a thin wall and grey-coloured mucous membrane containing numerous glands which, however, only secrete mucus; the fundus or central region has a wall three times as thick as that of the cardiac region, with mucous membrane of a mottled brown colour in which are numerous glands that secrete most of the juice containing acid and pepsin; and the pyloric region, somewhat thinner and greyer than the fundus. Pyloric glands secrete copious mucus but only a little active juice. A thick muscular projection lies across the pyloric valve, but its function is not known.

The Horse's Stomach is relatively small, hence horses eat little but often. The oesophagus forms a valve at the entry to the stomach, making it impossible for the horse to vomit or belch, and so the animal is very susceptible to digestive disorders. About half the stomach is purely muscular and is lined with plain white mucous membrane with a clear line of demarcation between it and the glandular half. In the glandular half three zones can be distinguished as in the pig, but they are not so clearly delineated.

The Ruminant's Stomach consists of four compartments, the first three of which may be considered as developments of the muscular, non-glandular gastric regions, or, possibly, as simple enlargements of the oesophagus. They are named Rumen, Reticulum, Omasum and Abomasum, but are collectively referred to as ' the stomachs '.

(1) *The Rumen* or Paunch is a large, blind sac occupying three-quarters of the abdominal cavity. It consists of a Dorsal Sac lying in the left upper quarter of the abdomen, and a Ventral Sac lying on the floor of the abdomen and stretching across it and along its whole length. In a full-grown ox it is capable of holding about 40 gallons,* in a sheep it is about 5 gallons. The mucous membrane lining is covered with papillae, some piliform, and some palmate (leaf shaped), but all having a curious dull green colour. In the camel the lining of the rumen is devoid of papillae and therefore quite smooth.

(2) *The Recticulum* or Honeycomb, is the smallest compartment, and holds about 2 gallons in the ox and 2 pints in a sheep. It lies in front of the rumen but on a lower level, so that it rests on the xiphoid cartilage of the sternum against the diaphragm opposite the pericardium. The mucous membrane lining is arranged in folds dividing the inner surface into hexagonal cellules, which are normally filled with fluid resembling saliva. The rumen and reticulum communicate with each other by a large orifice into which the oesophagus opens.

A deep groove bordered by flexible lips passes from the opening of the oesophagus across the reticulum to the third compartment or omasum. This is the ' Oesophageal Groove ' and, when the animal drinks anything but plain water the lips close, forming a tube continuous with the oesophagus. This carries the fluid direct to the omasum, so that the contents of

* After the organ has been removed from the carcase and the tissue distended to its fullest extent. In the living animal it is about half this volume.

the rumen are not affected by it. It is impossible to give a liquid medicine to take effect in the rumen unless something is given first to paralyse the lips of the oesophageal groove.

In the camel there are two additional reticula or 'water bags' at the front end of the rumen. In all three the cellules are deep and their openings can be closed by sphincter muscles preventing the escape of the saliva-like fluid. This mechanism was probably evolved to enable the animal to store fluid and so to keep the contents of the rumen and reticula moist during long absences from drinking water, but the story that during desert journeys camels can be killed and the contents of their stomachs drunk by humans is manifestly absurd.

(3) *The Omasum* or Manyplies, Book or Bible, is about twice the size of the reticulum, and lies somewhat above it and to the right. It is filled with about 100 folds of white muscle covered with a horny membrane studded with hard papillae. These folds run longitudinally to the reticulo-abomasal line. Both the entry from the reticulum and the exit to the abomasum are small.

In the camel, the abomasal leaves are quite smooth and devoid of papillae.

(4) *The Abomasum* or Reed corresponds to the glandular part of the stomach of other animals. It lies round the lower and posterior surfaces of the omasum, but is relatively small, having a diameter somewhat less than that of the reticulum. It has the same structure as the glandular part of the stomach of a non-ruminant animal.

A new-born calf or lamb (Fig. 47) has a rumen no bigger than its reticulum. The 'honeycomb' of the reticulum is only just visible, and the 'leaves' of the omasum are minute, barely visible ridges only. All three organs, however, develop rapidly in the course of the first month after weaning.

Rumination or 'Cudding' (Plate Xa). The grass, bush or scrub that form the natural diet of the various species of ruminant contain plenty of carbohydrate, but very little in the form of starch or sugar, the only carbohydrate that can be digested by mammals, and the fat content is negligible. When, however, these contents are well moistened and kept warm, they provide a medium on which bacteria can thrive, converting the indigestible carbohydrates into starch in the bacterial bodies. These conditions of moisture and warmth exist in the rumen, and in this organ there is therefore a rich growth of starchy bacteria. Feeding on these bacteria are numerous microscopical animals resembling leucocytes, but rather larger, each consisting of one cell only, and these convert some of the bacterial starch into fat. Thus, in effect, the bacteria and animalculae convert the straw into starch and fat, which the ox converts into meat. The rumen is never completely emptied, even after periods of prolonged starvation, and the residue of food left in it serves to re-infect the fresh food at the next meal. The bacteria can also build up most of the vitamins, hence cattle never suffer from vitamin shortage.

At each meal the rumen is filled, if possible, to about three-quarter capacity, seldom more, feeding being rapid and accompanied by the minimum of chewing needed to render swallowing possible. Then, during rumination, the rumen contracts rhythmically, kneading the mass of food together and mixing it thoroughly with saliva and the residue of the last meal. As the bacteria decompose or ' ferment ' the grass, they generate a large quantity of a gas called ' Methane ', and when this has accumulated sufficiently, the animal ' belches ' or draws it up into the mouth and expels it through the nose. A small quantity of saliva and grass is drawn up with the gas, but the saliva is expelled by pressure and immediately re-swallowed. The compressed grass or ' cud ' is chewed for about a minute and is then swallowed again, together with a quantity of fresh saliva that has been secreted during the chewing. Thus the contents of the rumen are gradually reduced to a fine chaff floating in a large volume of saliva. Note that the belch of rumination is brought about by suction in the oesophagus and mouth and thus differs from vomiting which is due to pressure on the stomach by the abdominal muscles. Rumination continues throughout the whole 24 hours, even during sleep, but naturally becomes less frequent as the rumen empties. If it is interrupted from any cause, the rumen becomes distended with gas and presses on the diaphragm so interfering with breathing. This condition, known as ' Bloat ' or ' Hoven ', is rapidly fatal unless dealt with promptly; but it can be remedied by driving a long knife into the left flank about 1 foot below the lumbar transverse processes, so that it pierces the rumen and allows the gas to escape.

The reticulum is kept full by the 'kneading movements' or contractions of the rumen which periodically force some of the rumenal contents through the wide rumeno-reticular orifice. The contractions of the reticulum take the form of lifting movements which result in most of the material being returned to the rumen, but each time some of the liquid and the smaller particles pass through the very narrow orifice of the omasum. Thus both rumen and reticulum are gradually

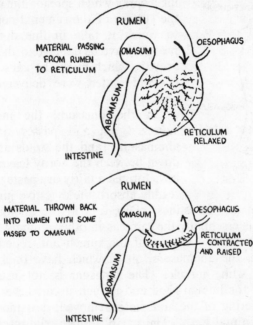

FIG. 46.—Movements of reticulum during rumination.

emptied. Heavy objects, however, such as whole grains, tend to sink to the bottom of the reticulum and remain there until they are dissolved; hence good farmers always crush or 'kibble' grain before feeding it to cattle. Occasionally strange objects such as pebbles, iron bolts and the like, are found in the reticulum, and there is often evidence that they have been there for years. Sharp objects, such as nails, will pierce the wall of the reticulum and the diaphragm against which it lies, and then, entering the pericardium and heart, will kill the animal.

The action of the oesophageal groove has only recently been discovered, by means of cine-cameras inserted into the rumens of living oxen. A suckling closes the groove completely when drinking, thus forming a continuous tube from the oesophagus to the omasum, so preventing the milk from entering the rumen, where bacteria might damage it. A weaned animal when drinking water only partially closes the groove, so forming a spray which spreads the water over the surface of the rumenal contents, on to which it falls in fine drops. This probably avoids damage to the bacterial growth, which might be caused if a jet of cold water were delivered in one place.

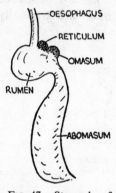

FIG. 47.—Stomachs of new-born calf.

In the omasum, the moisture is squeezed out and passes on to the abomasum; and the solids are ground down between the horny leaves till they have formed a fairly dry paste which will readily absorb the digestive juices in the abomasum and intestines. Digestion in the abomasum and intestines is essentially the same as in other animals.

' Edible Offals ' consist of the rumen and reticulum and, sometimes, the abomasum, all of which have thick walls of nutritious white muscle. The omasum is not usually considered fit for human food and though it can be eaten if the horny covering of the laminae is removed, it is more usually used for animal feed. The partly fermented contents of the rumen are usually used as a fertiliser for soil, but actually can be fed to pigs or poultry, who thrive on the micro-organic growth therein.

THE INTESTINES

The Pig. The small intestine, about 60 feet in length, lies for the most part on the right side of the abdominal floor in a series of intricate folds. The Colon, about 12 feet long, lies above it in a double spiral coil, conical in shape, with the apex pointing towards the centre of the right flank. The Caecum hangs over to the right side behind the colon, and is about a foot in length. Both colon and caecum have large diameters and are distinctly bulbous, and contain a rich bacterial growth. It is not known for certain if these bacteria play any useful part in digestion, but it is probable that they do. The mesenteric lymph nodes are found most easily in the folds of mesentery between the coils of the colon.

The Horse. The small intestine (70 feet in length) and the colon (25 feet) are convoluted together, but can be distinguished by the bulbous appearance of the latter. The caecum is very large and stretches from near the pubis to the xiphoid cartilage, thus occupying most of the abdominal floor. It is separated from the colon by a distinct constriction round a very small orifice. The caecum in life contains a large quantity of gas, and it is believed that a bacterial fermentation similar to that of the cow's rumen occurs in it, but this still awaits confirmation. Both horse and ass can maintain life on grass alone, but not on the bush and scrub that will support cattle, goats and sheep. The assumption is therefore that they depend, to some extent, on a bacterial ferment, but that this is not so efficient as in the ruminant.

The Ruminants (Plate XV). The entire intestine is about twenty times the length of the body. The small intestine lies coiled below the right edge of the ventral sac of the rumen. The large intestine, about one-quarter the length of the small intestine, and not much larger in calibre, occupies most of the space between the right side of the dorsal sac and the upper surface of the ventral sac of the rumen. It is devoid of sacculations, as its white muscle is evenly divided round the whole tube, but can be distinguished from the small intestine by its thin wall, through which the faecal material can be seen. The caecum is directed backwards, and the colon arranged in a flat spiral coil. The Mesenteric Lymph nodes lie in the mesentery, forming a semicircle about 1 inch away from the small intestine.

The intestines are generally used for casings, but the colons of sheep, and occasionally oxen, are split into threads and dried to make 'Catgut'. The caecum of the ox is split and dried and forms 'Gold-beaters Skin', on which thin sheets of gold are laid to be rolled off on to baser metals as a kind of plating.

LIVERS

The Pig. The liver is extremely coarse and hard compared with other animals, owing to the thickness of the trabeculae. It has a mottled appearance, as each lobule is distinctly shown, but the general colour may vary from a deep brown, almost black, hue to a pale pink, according to the amount of fatty infiltration. It is divided by three deep fissures into four distinct lobes of approximately equal size, the right outer lobe having a small additional lobe, the Caudate Lobe. The Posterior Vena Cava is entirely embedded in the liver substance.

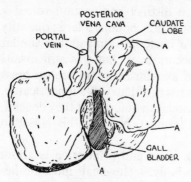

FIG. 48a.—Liver of pig.

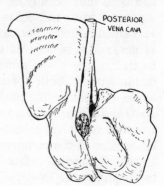

FIG. 48b.—Liver of horse.

(The human liver has a large right lobe and a smaller left lobe, with three other very small lobes. It is uniform in colour, the trabeculae being very thin.)

The Horse. The liver is somewhat soft, and has a uniform colour of a somewhat reddish hue, as the trabeculae are thin and cannot be seen with the naked eye. It is divided into three main lobes with a small caudate lobe attached to the right lobe. There is no gall bladder, though the bile ducts are large and store the bile to some extent but, as the horse feeds little and often, there is not much need for great accumulations of bile.

The Ox. The liver is practically in one lobe and lies on the right side of the abdomen against the diaphragm but extends along the abdominal floor for some distance. There is one small notch too small to be called a fissure at its lowest extremity called the Umbilical Notch. A fairly large square shaped caudate lobe or ‘Thumb Piece’ is attached to the right upper corner. The Posterior Vena Cava runs down the left or medial edge, but is only half embedded in the liver tissue. There is a large gall bladder.

In the calf, the liver is thicker, as the pressure of the omasum has not flattened it out. It is also redder in hue than in the adult. In a new-born calf, there is a small vein, the Ductus Venosus, leading from the entry of the portal vein direct to the Posterior Vena Cava, thus not all of the blood from the intestines enters the liver. The amount, however, that is by-passed through the ‘Ductus Venosus’ is very small, and it closes and shrivels up soon after birth.

The Sheep, Goat, and Deer. The liver resembles that of the ox, except that the umbilical notch is deeper and might be considered a fissure. The caudate lobe is triangular, or shaped like a three-sided

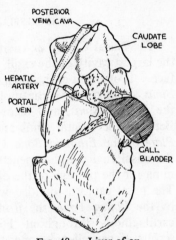

FIG. 48c.—Liver of ox.

pyramid. In these animals, the pancreatic and hepatic ducts unite and enter the duodenum at its origin.

Deer have no gall bladder.

The Camel. The liver consists of two lobes only, and has no gall bladder. The bile duct and pancreatic duct unite as in the sheep.

The Dog’s Liver has three large lobes and two small ones; five in all.

The Cat’s Liver has two large lobes, two about half their size, and three very small lobes, seven in all.

The Rabbit’s Liver has three large lobes and two smaller ones, five in all.

CHAPTER VIII

THE RESPIRATORY SYSTEM

The Respiratory tract; the Respiratory Process; Ventilation;
the Different Animals.

THE RESPIRATORY ORGANS

The Nasal Cavity or cavity inside the nose is, in animals,
the largest cavity of the skull, and forms the greater part of the
face. It opens at each side into a smaller cavity, the *Maxillary
Sinus* situated above the molar teeth, above and behind into
the *Frontal Sinus*, and below and behind into the Pharynx.
Between the frontal sinus and the pharynx is the *Cribriform
Plate* of the *Ethmoid Bone* which separates the cranium from
the nasal cavity and is penetrated with numerous small foramina for the passage of the olfactory nerves that detect scents.
The nasal cavity is divided wholly or partly into two nostrils
by the *Vomer Bone*, the front end of which usually remains
cartilaginous throughout life. Each nostril contains two
scrolls of cancellated bone, the Turbinate bones or Snuffles.
The whole of the nasal cavity and the sinuses (N.B. not ' sini ')
are covered with a moist mucous membrane that serves to
catch dust inhaled with the air. The dust laden mucus secreted
by it is further liquified by tears which enter the nostrils from
the inner corners of the eyes, and so runs down to be snorted
out or drawn back into the pharynx and swallowed. The whole
structure of the nasal cavity, especially the turbinates, tends to
set up turbulence or eddies in the inhaled air, which helps to
clear it of dust and, by delaying its passage, tends to warm it
before entering the pharynx.

The Pharnyx is the cavity beneath the cranium into which
opens the nose, mouth, the trachea or wind pipe and the
oesophagus or gullet, also a tube from each ear, the *Eustachian
Tubes*. It is lined with mucous membrane similar to that of
the nose. A loose flap of red muscle covered with mucous
membrane called the *Soft Palate* closes either the back of the
nose or mouth at the will of the animal, thus enabling it to

breathe through the mouth in hot weather or during exercise, and through the nose otherwise. During unconsciousness, the soft palate relaxes and may vibrate in the air currents causing 'snoring'. (The purr of a cat at ease is caused in the same way.)

The Larynx or Voice Box is the anterior end of the trachea and enters the pharynx just below the oesophagus. It is supported by the stirrup-shaped Hyoid bone which hangs down from the occiput. On the inner surface of the uprights of the Hyoid bone lie the two *Pharyngeal* or *Retro-pharyngeal Lymph Nodes*, just under the mucous membrane. The larynx is composed of several plates of cartilage, covered on the inside with mucous membrane and on the outside with loose areolar tissue. The first of these plates is the *Epiglottis*, which lies on the back of the tongue. During swallowing, the tongue thickens and is drawn backward and the hyoid bone and larynx are simultaneously drawn forward, and these two movements raise the epiglottis and press it over the orifice of the larynx so preventing food or water entering it. The next cartilage, the *Thyroid Cartilage*, is U-shaped, open above with the base of the U marked by a prominent ridge that forms ' Adam's Apple '. The *Thyroid Gland* consists of two oval, dark-coloured bodies lying on the outer side of the side plates of the cartilage and joined beneath by a thin band of glandular material. This gland produces the hormone ' Thyroidin ' that regulates growth, and faulty functioning of this gland causes either ' Cretinism ', resulting in the mis-shapen dwarfs known in cattle as ' Bulldog calves ', or ' Goitre ', an unsightly swelling in the neck; while excess of Thyroidin produces ' Glaucoma ' or bulging eyes. Behind the thyroid cartilages are a pair of loose cartilages, the *Arytenoids*, to each of which is attached a fold of mucous membrane, the *Vocal Cords*, though they have no resemblance to cords. Normally, the muscles of this region are tensed so that the cords are held well apart, when relaxed, the cords come together and obstruct the air flow producing the vibrations that cause the voice. It is the *relaxation* of muscle that produces voice, not, as one would expect, tension. Hence a completely unconscious animal may groan loudly and it usually does so when dying as all its muscles relax. In life, paralysis of these muscles causes involuntary voice and in animals is the cause of the trouble known to farmers as ' roaring ' or ' whistling '.

The Trachea or Windpipe consists of a series of incomplete cartilaginous rings joined into a tube of fibrous connective tissue. Outside this tube is a covering of areolar connective tissue and inside it is lined with mucous membrane that has a curious velvet-like feel when touched. This is due to the presence of innumerable microscopic hair-like projections, the ' Cilia ', that wave rhythmically during life in such a manner as to sweep the mucus secreted by the membrane up into the mouth for swallowing or expectoration. Any particles of dust in the air that reach the trachea are almost bound to settle on this mucous membrane and are thus removed with the mucus so that the air reaching the depths of the lung is practically pure.

The cartilaginous rings are not quite complete, but remain open at the top. Across this opening is a band of white muscle that, by contracting and relaxing, alters the size of the tube and so regulates the amount of air admitted to the lungs. The condition known as ' Asthma ' is a spasm of this muscle causing excessive contraction of the trachea, so reducing the amount of air below the minimum required. It is rarely seen in animals other than dogs.

The trachea runs down the neck under the cervical vertebrae from which it is separated by the *Longus Colli* muscle only. The oesophagus passes to the left of the trachea just behind the larynx and the two tubes run side by side into the thorax, passing above the heart between the two lungs. In the thorax, the trachea is partly embedded in the right lung and firmly attached to it until, about opposite the fifth rib, it divides into the two *Bronchi*, one of which enters each lung. In young animals, the thymus gland passes down the neck on each side of the trachea, and then passes beneath it, in the thorax as far back as the heart (see also Chapter VI, p. 104). This gland forms the best ' sweetbread '. The Middle Cervical Lymph Nodes in the neck lie on each side of the Trachea.

The ' Bronchial Tree '. The Bronchi have the same structure as the trachea, but immediately on entering the lung each divides into smaller tubes, the *Bronchioles* in which the cartilaginous rings are less complete. These bronchioles again subdivide repeatedly, becoming smaller and smaller with less and less cartilage, until they end as *Air-tubules* having no cartilage at all. The air tubules are about $\frac{1}{100}$ inch in diameter, and are comparatively short, each terminating in a cluster of about a dozen *Air-Sacs* or *Alveoli*. The resemblance of the whole structure to a tree in which the alveoli represent the leaves is obvious, and gives rise to the name ' Bronchial Tree '. The Bronchial Lymph Nodes lie above the bronchi at their point of departure from the trachea.

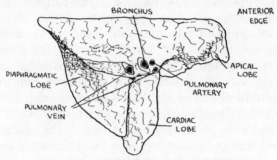

FIG. 49a.—Lungs of ox. Left medial view.

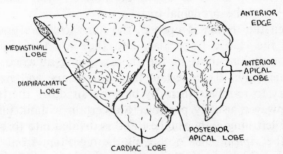

FIG. 49b.—Right lateral view.

The Lungs (Fig. 49, *a* and *b*). In a well-bled carcase, the lungs are pale pink, but in life they are red and in an animal dead from any cause other than haemorrhage (bleeding) the lung lying uppermost when death occurred is pink while that nearest the ground is purple, due to the accumulation of blood therein. Each lung is contained in a fibrous sac of yellow elastic tissue covered with a serous membrane called the *Pulmonary Pleura*. Through this can be seen the coarse trabeculae of yellow elastic tissue, dividing the organ into *Lobules* or irregular polygons with sides of about $\frac{1}{30}$ inch.

On section, the air tubules and alveoli can be clearly seen as holes about $\frac{1}{100}$ inch diameter giving the tissue a sponge-like look and feel. On crushing a cut portion, there is a copious exudation of lymph which forms a foam with the air from the alveoli. Healthy lung tissue will float on water.

Microscopical examination reveals that each lobule consists of an air tubule ending in about a dozen globular alveoli of about the same diameter, $\frac{1}{100}$ inch. These alveoli are formed by epithelial cells only one layer thick, pervious to gases but not to water or lymph. This is the *Respiratory Epithelium*. The lobule also contains a convoluted capillary blood-vessel attached loosely to the respiratory epithelium by a few white fibrils, the wide spaces between being filled with lymph. The trabecula contains a network of capillary blood-vessels, fed by the pulmonary artery, feeding the lobular capillaries, and finally discharging into the pulmonary veins ; a network of lymph ducts discharging into the *Mediastinal Lymph Nodes*, about a dozen in number, lying above the trachea; and the bronchial tree.

When the thorax is opened, the lungs collapse under the pull of the elastic trabeculae, and they are then found to occupy only one-third of the thorax, being attached to the backbone only. To ascertain their true shape and size, it is necessary to re-inflate them by blowing air down the trachea. It is, however, usually possible to ascertain without inflation, that the left lung is the smallest and is divided into three large lobes, the *Apical Lobe* occupying the region in front of the heart, the *Cardiac Lobe* lying about the heart, and the *Diaphragmatic Lobe*, the largest, lying against the diaphragm. The right lung also has an apical lobe, similar to that of the left lung, a cardiac lobe extending between the pericardium and the ribs and reaching as far as the sternum (N.B. It will be remembered that the pericardium touches the costal cartilages and ends of the ribs on the left side, but not on the right), and a diaphragmatic lobe and proceeding from the latter an *Intermediate* or *Mediastinal Lobe* extending over to the left side behind the mediastinal space above the pericardium. The Posterior Vena Cava runs between the mediastinal and diaphragmatic lobes of the right lung.

The Mediastinum or Mediastinal Space is the region between
the two lungs.   The lower half is occupied by the pericardium
and in front of this the thymus gland in a young animal or the
fatty deposit that replaces it in an adult, with the anterior vena
cava and the brachio-cephalic artery lying on it.   The upper
half contains a stout wall of fibrous tissue through which runs
the oesophagus and the trachea, with the mediastinal lymph
nodes lying on the upper surface of it and draining by ducts
running direct into the Thoracic Duct.   All these organs, as

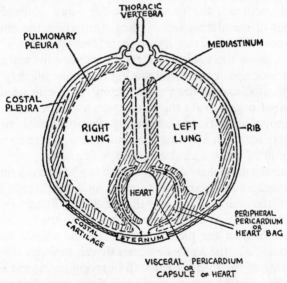

FIG. 50.—Diagram of pleura and pericardium.

well as the fibrous wall, are deeply embedded in fat derived
from the sub-pleural fat and covered with serous membranes
forming the Mediastinal Pleura.   In humans, the mediastinum
forms an impervious wall dividing the thorax into two completely separated cavities, but in farm animals the wall ceases
at the mediastinal lobe of the right lung, and here the two
cavities are in communication.

The Pleura (Fig. 50).   As mentioned above, the Pulmonary
Pleura forms an outer serous covering to the capsules of the
lungs.   It is continuous with the Mediastinal and Costal
Pleura lining the inside of the ribs and intercostal muscles,

and so forms a complete sac in which the lungs lie. T
membrane secretes lymph which reduces friction betw
lungs, the mediastinum and the ribs, and so may be con
as similar to the Peritoneal and Pericardial Membranes, both
in structure and functions.

Owing, however, to the pumping action of the heart, all
veins and lymph ducts in the thorax are in a state of suction
and as the pleural lymph flows direct into the thoracic duct,
which runs under the thoracic vertebrae to the anterior vena
cava, the pleural cavities are also kept in a state of suction or
' partial vacuum ', the pressure therein being noticeably less
than that of the atmosphere. Now, during life, the only communication between the atmosphere and the inside of the
thorax is down the trachea.   Hence, air enters the trachea and
fills the bronchial tree, thus inflating the lungs till they fill the
whole thorax, except the part occupied by the heart and the
mediastinal organs. As the diaphragm and ribs move, so the
lungs move with them, expanding the bronchial tree and
drawing in air, then allowing it to collapse somewhat under the
elastic pull of the trabeculae and expelling air.

When the animal is slaughtered and the bowels are removed,
the diaphragm is pierced in cutting out the liver. At this
moment, the inrush of air into the pleural cavity can be heard,
as the lungs collapse completely.   Thereafter, the lungs occupy
only one-third of the pleural cavity. If the animal has been
' *overstuck* ', i.e. the knife has been driven through the pleura
on the side of the mediastinal wall in trying to cut the bifurcation of the carotid artery, blood will have been drawn by the
vacuum into the pleural cavity and will have stained large
areas on the inner side of the ribs. This is known as ' Back
Bleeding ', ' Rib Splash ', or ' Oversticking '.

In human surgery, it is possible to put one lung completely
out of action by inserting a tube between the ribs. Air is
drawn in through this tube by the pleural vacuum and the lung
collapses and remains collapsed and resting as long as the tube
is in place, the patient in the meantime breathing twice as fast
with the other lung. As soon as the tube is withdrawn, the
two intercostal muscles which cross each other at right angles
close over the hole, the vacuum is restored and the lung comes
into use again. It is not possible to do this on animals, as

there is no complete division between the two sides of the thorax, so any attempt to do so results in collapse of both lungs and rapid death. Cattle were sometimes slaughtered in this way up to a hundred years ago.

RESPIRATORY PROCESSES

Respiration is the process by which air is drawn into and out of the lungs so that the blood contained in them can expel the carbon dioxide generated during muscular activity and acquire pure oxygen for circulation round the body. It will be as well first to consider the composition and properties of the air from which the oxygen is obtained.

A normal sample of air consists of

Nitrogen . . .	78·09 per cent.
Oxygen . . .	20·93	,,
Carbon Dioxide .	0·03	,,
Other gases . .	0·95	,,

These proportions do not vary greatly in the atmosphere anywhere, as all gases have a strong tendency to ' *Diffuse* ' or spread themselves out from regions in which they are highly concentrated to regions where their concentration is lower. If, for example, a flask containing pure oxygen is opened to the air, the oxygen molecules will rush out from their region of high concentration within the flask to the air around where their concentration is lower. Simultaneously nitrogen molecules will rush in from the air in which their concentration is high to the region inside the flask where their concentration is low. So, in a few seconds, equilibrium will be restored and the flask contain air of normally-mixed constituents. The same result will be obtained, though rather more slowly, if the flask is stoppered with a porous material or one through which gas can pass, such as cloth, plaster, or even cork, but then the time needed for completion will vary with the porosity of the stopper. Thus the constitution of the atmosphere, however altered, always tends to return to normality.

The gases mentioned above are all soluble in water and, when in solution diffuse in the same way, though much more slowly. If water be exposed to air, oxygen, carbon dioxide and nitrogen dissolve in it and diffuse, very slowly, throughout it. Thus, on the surface of a pond, oxygen from the air dissolves in the water until the concentration in the water equals that of the air. It then diffuses into the depths until their concentration is equalised with that of the surface. Thus, however deep the ocean, oxygen reaches its bed and life of various kinds is found, even at depths of five miles.

The lower types of animal life, the jellyfish and more primitive forms, have no active respiratory functions, as their skins are sufficiently delicate and porous to allow gases to diffuse through them readily. If the concentration of oxygen in their body fluids is low, more diffuses in from the surrounding water, and similarly if their concentration of carbon dioxide is high, it diffuses outwards into the water. The thin porous skin, however, is very little protection to the animal, and the area through which diffusion can occur is small. Higher animals therefore evolve some form of respiratory apparatus in which these disadvantages are overcome. In the mammalian lung the delicate respiratory epithelium is housed within the body out of harm's way, the air reaching it is cleared of harmful dust, and its area is enormous. In man, for instance, it is estimated that there are 2 million alveoli in the lungs, and that their total area is 100 times that of the surface of the body. This gives ample area for diffusion and allows for the surface of the body to be shielded by a thick skin that gives good protection even if it is impervious to gases.

It is interesting to note that the dormouse, during its hibernation or winter sleep, ceases to breathe, or at least ceases to move its diaphragm and ribs. Life is maintained, though at a very low level, by the diffusion of oxygen down the trachea and into the bronchial tree and alveoli, and the diffusion of carbon dioxide in the reverse direction, though the air in the trachea does not move. In active mammals, however, this would obviously be insufficient, so breathing occurs and most of the actual air in the bronchial tree is changed with each expansion and contraction of the thorax. This air that is changed is known as *Inhaled Air* when it is being drawn into the bronchial tree and *Exhaled Air* when it is being driven out. As, however, the ends of the bronchial tree are blind, it follows that there must remain a quantity of air therein that is not changed even when the lung is completely contracted. This is called *Residual Air*, and through this belt of residual air the gases diffuse in the same way that they diffused down the trachea of the sleeping dormouse.

The oxygen therefore diffuses from the Inhaled Air into the Residual Air, thence through the respiratory epithelium to the lymph, thence through the capillary walls to the plasma, and thence into the red blood cells for carriage to the tissues. In the tissues, it diffuses from the red blood cells to the plasma, thence through the capillary walls to the lymph, and thence to the tissue cells. The carbon dioxide diffuses in the opposite direction, both gases always moving from regions of higher to regions of lower concentration. This may be tabulated as follows:—

Oxygen Concentration	Per Cent.	Carbon Dioxide Concentration	Per Cent.
Inhaled Air . . .	20	Blood in Pulmony Artery . .	48
Exhaled Air . . .	16	Blood in Pulmonary Veins . .	44
Difference diffused in Blood	4	Difference diffused to Expired Air	4
Red Cells in Pulmonary Artery . . .	10	Expired Air	4
Red Cells in Pulmonary Veins . . .	14	Inspired Air . . .	Trace

Note that the blood is not freed entirely of carbon dioxide. It is necessary that some should remain even in the arterial blood.

The oxygen and carbon dioxide exchange are the most important part of the respiratory function, but some other gaseous materials are also excreted by the lungs by the same process of diffusion. The aromatic volatile oils and gases in certain foods such as onions and turnips pass out of the blood stream during the first hour or two after eating, so also do certain products of the bacterial activity in the large intestine, causing foul breath when in excess due to constipation. Very noticeable also is the excretion of water vapour by this route, which may amount to 8 or 9 per cent. of the expired air, though it varies considerably with the humidity of the atmosphere and the heat of the day. Water excretion by the lungs is probably incidental, but may be beneficial in keeping the mucus in the respiratory tract sufficiently moist for it to be moved easily by the cilia. If exhalations were quite dry, the mucus might also become too dry and sticky to move.

Respiration also plays a part in regulating the temperature

of the body, particularly in sheep and goats, the non-sweating animals. In hot weather the breathing is more rapid, so the mouth, pharynx and the top of the trachea receive a cooling draught more frequently. It is, however, shallower and the inhaled air is therefore not drawn so far into the bronchial tree. Thus there is a wider belt of residual air, and diffusion continues in it though it takes longer. The rate of breathing and the depth thereof are kept in balance so that the blood still receives the correct amount of oxygen and delivers the correct proportion of carbon dioxide in spite of the more rapid breathing.

The movements of the diaphragm and intercostal muscles that cause respiration are under the control of the *Respiratory Nervous Centre* situated in the medulla oblongata between the third and fourth cervical vertebrae. Being red muscles they are to some extent voluntary or under the control of the will, and the animal is conscious of their movements, but normally they act automatically like white muscle. The respiratory centre is stimulated by carbon dioxide (hence the need for retaining some in the blood, as if its concentration falls too low, breathing stops). As the concentration rises, breathing becomes deeper and *vice versa*, so that the carbon dioxide is always kept at a definite level, 48 per cent. in the veins and 44 per cent. in the arteries. If one enters a room in which carbon dioxide is leaking into the atmosphere, as sometimes happens in refrigeration works, one immediately breathes deeper automatically for as the difference between the concentrations of carbon dioxide in the blood and the air becomes less, the diffusion rate is slower, more accumulates in the blood, and breathing becomes deeper in comparison. In fact, carbon dioxide in the blood may be said to act as a hormone regulating the rate of respiration.

Ventilation. The normal concentration of carbon dioxide in the air is 0·03 per cent., but inside buildings it may rise to 0·05 per cent. without visibly affecting the breathing of men or animals. If it rises much above this percentage, the air is said to be ' polluted '. Ventilation problems are solved by measuring the amount of carbon dioxide exhaled by each species of animal and calculating from this the amount of air that it will diffuse in without raising the concentration above 0·05 per cent. For example, a fat ox exhales about 6 cubic feet of carbon dioxide per hour, which, when diffused into 30,000 (thirty thousand) cubic feet of air, will amount to 0·02 per cent., but there is already 0·03 per cent. in the air, so the total concentration will be 0·05 per cent., the limit allowable in ' non-polluted ' air. In a shed of 3,000 (three thousand) cubic feet, arrangements must be made by ventilators and fans to ensure that the air is changed ten times in an hour if one fat ox is to be stalled therein in comfort.

The figures given for the various animals are:—

Fat cattle and cart horses, etc.	6	cubic feet of carbon dioxide exhaled per hour.		
Light cattle, van horses, etc.	3	,,	,,	,,
Swine	1·5	,,	,,	,,
Sheep and Goats	1	,,	,,	,,
Fowls	0·03	,,	,,	,,
Man	0·6	,,	,,	,,

Ventilation, however, should only be calculated on these lines when absolutely necessary. Whenever possible sheds should be designed with open walls that allow unlimited air to enter and leave. There is ample evidence showing that excess carbon dioxide is not harmful, but that excess moisture in the air, due to exhaled breath, is definitely deleterious, and this excess moisture can only be dispersed by free air.

THE DIFFERENT ANIMALS

The respiratory organs of various animals can best be differentiated by examining the mediastinal fat, so the following points are more of theoretical interest than practical use.

In the Ruminant (Fig. 49, *a* and *b*). The trachea has the free ends of the rings upturned, so that they come together on closure and only a limited reduction of the lumen is possible. When closed as much as possible, these ends form a ridge running down the upper side of the tube. There is a small additional bronchus leaving the trachea about the level of the second rib, dividing into two and entering both parts of the right apical lobe. The right apical lobe is divided by a deep fissure, so that the right lung has five lobes, anterior apical, posterior apical, cardiac, diaphragmatic and mediastinal.

In Deer the tracheal rings are not complete, so that there is a wide gap at the back closed by white muscle and mucous membrane only.

In the Camel the lungs have no distinct lobes, each being in one piece. There is, however, the additional apical bronchus to the right lung.

In Swine the free ends of the rings of the trachea overlap, so that the tube can be closed almost completely. There is a small additional bronchus leading to the right apical lobe, as in the ox. The left lung has only two lobes, an apical and a diaphragmatic lobe.

(In the human trachea the ends of the rings do not meet at the back, the space being closed by white muscle and mucous membrane.)

In Horses. The soft palate cannot be lifted clear of the root of the tongue, and is only pushed up by the bolus of food during the act of swallowing, so breathing, and even neighing, must be performed entirely through the nose. The tracheal rings have the free ends overlapping, as in the pig, for that portion of the tube that lies in the neck, while in the thorax the ends of the rings do not meet but leave an unprotected gap closed by white muscle and mucous membrane only. There are two bronchi only, each entering a diaphragmatic region. The lungs are devoid of deep fissures, so that each forms a single block of tissue instead of separate lobes, but the parts can still be recognised as the apical region in front, the cardiac region with the recess for the heart, very large in the left lung, the diaphragmatic region, and a mediastinal region arising from the diaphragmatic region of the right lung. Compared with the ox, the horse's lungs are noticeably elongated.

In all these animals, the lung tissue is of very little nutritious value, owing to its large proportion of yellow elastic fibre which is practically indigestible. It can, however, be eaten as the respiratory epithelium, the capillary blood-vessels and the lymph supply some slight nutriment, and the remainder forms good ' roughage ' or indigestible matter that keeps the bowels distended.

CHAPTER IX

THE URO-GENITAL SYSTEMS

Urine and the Main Urinary Organs; the Accessory Organs; Male
Genital Organs; Castration; Recognition of Male Carcases; Female
Genital Organs; Recognition of Female Carcases; Tables of
Oestrum, Pregnancy and Puberty.

THE MAIN URINARY ORGANS

Urine is the watery secretion from the kidneys that carries
with it urea and other waste and surplus matter from the blood.
In composition it does not differ materially from sweat, but
the excretion of sweat is regulated by the temperature of the
atmosphere, while the excretion of urine is regulated by the
water content of the blood and lymph stream. To some extent,
sweat and urine are interdependent, for in hot weather or during
heavy muscular work, more water is required for sweat and
less is available for urine; similarly in cold weather and during
muscular idleness more urine is formed and less sweat; but
whatever the conditions, neither process ceases entirely as long
as the animal is living.

Both sweat and urine contain *Urea*, which is compounded
in the liver from broken down protein. The quantity is, of
course, variable, but in a fat ox it may amount to about
4 ounces a day. On being voided, urea is broken up by
bacteria into carbon dioxide and ammonium carbonate, the
latter being a valuable addition to the soil for crops of all
kinds. Urine also contains various salts of minerals either
received in the food and not used by the animal, or broken off
the protein molecules as they wear out, and it may also contain
a small quantity of sugar, especially after a meal, but it is very
small in healthy animals. The colour of urine is due to a
pigment derived from the free haemoglobin in the plasma, and
it varies, therefore, with the state of the blood, and also with
the bile-forming activities of the liver, since most of the haemoglobin in the plasma is used in the composition of the bile.
Finally, urine contains small quantities of albumen and mucus

from the mucous membrane of the uro-genital tract, sufficient to enable it to form a foam.

The Kidneys (Fig. 51, *a* and *b*) are a pair of organs, brown in colour, lying close beneath the lumbar vertebrae, each embedded in a pad of fat, the *Renal Fat* or *Kidney Knob* whose lower, or abdominal surface is covered with the peritoneal membrane. The right kidney is always immovable, but the left is, in some animals, ' floating ' or loosely attached to the backbone and free to change its position as the stomach becomes distended or collapses. On the medial edge, each kidney has a depression, the *Hilus*, into which runs the *Renal Artery*, and from which emerges the *Renal Vein*, the Renal Lymph Duct and the *Ureter*, a delicate tube leading to the bladder. The *Renal Lymph Node* lies close to the artery, between the kidney and the aorta, and the *Adrenal Body* (frequently mistaken for the renal lymph node, though quite unlike a lymph node in colour and shape) lies on the anterior inner corner of the kidney. In other respects the structure of the kidneys differ somewhat in the different animals, and they are best dealt with separately.

The Ox. The kidneys weigh about 20 to 25 ounces each, and each is composed of about twenty *Lobes* or *Pyramids*, lying with the apices pointing inwards, and separated by deep fissures, usually filled with fat. The right kidney lies just behind the upper edge of the liver beneath the first, second and third lumbar transverse processes, its lobes being so arranged that the whole organ has an elongated oval form. The left kidney is roughly pyramidal in shape, and is floating. In life it lies on the right of the vertebral column just behind the right kidney, being held there by the bulge of the rumen, but when the animal is killed and disembowelled, it swings over to the left side. Butchers call the left side of the carcase with its moveable kidney, the ' *Open Side* ', and the right side the ' *Closed Side*.'

On section (Fig. 51, *g* and *h*), it is seen that the apices of the lobes or pyramids penetrate the walls of a tube of thick white fibrous tissue, lined with mucous membranes, the *Renal Pelvis*, out of which the ureter leads. The apex of each lobe and its central part consist of a pale red material, the *Renal Medulla*, and surrounding this, forming the base and the outer parts of the sides of the pyramid, is a brown material, the *Renal Cortex*. The outer surfaces are covered with a firm, fibrous capsule from which barely perceptible trabeculae arise to run throughout the organ.   A bright red zone lies between the cortex and medulla, the Intermediate Zone. The inner portion of the cortex is radial in appearance, and at intervals rays of medullary substance may be seen in it, while the outer portion

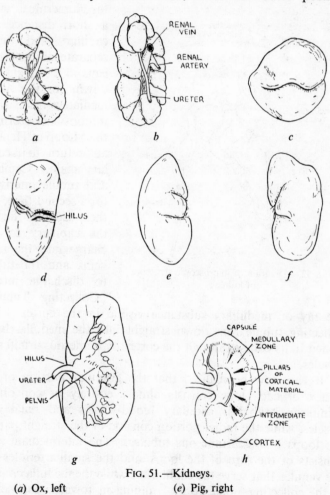

FIG. 51.—Kidneys.

(*a*) Ox, left   (*e*) Pig, right
(*b*) Ox, right   (*f*) Pig, left
(*c*) Horse, right   (*g*) Section of pig's kidney
(*d*) Horse, left   (*h*) Section of sheep's kidney

is more granular and contains numerous minute spots, only just visible to the eye. These are the *Renal Corpuscles* or Malpighian bodies.

Each corpuscle (Fig. 52) consists of a *Glomerulus* or tuft of capillary blood-vessel tightly coiled so as to resemble a knot, surrounded by a capsule (Bowman's Capsule) from which leads a *Uriniferous Tubule* convoluted with a capillary from the glomerulus. After a short distance, the capillary and tubule separate, and the latter runs in a straight line down to the intermediate zone, in which it loops back (forming the ' Loop of Henle '), and returns to its capillary again. Capillary and tubule intertwine for a second time, and then separate finally, the capillary to discharge into the renal veins and the tubule to discharge into a ' Collecting Tubule ', the ray of medullary substance visible in the cortex. This collecting tubule runs down straight into the medulla, being joined in its course through the cortex by numerous uriniferous tubules.

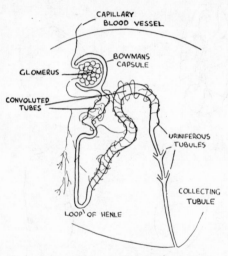

FIG. 52.—Diagram of microscopic structure of kidney.

It can now be realised that the granular portion of the cortex of each lobe consists almost entirely of convoluted uriniferous tubules, capillary blood-vessels and renal corpuscles, while the radial portion consists of the straight part of the loops of the uriniferous tubules. The intermediate zone consists of the turn of the loops, and the small arterioles and the venules that serve the capillaries, while the medulla consists of the collecting tubules only, running in towards each other and sometimes joining together, to discharge into the pelvis at the apex of the lobe.

Water and salts and excess sugar are discharged from the glomeruli into the tubules. Urea and a little albumen are excreted by the convoluted portions of the tubules and the completed urine then passes down the collecting tubules to the pelvis. There are about 4,000,000 (four million) corpuscles in the two kidneys of the ox, but it is probable that only about 1 million of these are active, since three-quarters of the entire kidney substance can be destroyed by injury or disease without causing the death of the animal.

The Sheep, Goat, Deer and Camel (Fig. 51). Each kidney is an oval body weighing about 4 ounces. In the foetus, the kidneys resemble those of the ox, but shortly after birth, the ten or twelve pyramids or lobes of each kidney fuse together to form one organ. On section, however, the divisions between the original lobes (about a dozen in each kidney) can be made out, as bars or *Pillars* of cortical material running into the medullary zone. The pelvis is wide and elliptical in shape. The left kidney is only slightly movable.

[The human kidney is identical with the sheep's in size and outward appearance, but could be distinguished by the yellow fat at the hilus. On section, it would be seen that the pillars dividing the lobes are much more pronounced in the human than the sheep. The dog's kidneys are more spherical than the sheep's, but resemble them otherwise. The left kidney is usually distinctly floating.]

The Pig (Figs 51, *e*, *f* and *g*). Each kidney is a flattened oval body weighing about 10 ounces, about twice as long as it is broad, and rather paler in colour than in other animals. In the foetus, the kidneys are lobular as in the ox, but before birth the ten or twelve lobes fuse together, forming three large lobes not very clearly divided, but on section the outlines of the original pyramids can be clearly seen. The pelvis is long and tubular. Both kidneys are immovable.

The Horse (Fig. 51, *c* and *d*). The right kidney is heart-shaped and the left bean-shaped, and neither show any lobes, but the foal has lobulated kidneys like the ox. At about one month old, the lobules fuse together but the original pyramids can be distinguished, though not very readily, throughout life. The pelvis is hollow and elliptical in shape. Both kidneys are immovable.

The Cat (Fig. 53*a*) has almost spherical kidneys fixed immovably on the same level beneath the second-fifth lumbar transverse processes. Their surfaces are covered with large, clearly visible veins. There is usually ample renal fat, but it does not completely cover the kidneys or form a knob.

The Rabbit (Fig. 53*b*) has kidneys similar in shape to those of the cat, but the left kidney is floating and varies its position according to the fullness of the stomach when the body cooled. It is, however, invariably further back than the right kidney, which touches the liver. There are no veins visible on the surfaces and, in wild specimens, there is very little kidney fat.

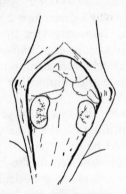

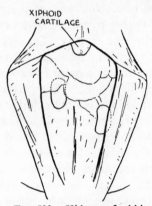

FIG. 53*a*.—Kidneys of cat.　　FIG. 53*b*.—Kidneys of rabbit.

The kidneys thus provide an easy means by which cat and rabbit carcases can be differentiated.

Urine itself is poisonous, but the amount left in the kidneys after death is negligible, and they are very nutritious owing to their high protein content.

THE ACCESSORY URINARY ORGANS

The Adrenal Bodies are not actually connected with the urinary system, but it is convenient to consider them now. They are about the same size as a lymph node but are brown in colour and firm to touch. They are sometimes heart-shaped and sometimes bean-shaped. Each lies on the inner anterior corner of the kidney.* They provide a hormone, Adrenalin,

* In the rabbit the left adrenal body lies just behind the centre of the liver and apparently does not touch the kidney.

which stimulates the sympathetic nervous system and causes contraction of white muscles. It is released into the blood stream in large quantities during excitement or fear, and causes erection of the hair (especially in cats and dogs), constriction of the arterioles of the skin, thus causing pallor and a sensation of cold, and abnormal movements of the bowels and bladder. The heart beat is also increased. Adrenalin is used in medicine to produce these effects, or it can be applied locally to check bleeding by constricting the arterioles of the part.

The Renal Artery comes directly from the aorta, half way between the anterior mesenteric and posterior mesenteric arteries. It is nearly as large as the femoral artery of the leg, showing that the kidney receives approximately the same amount of blood as the leg, namely about one-twelfth of the total circulation. The *Renal Vein* contains blood that is free of urea but has nearly the same amount of oxygen and carbon dioxide as arterial blood, as the cellular activity and consumption of oxygen in the kidney is very slight.

The Ureter (pronounced Ūr'ter) is a fine tube leading out of the renal pelvis through the hilus, and thence backwards over the abdominal face of the psoas muscles and ilium, finally passing round the rectum to enter the neck or posterior end of the bladder close to its fellow. The entry is made at a sharp angle so that it forms a valve preventing the return of urine up the ureter. The tube is composed of white fibrous tissue lined with mucous membrane.

The Bladder (Fig. 54) is a sac of thick white muscle lined with pleated mucous membrane, lying on the pubic bones of the pelvis, immediately below the rectum of the male and the uterus (womb) of the female. Its posterior end forms the ' neck ' or opening surrounded and normally kept closed by a strong sphincter muscle just behind the points of entry of the ureters. Its anterior end lies against the peritoneal membrane but is connected to the umbilicus (or navel) by a ligament, the vestige or remnant of the Urachus, the tube through which the urine passed during foetal life. When empty, immediately after urination, the bladder lies entirely within the pelvis, but it fills gradually and protrudes into the abdomen until it has almost reached the umbilicus. Then its wall of white muscle starts to contract spasmodically causing discomfort until the sphincter is relaxed and the urine discharged. The wide pelvis of the female allows for greater expansion of the bladder as long as she is not pregnant, hence non-pregnant females urinate less frequently than males.

The Urethra (pronounced URĒĒTHRA) is the thin tube of white muscle lined with mucous membrane leading from the bladder, and, in the male, running down the penis and, in the female, entering the vagina.

The accessory urinary organs have very little food value and, though sometimes used as casings, are more usually rendered down for gelatine, in which they are very rich. Pigs' bladders are used for storing lard and ox and sheep bladders used to be prepared as a very inferior writing parchment, but the demand for this has now ceased.

THE MALE GENITAL ORGANS

The Testicles (Fig. 54) are a pair of oval glandular bodies that produce the *Spermatozoa* or male reproductive cells and the hormones that produce growth of the male characteristics. Each testicle is rather larger than the corresponding kidney, and consists chiefly of a mass of tubules lined with generative Epithelium. When the animal is *Pubic* or about half grown, and in good health, this epithelium multiplies and sheds its surface layer in much the same manner as the epithelium of the skin and mucous membranes. The shed cells float free in the tubules, and again divide, forming two equal halves, each half containing only half a nucleus. They then grow long flagellae or tail-like processes, giving them somewhat the appearance of tadpoles. These flagellated, half nucleated cells are the Spermatozoa (Plate XIII).

In foetal life, and for a short time after birth, the testicles are situated just behind the kidneys, being served by the *Spermatic Artery and Vein*, which leave the main blood-vessels just behind the posterior mesenteric artery. A duct, the *Seminal* or *Spermatic Duct*, leaves the posterior end of each testicle, and passes backward parallel with the ureters to the neck of the bladder, where it terminates in the *Seminal Vesicles*. Shortly after birth, each testicle moves round the side of the abdomen to the abdominal floor, and passes through the corresponding *Inguinal Canal* between the abdominal muscles and the front edge of the pubis, to hang, one on each side of the penis, in the *Scrotum* or ' *Purse* ', a loose fold of abdominal skin. In its course, the testicle becomes involved with two folds of peritoneal membrane which surround it and line the scrotum, thus allowing the testicle to move freely within it, and with a thin strand of red muscle, the *Cremaster Muscle* (a branch of the internal oblique abdominal muscle) which raises it in cold weather or during sexual excitement. Thus, the testicle is

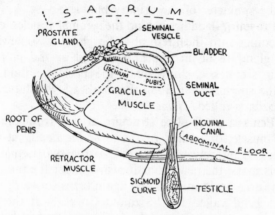

Fig. 54.—Genital organs of bull.

suspended in the scrotum by the ' *Spermatic Cord* ', consisting of (*a*) The spermatic artery and vein in front; (*b*) the spermatic duct behind; (*c*) the two folds of peritoneal membrane, called the *Tunica Vaginalis*, surrounding both, and (*d*) the strand of red muscle called the *Cremaster Muscle* on the outer side. The Superficial Inguinal Lymph Node lies behind the cord at the outer end of the inguinal canal, and the Deep Inguinal Lymph Node at the internal end of the canal.

The Seminal Duct leads from the lower pole of the testicle. At its origin it consists of several tightly-coiled tubes into which the tubules of the testicle empty. The main duct runs up behind the testicle, through the inguingal canal in the spermatic cord and over the top of the bladder, where it enters the seminal vesicles beside its partner. Besides conducting the spermatozoa from the testicle to the seminal vesicles, the ducts, at their origin, produce hormones which, together with hormones from the testicles, give the animal its male growth and character. A small, Y-shaped body may be found on top of the bladder between the latter portions of the ducts, this is the Male Uterus.

The Seminal Vesicles are bladders of various size and shape lying above the sphincter of the urinary bladder. The spermatozoa which are being formed slowly but continuously assemble in the seminal vesicles, so that vast numbers are available at the moment of mating. The vesicles are entered by the seminal ducts and discharge into the urethra at its origin just behind the sphincter of the urinary bladder.

The Prostate Gland lies behind the seminal vesicles, covering their openings into the urethra. The gland is somewhat like salivary gland tissue in appearance, and at the moment of mating it secretes a slimy fluid, the prostatic fluid, which washes the spermatozoa along the urethra. Prostatic fluid + spermatozoa is called ' *Semen* '.

The Penis is a rope-like structure arising from the Bulbo-urethral muscle, or ' *Bulb* ' or ' *Root of the Penis* ', a mass of red muscle lying between the ends of the two ischial bones. From this mass, the penis runs forward under the pubic bones and then turns back on itself and again turns forward, forming an S-like bend called the ' Sigmoid Curve '. It then passes between the two spermatic cords and terminates just behind the umbilicus. Except at the scrotum, it lies immediately below the skin, being held in place by the subcutaneous areolar tissue, which in this region is free of fat (in the entire male) to allow for expansion of the organ during erection. On the skin over the portion anterior to the scrotum are two, four, or sometimes six nipples. The extreme end of the penis is covered with a short tube of skin lined with pleated mucous membrane, the *Prepuce* or ' Foreskin ', which normally contains a quantity of dried mucus, the *Smegma*. A thin red muscle runs from the root to the lower end of the sigmoid curve, the *Retractor* muscle. The urethra enters the root and runs down the penis close to its outer surface. Its orifice, at the end of the penis, is closed with two small lips and above them lies a small depression that is frequently mistaken for the orifice but is, in fact, a blind pit.

There is no sigmoid curve in the penis of the horse.

The urethra of the ram and billy goat (Fig. 55) protrudes beyond the penis for three or four inches, forming the ' Urethral Process ' or ' Worm '. If this is damaged the animal is incapable of successful mating.

The penis itself contains a quantity of cavernous erectile tissue consisting of a mass of fairly large blood spaces. These are filled by branches of the internal iliac artery entering the organ between the root and the sigmoid curve, but they all drain into two veins that pass through the root. When the root is contracted under sexual excitement, these veins are compressed and the flow of blood out of the organ is obstructed. So it becomes engorged with blood under high pressure from the arteries and enlarges or becomes ' erected '. The sigmoid curve is straightened out and the organ protrudes from the prepuce. On the erection subsiding, the organ is withdrawn by the retractor penis muscle and the prepuce closes over the end again. Although full erection is normally associated only with sexual excitement, there is a slight erection each time the animal urinates.

Fig. 55.—Penis of ram.
(After Böhm.)

In certain animals, namely camels, llamas, deer and elephants, there are definite ' Rutting ' seasons, and erection and breeding can only occur during these periods. In camels and llamas rut is shown by the elongation of the uvula (a process of the soft palate) which protrudes from the mouth, in deer by the shedding of the epithelium of the antlers, and in elephants by a discharge from two sebaceous glands in the forehead. Probably rut is always a matter of better feeding at certain seasons than any actual period of time.

Castration or ' Gelding ' is the operation of removing the testicles. If carried out as soon as possible after birth, it results in the complete absence of male characteristics, the hard dark muscle with a strong, urinous odour, heavy bone, and a restless truculent temper. These characteristics are developed as a result of the activities of the hormones developed by the testicles and the part of the seminal ducts attached to them. The longer castration is delayed, the more these characteristics will develop, thus horses, working oxen and camels, in which muscle and bone are desirable, are not castrated till fully grown, while meat animals are castrated as soon as possible after birth.

The usual method of castration is to slit the scrotum and the peritoneal folds within with one long deep cut, so that the testicle falls out. The tissues of the spermatic cord except the artery are cut through with the second cut ; and the artery is torn or crushed through so that it clots almost immediately, for a clean cut of the artery would allow serious bleeding. When the second testicle has been removed, the animal is set free and usually feeds within a few minutes for, if done quickly, the operation is not very painful, as the second cut that severs the tissues of the cord cuts the nerve and renders the part numb or insensitive.

Losses are usually negligible, but some may occur from bleeding if the artery is not properly closed, or from infection of the wound. As the peritoneal membranes have been cut through, such infections may give rise to a fatal peritonitis, but the resistance of farm animals generally to wound infection is so great that this rarely occurs. Usually, castration is performed on all except adult horses by a shepherd or cowherd who takes no special precautions to prevent infection. Adult horses are more usually castrated by a veterinary surgeon with every possible care, as they are more liable to heavy bleeding or serious infection than young cattle, sheep, or swine.

The Italian or Burdozzo method of castration is now gaining popularity. In this, the neck of the scrotum is seized with a pair of heavy pincers and squeezed so that the artery is crushed and the blood clots therein, and the testicles, deprived of blood, die and degenerate into fat. There is no open wound to allow infection, nor can the animal suffer from serious bleeding, but the method is not absolutely certain as, occasionally, blood breaks through the clot and the testicle revives instead of dying. It is therefore necessary to examine all animals castrated by this method a month after the operation, and to repeat it where it has been unsuccessful.

Other methods are used in different countries, according to the customs of the inhabitants, but they are all inferior to the methods outlined above. Some experimental work has been done on injecting young males with female hormones but, so far, it has only proved commercially successful with birds.

Recognition of Carcases. Dressed carcases with the sex organs removed, can be recognised as follows:—

The carcase of *an entire male* has a definite urinous odour, especially in the hind-quarters, most noticeable in the boar and mildest in the bull. The inguinal canals are open, and may have remnants of the cords hanging in them. The root of the penis and the retractor muscles are large; there is very little cod fat; the neck and shoulders are heavy. The musculature generally is dark and the bones thick. Heads have broad foreheads with short, thick horns. The boar develops a thick 'shield' of cartilage in the skin over the scapula, and this can be used for brawn.

The carcase of an *animal castrated early in life* has light bone and paler muscle. The shoulders are light and the forehead narrow with long thin horns. The pelvis is narrow, as in the entire male, but the inguinal canals are closed as in the female. The root of the penis and the retractor muscles are small and the channel of the penis is surrounded (but not, of course, filled) with fat, as the organ no longer erects. In cattle and sheep there is usually a large quantity of cod fat, in place of the testicles, which forms lobules (udder fat in the female is unlobulated) but the actual quantity varies with the animal's condition.

'Stag' carcases are those from animals castrated late in life that show a varying amount of male characteristics. Usually the inguinal canals are closed, but the closure may be only fatty and the finger can be pushed through them. A very recent castrate will have the canals fully open.

'Rigs' or 'Steer-Bulls' are *Cryptorchids* or animals in which one or both testicles have failed to pass through the inguinal canals and remained in the abdomen. Such animals can only be castrated by an intricate operation and are usually left entire. They show all the characteristics of entire males.

'Cut Proud.' If the castrator allows the spermatic duct to separate from the testicle, its initial portion may not be cut off, and may return to the abdomen. As this initial portion of the duct produces some of the male hormones, the animal develops many of the male characteristics and the carcase is usually 'staggy'.

Inguinal Hernia occurs when a portion of the intestine descends through the inguinal canal into the scrotum. The condition is usually detected during castration and remedied then, but may recur. Except for the failure to develop cod fat on the ruptured side, such animals usually appear normal and make good carcases.

THE FEMALE GENITAL ORGANS

The Uterus or Womb (Fig. 56a) is shaped somewhat like a Y. The *body*, corresponding to the upright of the Y, lies between the rectum and the bladder in the anterior half of the pelvic cavity, with its posterior end protruding into the vagina and closed with a strong sphincter, forming the *Os uteri* or *mouth* of the uterus. The *Cornua* or *Horns* corresponding to the arms of the Y, lie across the anterior entrance to the pelvis between it and the abdomen, and are attached by the Broad Ligament of the Uterus to the front edges of the Ilia. During pregnancy they protrude into the abdomen between the intestines and the abdominal floor. The organ consists of a thick white muscular tube lined with pleated mucous membrane and, in farm animals, none of this membrane ever desquamates or peels off; that is to say, they have no periodic discharge of blood.

The Vagina, in the posterior half of the pelvis, is also a tube of white muscle lined with mucous membrane. Its lumen is rather larger than that of the uterus which protrudes into it for an appreciable distance and is thus surrounded by a gutter filled with mucus. In its posterior half, the vagina enlarges gradually to its posterior end, which is closed by a pair of lips of erectile tissue covered with mucous membrane inside and skin outside, forming the *Vulva*. On the floor of the vagina, just inside the vulva, is a small erectile body, the *Clitoris*, the vestige of the male penis, and, just behind this, the entrance of the urethra closed by a pair of minute lips.

The Oviducts or Fallopian Tubes. These may be considered as continuations of the horns of the uterus. Each is a thin membranous tube that takes a tortuous course from the end of the uterine horn to the site of the ovary. Here it broadens into a cup that envelops most of the ovary and a small aperture in the side of this cup gives access to the peritoneum. Thus, the female peritoneum is in direct communication with the uterus and forms the only exception to the rule that serous sacs have no openings.   Owing to this communication, infections of the uterus may lead to infection of the peritoneum and, conversely, infection of the peritoneum, notably tubercular peritonitis, may lead to infection of the uterus.

The Ovaries.   These are a pair of spherical organs, about half the size of the testicles of the male of the same species, and they produce the *Ova* or female reproductive cells.   Like the testicles, the ovaries are developed behind and close to the kidneys, but by the time the animal is *Pubic* or capable of

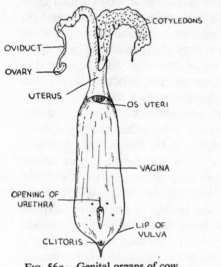

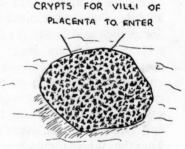

FIG. 56a.—Genital organs of cow.
(from Leisering's Atlas).

FIG. 56b.—Cotyledon from uterus of pregnant cow.

breeding, they move their position somewhat, and are found in different places in the different species.   Each ovary is almost entirely surrounded by the cup at the end of the Oviduct.

On examining the ovary of a pubic, but not pregnant, female, a number of vesicles or blisters will be found on the surface.   These are the *Graafian Follicles*, each of which contains one ovum.   Occasionally some of these follicles have burst and discharged their ova, their place being shown by blood spots.   There will also be some yellow, scar-like bodies of different sizes, the *Corpora Lutea*, but if the animal is pregnant, only corpora lutea will be found.   The ova are very large cells, about $\frac{1}{300}$ inch in most mammals, and therefore visible to the naked eye. Usually they are spherical, but are capable of assuming any shape like the leucocytes or white blood cells and, like them, can travel by amoebic movement. Like the spermatozoa, the ova have only half-nuclei.

The Oestral or Sexual Cycle. At periodical intervals, the Graafian follicles on the surface of the ovary burst and the ova come out and enter the oviducts, travelling down them towards the uterus. Meanwhile, the liquid contained in the follicle enters the peritoneum through the apertures in the cups of the oviducts, and so mixes with the lymph and, later, the blood stream. The empty follicle fills with blood which clots almost immediately. This state is called ' Oestrum ', and, in farm animals, successful mating is only possible during or soon after oestrum, as their ova are very short-lived and will die if not mated within a day or two of discharge. If the animal is well fed and normal in all respects, the follicular liquid that enters the lymph acts as a hormone that stimulates desire, and she will show excitement and call for and seek a mate. She is then said to be ' *On Heat* '. Meanwhile the blood spots on the ovaries are being replaced by the yellow, scar-like corpora lutea, and as soon as these are formed, heat ceases and successful mating becomes impossible. After a definite period, the corpora lutea diminish in size and, while they are so doing, fresh follicles rise to the surface of the ovary, to ripen and burst when the corpora lutea have finally disappeared. Thus the cycle of events, the Oestral or Sexual Cycle, is repeated.

If, however, the animal is successfully mated during oestrum, the corpora lutea persist, so no fresh follicles rise to the surface and the whole cycle ceases for the duration of pregnancy. As pregnancy nears its end, the corpora lutea gradually disappear and labour and parturition occur as soon as they have vanished. The oestral cycle is restored soon after, though usually the animal does not show outward signs of heat for several periods later.

Except for interruptions due to pregnancy, the cycle continues throughout life, for no farm animals show anything equivalent to the ' Change ' in women. Outward signs of heat, however, may be missing occasionally, as when food is scarce or conditions generally are unfavourable, and such changes in conditions bring about the ' Breeding Seasons ' in wild animals. Farmers can usually arrange breeding seasons for their stock by feeding liberally or withholding food so as to stimulate or suppress desire.

The Mammary Glands or Udder (Fig. 57). These glands lie between the skin and the abdominal wall, and are considered as developments of the sebaceous glands. Each gland lies on a deep pad of laminated fat, the ' *Dug Fat* ', the gland itself being composed of a mass of tubules lined with a special excretory epithelium. The tubules open into a labyrinth of cavities, called ' *Milk Sinuses* ', and these all empty into a large ' *Milk Cistern* ' inside the teat and extending a short way above it. The end of each teat has one or two ducts, guarded by small sphincters, from which the milk exudes.

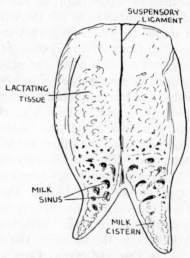

Fig. 57.—Udder of cow. Transverse section.

The period after parturition during which milk is secreted is termed a ' *Lactation* '. During the first half of lactation, the glandular tissue invades the fatty tissue and, to some extent, replaces it, with the result that the milk flow increases gradually as the suckling grows. During the latter half and between lactations, the fat returns to some extent, but never completely. As a result, following each lactation, there is less and less fat, and more and more glandular tissue, and the udder therefore becomes more and more pendulous.

THE GENITAL ORGANS OF THE DIFFERENT ANIMALS

The Cow (Fig. 56, *a* and *b*). The ovaries lie on the front edge of the pubic bones and the horns of the uterus are recurved so as to approach them. The mucous membrane lining of the whole uterus shows about thirty button-shaped protuberances about 1 inch diameter, the *Cotyledons*. The surfaces of the cotyledons are spongy to the touch, due to the presence of numerous crypts. In an animal more than four weeks pregnant, the *Placenta*, or membrane in which the foetus develops, lines both horns and the body of the uterus, and sends villi or projections into the crypts of the cotyledons from which it sucks nourishment. If, as is normal, only one foetus is formed, it develops in the right horn, which therefore becomes noticeably larger than the left horn, and by the third month the difference can be felt through the wall of the rectum and is a means by which pregnancy can be diagnosed.

The Udder (Fig. 57) consists of four glands or ' Quarters ', adjacent to each other and situated in the inguinal region or groin. A strong sheet of ligament separates the right and left sides, and being attached to the pubic bones and linea alba, supports the organ. There is no clear division between the fore- and hind-quarters of the udder, but inflation of one quarter does not affect the other and so proves that they do not communicate. The teat has only one duct.

The super-mammary lymph nodes are found at the posterior upper corner of the udder. The udder is supplied by branches from the internal iliac artery, and is drained by a similar vein and also by the large ' milk vein ' running forward along the abdomen to the thoracic system.

The Ewe and Nanny Goat have similar shaped uteri, with similar cotyledons. There are only two quarters in the udder and the teats have two ducts each.

Camel. There are no cotyledons in the uterus, but in other respects it resembles that of the cow. The udder has four quarters.

The Mare. The horns of the uterus point forwards, and the ovaries lie beneath the kidneys. There are no cotyledons, and the villi of the placenta enter crypts diffusely scattered throughout the whole uterus. The udder has only two quarters and each teat has two ducts.

The Sow. The uterus is continuous with the vagina and there is no ' os uteri ' or division between the two organs. When not pregnant, the horns of the uterus are recurved, as in the cow, but extend forwards during pregnancy. There are no cotyledons, the villi of the placentae and the crypts of the mucous membrane being diffuse, as in the mare. There are six pairs of udders, each a separate organ; four pairs lying on the abdomen and two on the thorax. Each teat has two ducts, closed with strong sphincters, over which the animal seems to have conscious control, so that a sow cannot be milked by any but its own young.

The Female Sex Hormones. The ovaries have less influence on growth than the testicles, and therefore their removal does not add appreciably to the value of the carcase. '*Spaying*' or removal of the ovaries is not practised normally, but is sometimes done for surgical reasons not connected with meat.

	Cow	Ewe and nanny	Buffalo	Camel	Sow	Mare
Oestral Cycle .	21 days	17 days	28 days	—	15-30 dy.	28 days
Duration of Heat .	5 hours	2 days	2 days	—	1-2 days	4 days
Duration of Pregnancy . .	283 days 40 weeks	147 days	310 days	315 days	116 days 3 mths. 3 weeks 3 days	340 days
Female Puberty .	12 mths.	8 mths.	15 mths.	5 years	8 mths.	18 mths.

The oestral cycle is stimulated by hormones˙ produced by the Pituitary Body in the brain (see Chapter V, p. 82). In a normal, pubic female these hormones cause the Graafian follicles to ripen and burst; but, if corpora lutea are present, they are sidetracked into the urine. So the persistence of corpora lutea during pregnancy prevents the occurrence of oestrum.

The Zondek Ascheim Test or '**Mouse Test**' for pregnancy consists of injecting urine from the female under test into immature, non-pubic mice or rabbits. If the hormone is present, the oestral cycle is started in the mouse, and it can then be deduced that the female under test is sidetracking her hormones into her urine and is therefore pregnant. Preparations of these hormones are also used to bring sluggish heifers on to heat and to correct other sexual abnormalities.

Recognition of Carcases. The female carcase with the sex organs removed can be recognised by the wide pelvis, wider if the animal has borne young than if it was virgin, the sharp anterior edge to the pubic bones, the large, bean-shaped section of the gracilic muscle, and the absence of the retractor penis and the muscle at the root of the penis. Udder fat is laminated or laid down in layers, while cod fat is lobulated (but both of these can be 'faked' or modelled with a warm iron). If the udder fat is removed, the oval patch where it lay will be visible, as well as the remains of the suspensory ligament.

In the camels and llamas oestrum and heat only occur when males 'in rut' are present. Their company apparently stimulates the production of oestrogenic hormones. The same holds good for rabbits and hares.

CHAPTER X

REPRODUCTION

The Formation and Development of the Foetus; Foetal Anatomy;
Parturition; Twins; Artificial Insemination; Heredity; Chromosomes; Determination of Sex; Popular Fallacies.

As stated in the previous chapter, a cow will not mate unless
she is ' on heat ', which term implies that she is in oestrum so
that at least one ovum, sometimes two or more ova, have left
her ovaries and are proceeding down the oviducts to the cornua
of the uterus.   These unfertilised ova are very short-lived, and
unless they are fertilised within two days of liberation they
will die and disintegrate,* but at some time during these two
days, for a few hours only, the cow will experience desire,
owing to the hormones liberated from the ruptured Graafian
follices, and she will therefore seek a bull and allow him to
mate her.   A normal bull will not attempt to mount a cow
that is not on heat.

In mating, the bull ejects about five million spermatozoa,
most of which enter the uterus.   These also are normally short-
lived, and unless they can find ova with which to unite, they
will die within a day and disintegrate.*   Normally one spermatozoon, presumably the quickest and strongest, combines with
the ovum by plunging into it, leaving its flagellum outside.
The half-nucleus in the head of the spermatozoon then unites
with the half-nucleus in the ovum, to form a complete nucleus,
and the ovum is ' fertilised ' or converted into a ' Germ Cell '.

The germ cell feeds on the mucus and albumen in the
uterus and multiplies with great rapidity by repeated division.
In the cow, a mass the size of a mulberry is formed in 48 hours,
which mass is called a ' Morula '.   When it has reached this
size, the cells in the centre find difficulty in obtaining nourishment, and so they rearrange themselves as a bladder with
walls made of two layers of cells and a lymph-like liquid
within.   Nutriment can then be absorbed by the outer cells,
passed by them to the inner cells, and by them to the liquid in

---

* This is not the case in human beings.

which it will diffuse ensuring that all parts of the bladder get an equal supply either from without or within.   Such a bladder is called an ' *Embryo* '.

The embryos continue to grow rapidly, and the strongest, if more than one be present, smothers the others, but continues its own growth until it has lined the whole uterus, stretching from the extremities of the cornua down the body as far as the Os, which it occludes completely, forming the *Uterine Seal*. (Should this seal be ruptured, the embryonic liquid will escape, and the pregnancy be terminated violently, probably with serious if not fatal consequences for the mother, but as cows

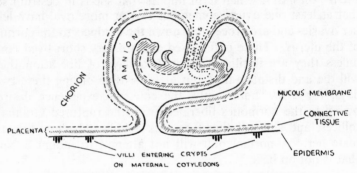

FIG. 58.—Diagram of embryo with half developed foetus.

will not mate except when on heat, this accident is very rare with them.)   This embryonic bladder is only attached to the walls of the uterus at the cotyledons.   Elsewhere there is a small space filled with mucus between the uterine wall and the embryonic wall.

Opposite each cotyledon, the embryo produces villi or small projections that enter the crypts on the cotyledonary surface.   These villi not only hold the embryo in place, but also drink in nourishment from the crypts, in the form of a liquid termed ' Uterine Milk '.   This ' milk ' contains all the essentials for building a body, namely carbohydrate, protein and a little fat, and also all the oxygen required by it.   The carbon dioxide formed by the embryo also diffuses out through this milk into the mother's blood for her to get rid of.

About the third week of pregnancy, the embryo develops an additional layer of cells, between the outer and the inner layer, but this new layer is composed of spindle-shaped cells, whereas the other two are made of flat or ' round ' cells. At the same time, a tubular depression with a raised centre appears in a part of the embryo lying within the right horn of the uterus. The raised centre of the tube is called the *Foetus* and will become the young calf, while the remainder of the embryo is called the *Placenta*. The outer layer of round cells of the foetus will become the Epidermis or outer covering of the skin,* the inner layer will become the mucous membrane lining the alimentary canal, the bladder and the trachea and bronchi, and the middle layer of spindle cells the connective tissue that builds up most of the body (Fig. 58).

As the foetus grows within the cow, the walls of the tube in which it lies enlarge to accommodate it, but the outer end of the tube closes and the inner end remains small and later forms the *Umbilicus* or navel. The foetus is now lying within two bladders of placenta, the outer one, called the *Chorion*, lining the uterus and adhering to the cotyledons, and the inner one, called the *Amnion*, formed from the walls of the tube covering the foetus but not adhering to it except at the umbilicus. A third bladder, the *Allantois*, soon protrudes from the umbilicus and is connected with the foetal urinary bladder by a wide tube, the *Urachus*. The Allantois stores urine secreted by the foetus during its uterine life. As the foetus has negligible muscular activity in this period, the secretion of urine is very slow, and can be accumulated in the allantois until birth.

About the seventh week of pregnancy the foetus begins to make its own blood and to build up a heart and blood-vessels to circulate it. This blood is sent by blood-vessels passing through the umbilicus to the chorion where it picks up nutriment and oxygen from the villi, and thereafter it returns to the foetus and circulates throughout it. *At no time does the foetus receive any blood direct from its mother*; it makes its own blood in the same manner as does the chicken within the egg. The mother supplies only the raw material from which the foetus builds up its blood.

At the eighth week, the foetus is about 3 inches in length from forehead to anus, and is clearly recognisable as a calf.

* Actually the nerves are also derived from this layer, although they become deeply buried in the body.

It doubles itself in length approximately every fourth week until the sixteenth week, at which time the hairs begin to form. Thereafter, the growth becomes slower, till between the twenty-eighth to thirty-second week it only increases by one-fifth. It is a complete calf, ready for delivery, at the thirty-fifth week, and can survive if born then, though normally it is carried to the fortieth week. There are, however, certain points of interest in the anatomy of the unborn calf that may well be considered. Most are due to the fact that neither the faeces nor the urine, nor the carbon dioxide, can be voided in the normal way, nor can the lungs oxygenate the blood.

The Foetal Heart (Fig. 59*a*). There is an opening in the septum between the auricles guarded by a valve so that blood can pass from the right auricle to the left auricle but cannot return. Thus, only half the contents of the right auricle are discharged into the right ventricle, the remainder passing into the left auricle where it mingles with the trickle of blood from the lungs to be circulated round the system. This opening is the *Foramen Ovale*.

A duct puts the pulmonary artery in communication with the aorta, so that most of the blood from the right ventricle joins that in the aorta for systemic circulation and only a trickle goes on to the lungs, sufficient to enable them to grow. This duct is the *Ductus Arteriosus* or arterial duct.

When the calf is born, the first deep gasps for breath cause a partial vacuum in the thorax and draw quantities of blood into the pulmonary artery, so allowing the valve of the foramen to close. Subsequent sealing of the valve is rapid and should be complete in 10 or 20 minutes. If sealing is not complete, ' *Congenital Heart* ' (as in ' blue babies ') results, and the calf never thrives and dies in infancy. Normally it closes and the arterial duct shrivels up in the course of a few days and becomes a ligament.

The Circulation (Fig. 59*b*). Some confusion is often ex-perienced by students who fail to realise that the blood leaving the foetal heart is rich in carbon dioxide but has comparatively little oxygen, nevertheless it still runs through arteries for, by definition, arteries are blood-vessels that lead away from the heart. As shown above, only a trickle passes through the lungs, and the rest leaves by the aorta for distribution through

the system.   Each internal iliac artery near its point of departure from the aorta sends a branch down to the umbilicus.
These two *Umbilical Arteries* pass through the umbilicus and
out to the chorion or outer layer of placenta.   In the chorion
they divide into numerous smaller branches which break up
into capillary vessels that enter the villi.   In these capillary
vessels, the nutriment and the oxygen from the uterine milk
are absorbed and carbon dioxide is removed.   After leaving
the villi the capillaries join together to form veins and these

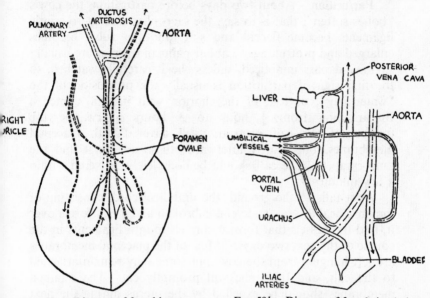

FIG. 59a.—Diagram of foetal heart.   FIG. 59b.—Diagram of foetal circulation

assemble to form one large *Umbilical Vein* which, though a
vein, since it runs towards the foetal heart, carries enriched and
oxygenated blood back to the foetus.   The umbilical vein
passes through the umbilicus and joins the portal vein,* so that
nutriment received from the mother is first delivered to the
liver, where it is dealt with as in the living animal.   It should
be noted that, despite the inactivity of foetal muscles, no fat
is formed in them, and very little elsewhere in the body other
than a few small patches round the kidneys.

* In a foetal calf, but not in other animals, a special vein, the Ductus venosus,
connects the portal vein to the Posterior Vena Cava, so that only part of the
umbilical blood passes through the liver.

Although the foetus has had no solid food, a faecal-like material, *Meconium*, forms in the intestine, composed of epithelial cells, dried mucus and a certain amount of bile. It has a greenish brown colour and a strong faecal smell, and when birth is due it completely fills the colon.

As stated above, the urine is discharged from the front end of the bladder down a wide tube, the *Urachus*, leading through the umbilicus to the *Allantois*. As birth approaches, this allantoic sac nearly fills the unoccupied portion of the uterus.

Parturition. About two days before parturition, the cow's ' bones soften ', that is to say, the sacro-iliac and sacro-sciatic ligaments become flaccid and soft, and the vulva becomes enlarged and protruding. Labour pains in the cow are usually slight and pass unnoticed, unless she is carefully watched, so the first sign of parturition is usually the protrusion of the ' water bag ', or fold of the chorion with its fluid contents. In anything from $\frac{1}{4}$ hour to 3 hours afterwards, the forefeet of the calf protrude, still covered with placental membranes, but shortly afterwards these are burst and the fluid escapes. The calf should be completely delivered within a few minutes.

As it falls to the ground, the umbilical cord, consisting of the umbilical arteries and vein, is broken and a clot forms over it, and the vessels that form it shrivel up into ligaments in the course of the next two days. Most of the placental membranes are left hanging from the cow, but some may remain attached to the calf, and these she will promptly eat. The retained membranes should be expelled by the uterus during the next few hours, but they may remain for several days, and only drop clear when putrefaction is well advanced. Such putrefying membranes are a source of grave danger, both to the cow and to persons who handle them without due precaution, so no cow should be slaughtered for 10 days after calving, by which time she is either completely ' cleansed ' or the presence of putrefaction is clearly manifested in other ways.

(Neither in the cow, nor in any farm animal, is any part of the uterus shed with the placenta at parturition, hence there is no haemorrhage or bleeding following a normal birth.)

A healthy calf will stand within 20 minutes of birth, and its feet, until then covered with soft, yellow horn and shaped like long claws, will open up and become hoof-like. It suckles during its first hour. The first milk given contains a special protein, ' *Colostrum* ', that acts as a laxative and helps the removal of meconium. It is extremely important to allow the calf to have all this colostrum from his own mother as, apart from its laxative effect, it contains a number of the antibodies against bacteria that have developed in his mother's serum, and it therefore helps to protect him against diseases that he might catch from her. Milk containing colostrum will clot on heating, forming a custard-like material, and on farms it is sometimes used thus, under the name of ' Beastings ', but its sale to the public is illegal. Pure milk, free from colostrum, does not appear normally until the seventh day after calving; but this period can be shortened by ' Pre-milking ', i.e. drawing milk and colostrum from the udder for 3 or 4 days before parturition. This practice deprives the calf of some colostrum and is to be deprecated, but nevertheless it is frequently done.

Foetal Carcases and Flesh. A foetal carcase that has been cut out of a slaughtered cow presents the following points:—
The umbilicus is open and the ends of the blood-vessels and urachus show inside it or may hang through it.

The lungs are solid to touch and dark purple in colour, but this appearance is also given by lobar pneumonia, a common cause of death in the new born when conditions are unfavourable, as when birth occurs in railway trucks or lairages.

There is a very large amount of lymph in the peritoneal and pleural cavities.

There is meconium, not faeces, in the colon and rectum.

The stomach is empty, but the calf may have been born alive but not suckled.

The hoof is long, yellow, and claw-like, but the calf may have been born alive and never stood up.

There is no rigor mortis, but this may be due to fever.

There is no fat in the musculature, but fat does not accumulate till the second week of life.

If the meat has been minced, it should be tested for the presence of large amounts of glycogen. An unborn calf has not got sufficient oxygen in its system to convert the glycogen into sarco-lactic acid, and therefore there is no rigor and the glycogen remains unchanged.

It may be mentioned that the objection to eating foetal flesh is purely aesthetic. There is no objection from the nutritional or sanitary point of view, and in many countries it is looked on as a delicacy.

TWINS, TRIPLETS, ETC.

These may be either ' *Identical* ' or ' *Non-Identical* ' according to which of two quite different processes produced them.

Identical Twins or Triplets are produced when two or more foetuses start to grow within the same embryo, usually one in each horn of the uterus. As they have been produced originally from the same spermatozoon and ovum, they are identical in sex and in all inherited traits such as colour and conformation. Otherwise they are quite normal animals, but may be rather small at birth.

Non-Identical Twins or Triplets, etc., are produced when two or more embryos of approximately the same strength develop instead of one smothering the other. Such embryos are produced by different spermatozoa and ova, and may therefore differ in sex and probably will differ in other inherited traits.

The tendency to produce twins of either type is undoubtedly inherited, and good twinning strains of goats and sheep are much sought after by farmers, but they are not liked in cattle as help is always needed in delivering twins, and there is another grave objection to them. If a cow has non-identical twins of opposite sex, the placental membranes will sometimes fuse together before development of the sex organs is complete, and in that case, the development of the female twin is checked somewhat by the hormones formed by the male twin and distributed by his blood through both the fused placentae. As a result, the female calf becomes incapable of female behaviour, and will not breed. Such animals are called ' Freemartins '. Usually they appear normal, but sometimes they may develop one or more male characteristics, such as a penis or a scrotum. The male twin is usually less affected by the female hormones, but may be effeminate, and is never used for breeding.

Not all non-identical twin calves are freemartins, probably not more than one in eight, but the phenomenon is sufficiently common for farmers to dislike cattle of twinning strains.

Freemartins also occur occasionally among sheep and goats, but not sufficiently frequently to outweigh the advantages of twinning.

OTHER ANIMALS

Sheep and goats reproduce in much the same manner as cattle.

In the **Mare** and the **Camel** the uterus has no cotyledons and the villi of the chorion enter crypts in the uterine wall at different points over a large area. This is called a ' *Diffuse Placentation*', as opposed to the 'Cotyledenous Placentation' of cattle, sheep and goats. Retention of the placental membranes is rare in animals with diffuse placentation, but in other respects reproduction is similar to that of Cotyledenous Placentation.

In the **Sow** there is also diffuse placentation. Several ova are released at a time and a pigling develops from each one, their actual number being determined by the inherited fecundity of the sow and her nutritional level when mated. Each pigling normally develops within its own placenta, as do non-identical twins, but ' identical ' twins or triplets in one placenta sometimes occur. Occasionally two or more placentae fuse together, producing freemartins showing organs of both sexes.

(In the woman, the placentation is ' Deciduous '. This means that part of the true placenta becomes closely adherent to part of the wall of the uterus. At childbirth, this part of the uterine wall, known as the ' Deciduum ' or ' Deciduous ' placenta is torn away and expelled with the ' True ' or ' Foetal ' placenta. A bleeding surface is left in the uterus that is very liable to admit bacterial injection if unsterilised instruments have been used. Deciduous placentation does not occur in any domestic animal.)

ARTIFICIAL INSEMINATION

This practice is gaining popularity among cattle breeders, as it eliminates the danger of venereal disease and considerably reduces the number of bulls needed, and bulls are expensive to rear and keep, and their carcases are of very little value when their breeding life is over. Artificial Insemination can be practised with any mammals or birds, but there is less demand for it for farm animals other than cattle.

The most common method of obtaining semen is the use of the Artificial Vagina. This is a rubber tube ending in a glass phial with graduations marked on it, both being surrounded by a water jacket containing water at blood temperature. The inner surface of the apparatus must be completely sterilised. A cow on heat is placed in stocks, and the bull is led up to her by his nose ring. As soon as he is in erection, but before he actually mounts, the artificial vagina is slipped over his penis so that he ejaculates into it. On removal of the apparatus the semen runs down into the phial and its quantity can be measured and its appearance noted. It is then carried carefully to the laboratory and, after a brief microscopical examination, it is sealed with paraffin to exclude oxygen and placed on ice in a dark cupboard. The absence of light, oxygen and warmth reduces the spermatozoa to a state of suspended animation, and they will remain alive but dormant for more than two months. The phials, stored on ice, can be sent by car, ship or aeroplane round the world if necessary, though jolting (as in trains) must be avoided, as it tends to injure the spermatozoa.

For use, the phial is warmed to blood temperature and the semen drawn out by sterilised pipettes in quantities of one cubic centimetre or less. The filled pipette is inserted by hand into the os uteri of a cow on heat and its contents injected with a fine plunger.

The bulls are kept at the artificial insemination centres in different parts of the country. They are under constant veterinary supervision, and this, combined with the fact that they are never in actual contact with a cow, completely eliminates any risk of venereal disease. One bull will ejaculate more then 5 cubic centimetres of semen at each service, and as only 1 cubic centimetre is needed for each cow, this obviously increases the bull's output five times. Actually, the semen can be diluted in suitable media about fifteen times, so that the output of each bull is really multiplied by seventy-five.

Pure-bred calves of dairy strains have very little value unless needed to increase the size of a herd or to replace wastage. Usually this means that only one such calf in eight is needed for rearing, and the remaining seven having been conceived solely to bring their dams into milk, are discarded as soon as possible. If, however, they have been got by a beef bull, they will make good, though not first-class carcases. Few dairy farmers can afford to keep two bulls, one to get pure-bred dairy calves and one to get half-bred beef calves, but if they are in touch with the artificial insemination centre they need not keep any bull at all. They simply send for the type of semen required whenever a cow comes on heat.

HEREDITY

The fact that certain traits are passed on from parents to children has been recognised from the earliest times, but it was not until the middle of last century that a theory was advanced that showed how these traits are inherited, and what happens when children are born to parents whose traits are dissimilar and cannot mix. This theory is called the Mendelian Theory, and the traits with which it deals the *Mendelian Traits* or *Characteristics*, after the Austrian monk, G. R. Mendel, who formulated it.

It is first necessary to realise that Mendelian traits are always passed on in a pure unmixed state. Though the parents may be cross-bred, the sperm or the ova produced by those parents are always pure-bred.

Taking for our example the red roan coat colour of certain cattle, which is produced by mating red-coated bulls with white-coated cows or red-coated cows with white-coated bulls. Now the roan bull will produce spermatozoa exactly half of which carry the red coat trait and exactly half of the white coat trait, but not a single spermatozoon will carry both traits. Similarly, the roan cow produces ova exactly half carrying the red coat trait and exactly half the white coat trait but not a single ovum carrying both. If, then, two roans are mated, there are the following possibilities:—

A ' red ' spermatozoon may unite with a ' red ' ovum; result, a red calf.
A ' red ' spermatozoon may unite with a ' white ' ovum; result, a roan calf.
A ' white ' spermatozoon may unite with a ' red ' ovum; result, a roan calf.
A ' white ' spermatozoon may unite with a ' white ' ovum; result, a white calf.

Thus the chances are that when red roan cattle are mated together, half of the calves will be red roan, one-quarter red and one-quarter white. It is, however, a matter of chance, but there is an invariable law that the more often a chance is taken, the more often it occurs. If a farmer breeds 4 or 8 calves only, he is unlikely to get these proportions, but if he breeds 100, he will get within one or two of the figures, 25 red, 50 roan, and 25 white (Fig. 60).

The red calves are pure-bred red and produce only 'red trait' sperm and ova and the white calves are pure white, and produce only 'white trait' sperm and ova. If a red is mated to another red, only red calves are produced, despite the fact that the ancestors may have been roan. Similarly, white mated to white produces only white calves. This is not a matter of chance, but of certainty.

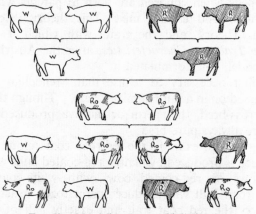

FIG. 60.—Mendelian theory of inheritance.

If a red roan cow is mated by a red bull there are the following possibilities :—

Red trait spermatozoon unites with red trait ovum, result red calf.

Red trait spermatozoon unites with white trait ovum, result roan calf.

There are no other possibilities, as the red bull can only produce red trait sperm. Fifty per cent. of such calves will be red and fifty per cent. roan. Similar results will follow mating a roan bull with a red cow, for

Red trait spermatozoon may unite with red trait ovum, result red calf.

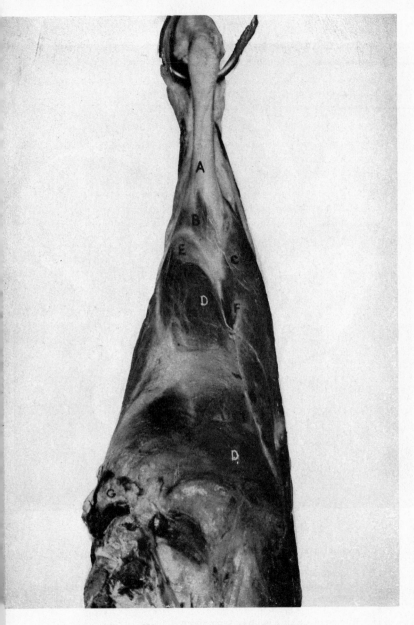

PLATE IX.—HINDQUARTER, BACK VIEW.

(*Hindquarter of cow carcase.*)

A. Achilles tendon
B. Gastrocnemius
C. Biceps femoris
D. Semitendinosus

E. Semimembranosus
F. Cut made for inspection of popliteal
    lymph node
G. Gracilis muscle

[*Facing page* 192.

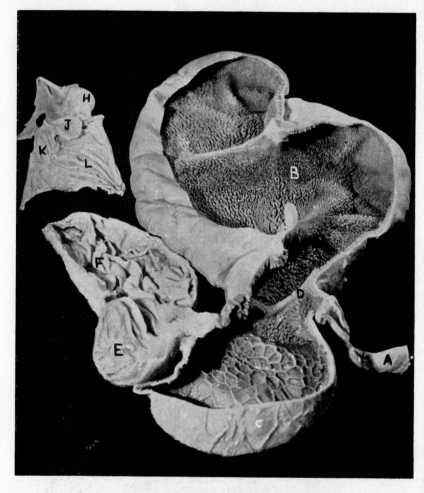

PLATE X*a*.—RUMINANT STOMACHS (SHEEP).

A. Oesophagus
B. Rumen
C. Reticulum
D. Rumeno-reticulo-orifice. The oesophageal groove has been removed
E. Omasum
F. Abomasum
H. Rumen of sucking lamb of same sheep
J. Reticulum of sucking lamb of same sheep
K. Omasum of sucking lamb of same sheep
L. Abomasum of sucking lamb of same sheep

In the actual specimen the 'honeycomb' of the reticulum at J can just be detected, though it does not show in the photograph, but the beginnings of the leaves of the omasum are quite visible at K.

PLATE X*b*.—THE OESOPHAGEAL GROOVE.

A′. Oesophagus
C′. Reticulum
E′. Omasum
G. The oesophageal groove

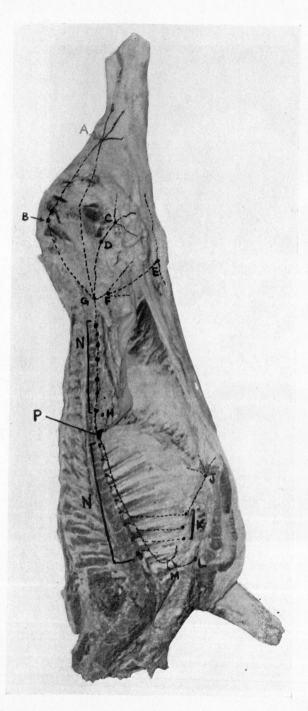

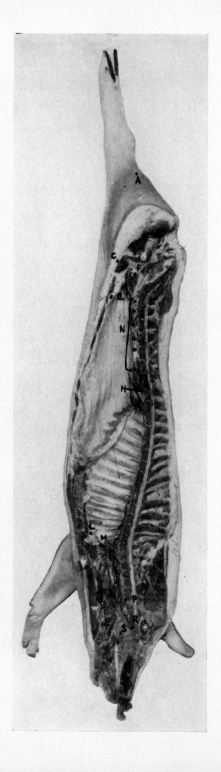

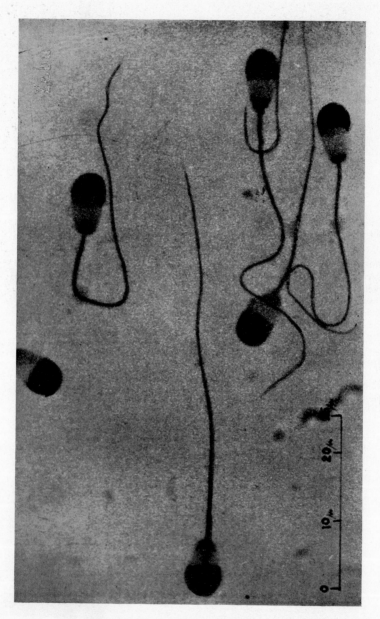

PLATE XIII.—SPERMATOZOA OF BULL.

The scale shows microns, or $\frac{1}{1000}$ parts of a millimetre.

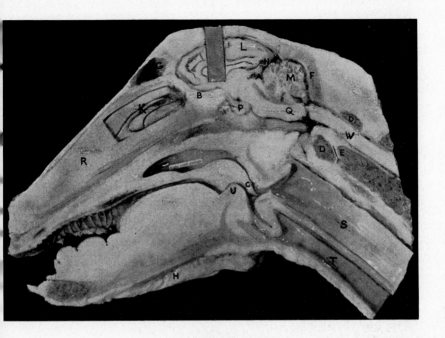

PLATE XIV.—HEAD OF SHEEP.

(Dissected and embalmed.)

The oesophagus (S) has been emptied of muscular tissue so that only the tube of connective tissue remains. The metal bolt in the cerebrum (L) indicates the correct position for a 'Captive Bolt' stunner; but actually the animal was killed by breaking the spinal cord; the point of rupture being visible to the right of the 'Q' on the medulla oblongata.

A. Position of pineal body
B. Ethmoid bone
C. Soft palate
D. Atlas
E. Dens of axis
F. Occipital bone
G. Frontal sinus
H. Sub-lingual salivary glands
J. Hard palate with piliform papillae
K. Turbinate bones
L. Cerebrum
M. Cerebellum
P. Pituitary body
Q. Medulla oblongata
R. Nasal septum
S. Oesophagus
T. Trachea
W. Spinal cord

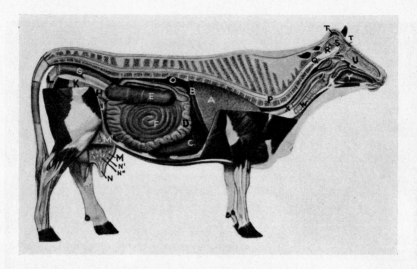

PLATE XV.—RIGHT ASPECT OF COW.

A. Lung
B. Muscular rim of diaphragm
C. Liver
D. Small intestine
E. Caecum
F. Colon
G. Rectum
H. Uterus, body
J. Right horn of uterus
K. Vagina
L. Vulva
M. Mammary or lactating tissue
M′. Mammary fat
N. Milk cistern
N′. Milk sinus (the white spots)
N″. Blood vessels (the black spots)
O. Right kidney
P. Spinal cord
Q. Medulla oblongata
R. Cerebellum
S. Cerebrum
T. Frontal sinus
U. Turbinate bones
W. Trachea
X. Oesophagus
Y. Tongue
Z. Soft palate

[*Facing page* 193.

White trait spermatozoon may unite with red trait ovum,
result roan calf,
and there are no other possibilities.

When two or more pairs of characteristics are being considered, the same rule applies, but the actual calculations of
the possibilities are increased. If black cattle are mated with
white, the offspring are blue roans, and if ' long horn ' cattle are
mated with polled (horned) cattle, the result is calves with
' scurrs ' or short, wrinkled horns. The results of large-scale
breeding of scurred roans are best set out in the form of a
Latin square in which

B = black trait sperm or ova.
W = white trait sperm or ova.
H = long horn.
P = polled.

Then BB means a black animal, caused by the union of
black trait sperm and ova; WW a white animal; BW or
WB a blue roan; HH a long horn; HP or PH a scurred;
and PP a polled animal.

	Long Horn	Scurr	Scurr	Polled
Blacks .	BB HH	BB HP	BB PH	BB PP
Roans .	BW HH	BW HP	BW PH	BW PP
Roans .	WB HH	WB HP	WB PH	WB PP
Whites .	WW HH	WW HP	WW PH	WW PP

The vertical columns show the coat colours, which are all
BB, BW, WB and WW. The horizontal lines show the horn
growths, which are all HH, HP, PH, PP.
There are thus 16 possibilities, namely:—

4 blacks, namely 1 long horn, 2 scurred and 1 polled.
8 roans, namely 2 long horn, 4 scurred and 2 polled.
4 whites, namely 1 long horn, 2 scurred and 1 polled.

Similarly, it can be shown that 3 pairs of characteristics will
give 64 or 2^6 possibilities and 4 will give 2^8 or 256, while

7

10 pairs of characteristics would give 2^{20} or 1,048,576 possibilities. In short, if $n =$ the number of traits, $2^{2n} =$ the number of possible variations.

It will be noted that only the corner squares of the figure above show the hereditary constitution of pure-bred animals. Animals with the constitutions $\frac{BB}{HH}$ are black and long-horned, and can only produce sperm or ova carrying these two traits, therefore if mated together they can only produce black long-horned calves, and the same holds good for the polled blacks in the top right-hand corner and the long-horned whites and polled whites at the ends of the bottom row. The farmer who is breeding scurred roans must be prepared to discard three-quarters of his calves as having either the wrong coat colour (BB or WW) or the wrong horns (HH or PP) or both.

Considering also the possibilities of the herd with ten pairs of characteristics, one in over a million will have a constitution differing from all the others, just as the $\frac{WW}{PP}$ in the bottom right-hand corner of the figure differ from the other fifteen. Such an animal may well cause surprise to its owner, and cause him to talk of ' it throwing back to a distant ancestor '. Such ' throw backs ' are well known to all large-scale breeders, and will occasionally cause disappointment to the small-scale man depending on a dozen or so cows only.

So far, we have been considering pairs of traits that are equally powerful. More often, however, one trait is more powerful than the other, and will conceal it, and in such cases the most powerful trait is said to be ' *Dominant* ' and the weaker one ' *Recessive* '. In cattle, black hair is dominant to red hair, which is therefore recessive, and if black cattle are mated with red cattle, the resulting cross-breeds will all be black in colour, and can only be recognised as cross-breeds when they have bred together, for the sperm and the ova will still be pure bred and the following results may be expected:—

Black trait spermatozoon + Black trait ovum = Pure Black calf.
Black trait spermatozoon + Red trait ovum = Cross-bred calf of the same black colour as the pure bred, for the red is dominated by the black.
Red trait spermatozoon + Black trait ovum = Cross-bred calf the same colour as the pure-bred, for the red is dominated by the black.
Red trait spermatozoon + Red trait ovum = Pure red calf.

I.e., one calf in four will show the recessive colour red, two in four will have the red traits in their constitution, but will look black; one in four will be pure black, both in constitution and appearance.

In such cases, if it is desired to build up a red herd, the reds can be mated with absolute certainty that only red calves will be born to them. The black animals, however, may be either pure bred black or cross-bred, and we can only tell which they are by mating them with reds, then the pure-breds will produce cross-breeds that all look black, and the cross-breeds will produce 50 per cent. reds, as follows:—

Red Pure Bred Produces	Black Cross Bred Produces	Result
Red trait sperm or ova +	Black ova or sperm	Black Cross-Bred
Red trait sperm or ova +	Red ova or sperm	Red Pure-Bred

In short, the animal showing the *recessive* trait is always pure bred in respect of that trait.

The animal showing the *dominant* trait may be either pure bred or cross-bred in respect of that trait.

CHROMOSOMES

The nucleus of every cell contains a number of thread-like bodies called ' *Chromosomes* ', arranged in pairs. There are a different number of pairs for each species of animal, thus the ox has seventeen complete pairs, while the horse has nineteen. When a spermatozoon or an ovum is to be formed, a cell detaches itself from the epithelium lining the tubules of the testicles or the follicles of the ovary, and then divides into two, in such a manner that each half contains one member of each pair of chromosomes. These half-cells become two spermatozoa or two ova, as the case may be, each with only half a nucleus, or rather half the number of chromosomes. After mating, when a spermatozoon unites with an ovum, the two half nuclei join together and form a complete nucleus with the complete number of pairs of chromosomes. One member of each pair has come from the male parent and one from the female parent.

It is believed that these chromosomes carry the factors of inherited traits. If a bull has developed from a germ cell containing in a pair of chromosomes a red factor in one

member of the pair and a white factor in the other, a red and
white or red roan animal results, but each one of the spermatozoon that it produces has only one member of the pair of
chromosomes, and can therefore only carry the red factor or
the white factor, but not both. Similarly, a cow developed
from a germ cell carrying both factors will herself be red roan,
but can only make ova carrying the chromosome for one factor
or the other but not both. It is clear also that both kinds of
ova and spermatozoa will be produced in equal numbers, and
the probabilities of the colour of their offspring will be as shown
above, one red, two roans and one white.

Now, as the ox has sixteen pairs of chromosomes, it follows
that there are only sixteen groups of characteristics that can
be inherited, and by the formula given above 2^{32} or somewhere
about 90,000 million different ways in which they can be
grouped in one ox.

It can be stated quite definitely that most of the stories of
cross-breeding between two widely different species of animals
are false.   Unless the animals have the same number of chromosomes of much the same shape, they cannot form pairs, and so
no germ cell can be formed.   Hence horses cannot breed with
cattle, nor can cats with rabbits, nor dogs with badgers.   Yet,
even in these days, the last two beliefs are widely held, and
malformed kittens and puppies are still accounted for in
country districts as having been sired by hares, rabbits or
badgers, and the author has been shown a book recently
published which gave the word ' Jumat ' as meaning the
offspring of a cow got by a stallion.

Determination of Sex. In mammals, the cells of the male
carry a single unpaired chromosome so, when the parent cell
of the spermatozoon divides into two, one-half carries the
unpaired chromosome and one-half does not. Thus, exactly
half the spermatozoa have an extra chromosome and generate
male offspring, while the remainder generate females. As
stated above, the ox has 16 pairs of chromosomes which
implies that all the cells of the body of a cow have nuclei
containing in all 32 chromosomes, while the ova she produces
each have 16 chromosomes, but the cells of the bull (or bullock)
have 33 (16 pairs + 1 unpaired) chromosomes, so half the
spermatozoon he produces have 17 chromosomes and half

16 chromosomes. If a 17 chromosome spermatozoon joins a 16-chromosome ovum, a male germ cell of 33 chromosomes is formed and a bull calf begotten ; but if a 16-chromosome spermatozoon joins a 16-chromosome ovum, a 32-chromosome germ cell is produced and a heifer calf begotten. In poultry the case is reversed, for the hen's cells carry the extra chromosome that forms a female and therefore exactly half the eggs she produces carry hen-forming ova and half carry cock-forming ova and the chances of mating make the odds still 50-50 for either sex resulting.

The value of this knowledge to breeders lies in the fact that purely female traits such as milk yield are inherited from both parents and the pedigree of the bull must therefore be considered as of equal importance with that of the cow if a good herd is to be built up, or, as old farmers say, ' The bull is half the herd '. But most beef characteristics are linked to the male traits, and therefore in building up a beef herd, the bull is more than half the herd. He plays the biggest part in making it a success. With poultry it is the reverse, for the purely feminine traits are inherited from the hen only, but the male traits are inherited from both parents. Hens with a dominant colour linked to their extra chromosome are valuable as their hen chicks will show this colour on hatching but not their cockerel chicks.

This knowledge disposes at once of certain old-time beliefs. It used to be held that the sperm of the right testicle was male and that of the left, female ; or that of the ova of one ovary was male and the other female, or that the ova released in alternate oestral cycles were male and female in turn. In mammals, both testicles produce male-forming and female-forming spermatozoa in exactly equal numbers, and the sex of the progeny is purely a matter of chance. In poultry, the male-forming ova and the female-forming ova are also produced in exactly equal numbers, and the rest is also a matter of chance. Research has been going on for some years now in the hopes of finding some method of reducing the number of male-forming spermatozoa and so increasing the chances of females being born, but so far with no success.

SOME OTHER POPULAR FALLACIES

Pre-natal Influence.   While it is obvious that the health of the dam during pregnancy may materially affect that of the offspring, it is equally obvious that the colour of the calf's hair cannot be influenced in any way by placing his mother in a whitewashed or tarred or otherwise painted shed while mating or during her pregnancy.   Similarly, though a bad fright may possibly affect a cow's health and therefore the health of her calf, it cannot distort the calf in any way.   ' Bull-dog ' calves are the result of a glandular deficiency in the make up of the calf, and are never due to the cow having been frightened by a dog.

Influence of Previous Sire.   This idea is more widely held by dog owners than any other breeders.   It is commonly held that, if a pedigree bitch is mated by a mongrel, she will continue to deliver mongrel pups for the rest of her life, even when mated by thoroughbreds, though it is never stated that a mongrel bitch mated by a thoroughbred will continue to have thoroughbred pups all her life.   It is impossible to conceive of any mechanism by which this phenomenon could occur and it has been disproved by countless experiments.

Inheritance of Acquired Characteristics.   This belief is not widely held nowadays, but at one time it was thought that by training the cows' horns in a certain way for several generations, calves would eventually be born that would develop the artificial horn growth of their mothers.   It should be realised that terrier dogs have had their tails docked since the time of the Norman Conquest, but they are still born with full-length tails. No injury or accidental or artificial alteration of the body is ever inherited.

Recently it has been shown that the inherited traits in plants can be altered by exposing the parents to gamma-rays but, so far, the exact alteration cannot be foreseen.   At the time of writing, it has not been successfully attempted with mammals or birds.

CHAPTER XI

THE FOWL

Skeleton; Muscles; Nervous System; Skin; Vascular System; Respiratory System; Digestive System; Uro-Genital Systems.

THE SKELETON (Fig. 61)

The Vertebral Column. The Vertebrae over the body are for the most part, fused together, and even the articulated bones are not capable of much movement, thus only the neck and tail are truly flexible, the former very much so. The *Cervical Vertebrae* number fourteen and resemble those of the mammal in all essentials, except for the *Atlas*, which is a simple ring with no wing-like processes. The *Thoracic Vertebrae* number seven, of which the second, third, fourth, and fifth are fused together, the first and sixth are articulated, but not very freely, and the seventh is fused to the first lumbar. The *Lumbo-sacral Vertebrae*, fourteen in number, together with the seventh thoracic and first coccygeal, are fused together. The remaining five coccygeal are articulated, the last being enlarged to form the Pygostyle or ' Parson's Nose '. Thus, though the vertebral formula is $C_{14} . T_7 L + S_{14} . C_6$, it is more practicable to consider it as Neck$_{14}$. Chest$_6$. Abdomen$_{16}$. Tail$_5$.

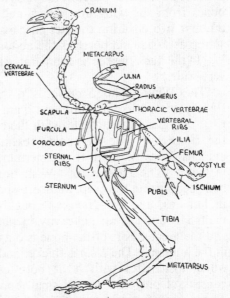

FIG. 61.—Skeleton of fowl.

199

(In the Duck the vertebral formula is $C_{15}T_9L + S_{12}C_6$. The thoracic and lumbar-sacral vertebrae are all fused together, but all six coccygeal bones are freely articulated.)

The Ribs. The first two pairs are ' floating', but the remaining five are joined to the sternum. These sternal ribs are jointed in the middle so that each is in two parts, a vertebral part and a sternal part, the latter corresponding to the costal cartilage of the mammal. The vertebral part of ribs 2-5 is joined to the rib behind by a short process.

(In the duck only the first pair of ribs are floating.)

The Sternum consists of a deep keel, surmounted by a longitudinal gutter that supports the thoracic and abdominal organs. There is an anterior process, the *Rostrum*, to which the coracoid bones from the wing are joined, and three lateral processes, the first two covering the sternal part of the ribs and the last acting as a side support for the abdominal organs.

(In the duck the keel is comparatively small, but the ' gutter ' very wide.)

The Wing. The *Scapula* is a narrow blade-like bone, slightly curved like a sabre, and lying over the tops of all the ribs. Its glenoid articulates with the coracoid, the furcula and the humerus. The *Coracoid* (absent in humans and farm animals) joins the limb to the sternum and supports the body in flight. The *Furcula* (or ' Wish Bone ') is a stirrup-shaped bone supporting the crop, and corresponds to the two clavicles in humans, and the *Humerus* roughly resembles that of the mammal, but has an air cavity in place of a marrow cavity, and the greater part of the bone is outside the thoracic skin, as in the human. The *Ulna* is thicker and longer than the *Radius*, which articulates with it at both ends. The *Carpal Joint* consists of only one row of small bones; there are two main *Metacarpals* fused at each end and articulated to a short digit, while an accessory metacarpal articulates with a digit corresponding to the human thumb. The wing membrane consists of a double fold of skin stretching from the top of the humerus to the tip of the main digit.

(In the duck, the furcula is thick and strong and curved backward.)

The Leg. The *Ilium* fuses with its fellow above the first six lumbo-sacral vertebrae. (In the duck, the ilia cover the last three thoracic vertebrae as well.) The *Ischium* is a broad plate of bone forming the side wall of the upper part of the abdomen. The *Pubis* is a thin strip of bone fused to the lower edge of the ischium and protruding behind it, but it does *not* fuse with its fellow. The *Femur* is similar to that of the mammal, but contains an air cavity instead of a marrow cavity. The bone lies within the abdominal skin except at its lower end. The *Patella* is a broad flat plate of bone. The *Tibia* and *Fibula* resembles those of the mammal, but are fused instead of articulated, and the lower end of the tibia fuses with the Astragalus forming one bone. There is no os calcis, and the remaining bones of the *Tarsus* fuse with the metatarsal bone, so that the tarsus forms a single joint. The *Metatarsal* bone supports three digits that point forwards and a shorter one that points backwards. In effect, the bird stands on the equivalent of the ball of the human foot.

The Skull. The *Cranium* lies at the back of the head, its front being considerably behind the eyes. It is surrounded by thick, bony plates, but its actual cavity is small, and there is no frontal sinus. The two orbits are separated by a thin bony plate, but the nostrils are only separated by cartilage and the turbinates remain cartilaginous throughout life. The jaw bones are light and thin, as the horny beak requires very little support. The *Hyoid* bone consists of two long, thin bars that bend forwards and join to form a thin process filling most of the tongue.

THE MUSCLES

The muscles as a whole are pale and lacking in intramuscular fat or 'marbling', but those round the leg are redder and firmer than elsewhere. Their general arrangement is similar to that of the mammal, but the following differences may be of interest.

The Diaphragm consists of a muscular rim with no tendinous centre. Thus there is no division between the thorax and abdomen which, therefore, form one cavity, the *Body Cavity*. This is lined with a continuous serous membrane, the *Pleuroperitoneal Membrane*. Respiration, defaecation, and the deposition of eggs are carried out by contraction of the rib and abdominal muscles only.

The Wing Muscles. The large *Pectorals*, which form the muscular mass popularly known as the ' Breast ', connect the keel of the sternum with the wing and bring about its downward beat in flight. The wing is lifted by the combined *Lattissimus Dorsi* and *Trapezius* muscles, which form most of the meat of the back.

The Leg Muscles. The Psoas is rudimentary and may be missing entirely. The *Adductors* join each other, instead of the pubic bone, and so strengthen the abdominal floor. The *Gastrocnemius* and the *Extensors* and *Flexors* of the leg are large, firm and red, and are attached by rods of cartilage instead of tendons, to the digits. In adult birds, these rods tend to ossify.

The Fat may be white or yellow, according to the breed. It accumulates in the body cavity especially on the abdominal floor, but is scanty in the muscular regions.

THE NERVOUS SYSTEM

This closely resembles that of the mammals. It is perhaps as well to emphasise that the brain lies at the back of the head and is relatively small, as it is common for laymen to kill birds by driving a knife through the face bones at the back of the nose and eyes. This causes death by haemorrhage and suffocation, but does not cause immediate unconsciousness. Birds can be ' pithed ' behind the head as can mammals, or the knife can be driven through the back of the mouth into the cranium. This is probably the best method, as it causes a spasm of the white muscles throughout the body, thus erecting the feathers and making subsequent plucking easier.

THE SKIN

There are no sweat or sebum glands in the skin. The feathers are produced by a process similar to the production of hair and horn, and are composed of tightly packed, completely desiccated, epithelial cells. They are oiled during ' preening ' with a fatty secretion that is spread by the bird itself with its beak from glands near the vent.

The Comb and **Wattles** remain uncovered, and contain cavernous erectile tissue that becomes engorged during excitement, especially in males.

The Spur is an extra claw developed by males after fledging. It is a horny growth on the skin only and has no bony core. The drake and the guinea cock have no spur.

THE VASCULAR SYSTEMS

The circulation of blood and lymph is essentially the same as in the mammal. *Lymph Nodes*, however, are only found in the mesentery but the bone marrow contains abundant lymphoid tissue. The *Spleen* is a rounded, red-brown body about 1 inch diameter, lying on the anterior right wall of the gizzard, and for some unknown reason, popularly referred to as the 'Kidney'. (The true kidneys are described below.) The *Red Blood Cells* are elliptical in outline and have large nuclei.

THE RESPIRATORY SYSTEM

The Larynx has no vocal cords and no epiglottis, hence the trachea cannot be closed and the head must be thrown well back in drinking. The rings of the *Trachea* are complete, so that its diameter cannot be altered. At its point of bifurcation into *Bronchi* there are membranous folds that serve the same purpose as the vocal cords and by vibrating in the air stream produce voice. The *Lungs* adhere to the ribs and are covered on their medial surfaces only with serous membrane which is continued into the abdomen, forming part of the *Pleuro-peritoneal Membrane*. There is thus no pleural cavity. The lungs themselves have no alveoli, but are penetrated by minute bronchioles which lead from the main bronchi to "*air cavities.*" These bronchioles are lined with respiratory membrane, similar to that lining the alveoli of the mammalian lung. Capillary blood vessels are wound round each bronchiole and gases are exchanged as the air passes to and from the air cavities.

Respiration depends partly on rib movement and partly on the movement of the walls of the air cavities which act as bellows, drawing air through the bronchioles. There are eleven such air cavities, three at the root of the neck, one under each wing communicating with the interior of the humerus, and six round the abdominal organs lying between them and the muscular walls and communicating with the interior of the femur. Each is lined with a thin mucous membrane lying on pelvic peritoneal membrane. In addition to their respiratory function, their purpose seems to be to provide the equivalent of sweating and cooling areas as external sweating would damp the feathers and interfere with flight.

THE DIGESTIVE SYSTEM (Fig. 62)

The tongue has a fairly sharp horny tip, and its base is furnished with a few piliform papillae directed backwards, lying just in front of the tracheal orifice.

The food is swallowed without chewing and accumulates in the *Crop*, a large sac lined with mucous membrane lying at the entrance to the thorax and supported by the furcula. In the crop it is mixed with saliva and is passed on slowly to the *Glandular Stomach*, a short, tubular organ that lies in the posterior part of the mediastinum and provides the gastric digestive juices. Material from the glandular stomach enters the *Gizzard* or *Muscular Stomach*, which is a strong, thick-walled organ of red muscle lined with a horny epithelium that is roughened with small hard papillae. This normally contains small grit that, in all probability grinds up the food and so act in place of teeth.* Some of the grit is broken up in time and dissolved by the digestive juices, so making good any mineral shortages in the food.*

The structure and function of the small intestine is similar to that of the mammal. The *Large Intestine* is straight as in cattle, not bulbous as in other mammals. It consists of two long *Caeca* that stretch the entire length of the abdominal floor, and a relatively short *Colon* which terminates in a short dilatable portion, the *Cloaca*, into which the uro-genital orifices also open. The terminal sphincter is referred to as the *Vent*. The walls of the caeca are covered with lymphoid tissue apparently corresponding to Peyer's Patches, and the contents are liquid and never gaseous. There is evidence that a considerable amount of absorption occurs through the caecal walls, as well as those of the colon.

The Liver lies in the anterior part of the abdomen touching the pericardium. Above it lies the gizzard and proventriculus and behind it the intestines. Below and beside it are air

---

* Each of these statements has been denied by various investigators, but both are still generally accepted by the majority of workers.

cavities. It is divided into two lobes. The ducts of the right lobe discharge into a small gall bladder which discharges into the small intestine. The ducts of the left lobe discharge into the left bile duct, which discharges into the intestine without a gall bladder.

1. Tongue
2. Piliform papillae·
3. Opening of trachea
4. Opening of oesophagus
5. Oesophagus
6. Crop
7. Proventriculus or glandular stomach
8. Left lobe of liver
9. Wall of gizzard or muscular stomach
10. Papillae and mucous membrane lining gizzard
11. Grits in gizzard
12. Gall bladder
13. Pancreas
14. Left caecum
15. Right caecum
16. Pancreatic duct
17. Right lobe of liver
18. Right hepatic duct (no gall bladder)
19. Large intestine
20. Genital papillae
21. Cloaca
22. Vent
23. Opening of ureters

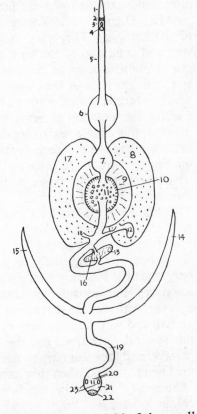

FIG. 62.—Diagram of digestive tract of cock.

The Pancreas is a long, thin strip lying in a fold of the small intestine into which it discharges by two ducts.

The Mesentery supports all the abdominal organs. It is usually free of fat. Parts of it are covered with mucous membrane that line the abdominal air cavities.

THE URO-GENITAL SYSTEMS

The kidneys, or 'soles', lie on each side of the backbone, stretching from the sixth rib to the centre of the lumbo-sacral vertebrae. Each is about 1 inch in length by one-third in breadth, and has four lobes, and each is fixed and normally buried deeply in fat. The *Adrenal Bodies*, about the size of a pea, lie at the anterior inner corners. The *Ureters* lead down to the cloaca to empty separately just within the vent, the urine being extruded with the faeces.

Male Organs. The Testicles lie beneath the anterior end of the kidneys. They vary in size according to the time of year and condition of the bird, and may only be the size of a pea in midwinter, or as large as a cherry in the spring. The spermatic ducts enter the cloaca by two small erectile papillae, which protrude during mating and enter the cloaca of the hen. Careful manipulation of newly hatched chicks will reveal these papillae and enable sex to be determined, but 48 hours after hatching they are too deep in the body to be exposed without injuring the bird.* In geese and swans there is only one papilla which becomes very large, and these birds can be made to protrude it by manipulation.

Removal of the testicles produces a lazy, fat bird, lacking most male characteristics and called a ' Capon '. Although the operation involves opening the abdomen, it is not particularly dangerous, and can usually be performed by a farm hand, but only when the birds are well grown and some of the male characteristics are already developed. Downy chicks can be injected with female hormones that will suppress all male growth and so produce a very much better table bird than will the surgical operation, but the injections are still rather expensive, and they can only be used when the sexes of the chicks are known, that is, when they have been sexed as day-olds, or in ' Cross-bar ' breeds in which male chicks have a different colour to females.

The Female Organs. Normally only the left ovary and oviduct develop, the right disappearing soon after hatching. The ovary lies close to the left kidney, and is connected to the cloaca by a long, flexuous oviduct of thin white muscle lined with thin mucous membrane. When a hen is about to come into lay, an ovum inside a Graafian follicle starts to acquire a ' yolk ' or food material and to swell, without, however,

* The manipulation should only be carried out by qualified operators, as unskilled persons injure and kill large numbers of chicks.

rupturing the follicle, which is enlarged with it. Another ovum starts to swell the next day. The swelling is at first slow, and it takes about 10 days for each yolk (really an enlarged ovum) to reach the size of a millet seed. Thereafter growth is rapid and in four days the yolk reaches its full size. It then breaks out of its follicle and travels down the oviduct, acquiring four layers of albumen in doing so. The shell is added about 4 hours before laying. Thus in the carcase of a hen in lay there will be a cluster of small yolks and three or four large ones and a complete or nearly complete egg. Should the bird be mated, the spermatozoa from the cock lie in the oviduct and fertilize the ova as they pass. These spermatozoa are comparatively long lived and will continue to fertilize eggs three weeks after the last mating. There is no equivalent to the periodical oestrum of the mammal, and eggs are formed whenever the bird is in good condition and the surroundings are suitable whether she is mated or not. At indefinite periods ' Broodiness ' develops and egg-laying is suspended, and it is also suspended when the hen is mothering chicks or when she is moulting. Cold or wet weather may also affect it in varying degrees.

The ovary can be removed by a surgical operation, but the resulting bird, the ' Poulard or Half-hen ' is not very greatly superior to normal table birds, and the operation is dangerous, and frequently results in death and total loss. It has, therefore, dropped out of use almost entirely.

The development of the fertile egg is similar to that of the mammalian embryo. A morula is first formed, expanding later into a membrane equivalent to the placenta that lines the shell and also surrounds the yolk. This membrane exchanges gases through the shell, which is porous, and acquires nutriment from the yolk. The foetus develops in one side of this membrane.

CHAPTER XII

DEATH AND POST-MORTEM CHANGES

Circulatory Failure; Rigor Mortis; Auto-digestion; Bloating; Fermentation; Putrefaction; Keratinisation; Adipocere; Freezing.

IN law a man or animal is considered to be dead when both the heart beat and respiration have finally ceased, but manifestly this is only a legal assumption, for the body being composed of a mass of cells each living its individual life, it is not truly dead until all its cells have perished. Comparatively inactive cells, such as those of the bones, teeth or roots of the hair and horn, whose oxygen requirements are slight, may live for a considerable time after the circulation and the respiration have stopped, and it is difficult to say when exactly such cells die. Epithelial cells may be considered dead when they allow the passage of moisture in both directions, for in life the epithelium of the cuticle will not allow the passage of moisture in any direction, and the epithelium of living mucous membrane may allow the passage outwards of moisture (excretion) or the passage inwards of moisture (absorption), but never both. Nerve cells may be considered dead when they finally cease to transmit sensations and stimuli to the muscles, but unless the muscles or the consciousness are still alive, we cannot say if the nerves have ceased to act. Muscle cells and connective tissue cells alone provide exact evidence of the moment of their death, for, in life, they always retain some tension, however slight it may be, while after death, they are completely relaxed. As their oxygen requirements are considerable, they always die very soon after circulation has ceased (and some may even be dead before this), and the complete relaxation of the body that results when all muscle is dead is usually accepted as the moment of its death. Nerve cells use, if anything, more oxygen than muscles, and may therefore be assumed to die earlier than muscles.

In nature, most animals die as a result of failure of the heart. The heart muscle can no longer maintain its regular and incessant beat owing to age or to poisoning by the products of disease or malnutrition due to actual starvation or to digestive disorders. As the failure is usually progressive, the muscle cells are already short of oxygen and nutriment, especially glycogen, when the final stoppage of the heart occurs, and they therefore die rapidly with no post-mortem movements and little or no rigor mortis, for rigor mortis requires abundant glycogen and a certain amount of oxygen. The mucous membranes and visible skin have a pale blue tint due to the de-oxidised blood therein. On opening the body, it is seen that the arteries are empty, for they live longer than the heart, and their last pulsations drive the blood out of them; but the veins, especially those on the lower side of the body, are full of blood clots and clear serum. The flesh and the organs, especially the lungs, are dark, owing to the engorged capillary blood-vessels, particularly on the side nearest the ground. Clotted blood is also found in the heart, for its last relaxation will allow it to fill, but its final contraction is too weak to empty it. Frequently the blood in the heart 'separates' before clotting, and a clot of clear yellow fibrin forms in a ventricle with a cap of red blood corpuscles on top. This is called an 'agony clot', but it has no connection with agony or pain, and is only found after a slow but peaceful death.

If the circulatory failure has been rapid, as a result of injury or accident, for example, the cerebrum dies first for its oxygen requirements are considerable, and thereafter the animal is unconscious. Next the cerebellum and medulla die and, just before their death, they seem to undergo a spasm of activity that promotes 'reflex actions' or 'post-mortem movements'. The body starts a regular galloping or trotting movement that may last 10 or 20 minutes. There is no conscious efforts in these movements, for the body does not attempt to rise and cannot maintain balance if it is raised. These movements can be brought to an end by destroying the cerebellum or medulla. Finally, the red muscles die, but also undergo a death spasm by contracting fairly firmly. This final death contraction starts at the head and slowly passes over the whole body, making it rigid, and in an ox this rigidity takes about 2 hours to complete, but in smaller animals it is not so long. Like all muscular contractions, this post-mortem contraction generates heat, and as there is no circulation to disperse this heat, the temperature of the dead body rises two or three degrees after its apparent death. In most cases, the rigidity of the dying muscle cells lasts until most of the glycogen has been converted into sarcolactic acid by the oxygen retained in them (see Chap. III, p. 53), and this acid coagulates their liquid protein, myosin, so establishing rigor-mortis.* In the course of about five days, the accumulation of acid converts the protein of the white connective tissue ' collagen ', into gelatine, a process that somewhat softens or ' ripens ' the meat.

If the animal was subjected to severe muscular activity before death, as in a hunted animal or one that had struggled hard before collapse, the tired muscle cells die sooner and the preliminary contraction starts earlier, and, as the glycogen store in the cells has been drawn on heavily, there is little sarcolactic acid formed and subsequent rigor mortis will be slight or absent altogether. In such animals it is said that ' rigor mortis starts early and passes quickly '. Really true rigor mortis has not been established at all.

In nature, dead bodies are usually consumed by the carrion-eating mammals and birds, of which there are far more, even in the English countryside, than is generally realised. Failing these, flies, beetles and similar forms of life consume them, while in rivers and ponds the fish and shrimps perform the same duty. If, however, it is not consumed, a dead body undergoes the following changes.

Auto Digestion. As soon as the mucous membrane of the alimentary canal dies, the digestive juices therein can enter the cells and dissolve their protein contents, so the walls of the bowel gradually turn black and become soft and easily torn. The juices may penetrate to the peritoneal membranes and stain and destroy the mesentery, omentum and the inner surface of the abdominal wall. Dark green, almost black, staining is due to this and is known as ' Bile Stain '.

Bloating. The large intestine of all mammals and the rumen of ruminants contain large numbers of bacteria that play parts of varying importance in digestion, and most of

---

* Research at present in progress at the Low Temperature Research Station, Cambridge, would seem to indicate that the current hypothesis of rigor mortis as given above may need modification, or even replacement. It is probable that the initial death spasm of the muscle fibrils is due to chemical activity; and this activity probably affects the subsequent ' setting ' of the meat.

these generate gases while multiplying. In life, these gases are absorbed into the system or passed out through the anus or belched out of the mouth, but after death, they accumulate and swell out the body, giving a tense, drum-like feel to the abdominal regions.

The bodies of birds do not bloat, as accumulations of gas pass through the intestinal wall into the abdominal air sacs, and thence pass out of the trachea.

Fermentation. The intestinal, but not the ruminal, bacteria occasionally penetrate the intestinal wall of the living animal and enter the blood and lymph streams, but these are dealt with by the leucocytes and lymph nodes. After death, these bacteria penetrate more rapidly and can spread along the lymph and blood-vessels without resistance. The gases they generate contain a large proportion of phosphoretted hydrogen which gives the flesh the smell known as ' bone taint ', since it is strongest in the large lymph spaces such as the synovial sacs in the joints between bones. Usually they enter the external iliac blood-vessels early, since these pass close by the bowels in the posterior end of the abdominal cavity. Hence the meat of the hind limbs served by these vessels is first affected. These bacteria do not attack solids, but decompose the lymph, blood, bone marrow, and the liquid contents of those muscle cells that have not undergone rigor mortis, and in blood they produce a ' *Green Stain* '. They are not, in themselves, harmful, nor do they generate poisons, but they render meat offensive to most people, though some folk like the ' gamey ' smell and flavour in venison, mutton, hare and wild birds. Domestic poultry do not appear to carry any fermenting organisms.

Fermentation can be delayed and reduced by the following means:—

(a) Ensure that all animals are in good health before slaughter, so as to ensure that any bacteria that invade the blood and lymph stream during life are dealt with by the body's defences.

(b) Ensure that they are well nourished and that they are well rested before slaughter, so that the glycogen content of the muscles will be high and good rigor mortis will set in, as solidified muscle will not ferment.

(*Note.*—This will not delay fermentation in organs unaffected by rigor mortis, i.e. brain, spinal cord, liver, spleen and bowels.)

(*c*) Ensure thorough bleeding, so as to reduce the possibility of bacteria spreading along blood-vessels.

(*d*) Remove bowels as soon as possible after slaughter.

(*e*) Remove all bruised flesh in which blood has clotted, as this will form a favourable medium for bacterial multiplication.

(*f*) Maintain strict cleanliness to prevent reinfection of the meat.

(*g*) Cool down the carcase as quickly as possible after dressing.

Putrefaction and Decay.   These are due to various bacteria (putrefaction) and moulds (decay) which, like the fermenting bacteria, can only migrate through moisture, though moulds require less moisture than bacteria.   Both bacteria and moulds will, however, attack all proteins, both liquid and solid, and reduce them to simple compounds that dissolve readily in water.   Putrefactive organisms abound in all soils, dust and unsterilised water, so, as soon as the epidermis of the skin has died and allowed water to enter the dermis, putrefactive organisms will enter with it and start their work of destruction. Many of them generate phosphoretted hydrogen, and so the smell of putrefaction is generally indistinguishable from that of fermentation, but the products of putrefaction are frequently poisonous, and some of the organisms can be highly dangerous when in an active state and invigorated by breeding on the meat proteins.   People therefore who eat fermented meat run the risk of eating putrefied meat without being aware of it and being poisoned thereby.

Putrefaction can be delayed by the same steps as those taken to prevent fermentation, with the additional one of hanging the carcase clear of the floor (which will obviously be either wet or dirty) before the skin has had time to die and become sodden.

In killing an animal, it is impossible to prevent the entry of some putrefactive organisms into the system unless the same care is taken as a surgeon does in operating.   The amount of such infection, however, can be reduced to a minimum by reasonable cleanliness and by avoiding, as far as possible, the opening of veins in which the blood would carry the infection back to the heart. If the brain has been penetrated in stunning (the usual practice) the animal should be bled as soon as possible afterwards, so that circulation ceases before the organisms have time to multiply.

Poultry are best kept in a dry, cool store without their bodies being opened, as opening the abdomen to draw the bird will also allow the entry of putrefactive organisms. As stated previously, poultry carcases do not ferment.

The prevention of auto-digestion, fermentation and putrefaction form the greatest problems in abattoir management and the storage and handling of meat. The outline given above is therefore dealt with more fully in the books on Meat Technology. It will, however, be of interest to follow somewhat further the changes of a dead body that has been left to the forces of nature.

In natural water, or even on normally moist ground, the body will absorb sufficient moisture to allow putrefaction to proceed, and it will proceed at all temperatures between freezing-point and about 120° F. (At 145° F. it is checked and, if kept at this level for some time, the organisms are killed, but the proteins of the meat undergo considerable alteration.) Therefore, in damp, warm or temperate climates, even a large body, such as that of an ox, is completely dissolved in a month, except for the hard material in the bones, and this, having no cartilaginous support, usually crumble away soon after, though occasionally, if there is much lime in the soil, this is deposited in the bones, forming 'Fossils'. If, however, the body is in dry surroundings, it will tend to lose moisture through the skin as soon as the epidermis has died, and it may become too dry for the putrefactive organisms to act. In time, 2 or 3 months at the least, the flesh is completely dried and the proteins undergo an alteration, forming a hornlike material, 'keratin', and the body has the shrivelled appearance of a mummy. Mummified bodies are found on arid deserts and in dry graves or in places where they have been packed round with quicklime. Partial drying of meat sufficient to check putrefaction, but not to keratinise it, has been practised from the earliest times, and until recently the product was known as ' biltong' or ' pemmican'. Nowadays it is called ' Dehydrated Meat ', but the process is essentially the same. Dehydrated meat retains most of the nutritious qualities of fresh meat, and will keep a long time, but not indefinitely. In its preparation care must be taken not to extract all the water or a keratinised product of no nutritional value results.

If the body is lying in an acid water, such as that found in most bogs, moorland or forest areas, it is converted into a fatty material called ' *Adipocere* ', which is quite useless as a nutriment. The process takes about 6 months in most places, and is so gradual that normally the original outline is maintained, and even features show little change. The bones are unaffected. A similar change sometimes occurs in parts of the living body as a result of disease or injury.

All processes of auto-digestion, fermentation and putrefaction are delayed by cooling, but they are not entirely checked as long as the temperature is above freezing. Chilled meat, therefore, will keep for a long time, but not indefinitely, for, in time, it will decay. Freezing, however, entirely stops all three processes, and frozen meat will keep for any length of time as long as its temperature remains below freezing-point. Indeed, bodies of animals known to have died more than 3,000 years ago are recovered from time to time from the Arctic ice, and are found to be in a state of perfect preservation. In bodies, however, frozen by the force of nature, the body fluids form large ice crystals that rupture the cell walls ; so, on thawing out, they tend to crumble away and the putrefactive bacteria destroy them with great rapidity. None has lasted long enough to be preserved as museum specimens.

The science of refrigeration studies how meat can best be frozen without damage to the tissues, and how it can be kept thus, unchanged in consistence and constitution, for indefinite periods of time.

THE LYMPH NODES

[The exact positions of the lymph nodes can only be learnt by actually detecting them on carcases and viscera. Illustrations and written descriptions can only act as aids, not substitutes, for this.]

As shown in Chapter VI (Circulation), practically all the lymph from the posterior half of the body collects in the *Chyle Cistern* at the top of the diaphragm. From there it runs through the *Thoracic Duct*, under the thoracic vertebrae parallel to the aorta, and enters either the anterior vena cava or the left jugular vein to join the blood stream. Lymph ducts from the anterior half of the body drain into this thoracic duct, usually directly, but sometimes a short Right Thoracic Duct collects a few of those from the right arm and side of the thorax and joins the Main Thoracic Duct just before its termination. Each subsidiary lymph duct passes through one, two, or sometimes several, *Lymph Nodes* before entering the chyle cistern or thoracic duct, and these nodes filter the lymph and add leucocytes. All lymph nodes are surrounded by fat. The positions of most of these lymph nodes are given with the descriptions of the organs and muscles, but they are repeated here for convenience of reference.

THE OX

The Abdominal Organs. Lymph from the intestines is enriched with fat obtained from food, and is called Chyle. It is collected from the intestines by minute lymph ducts called Lacteals, and most of these pass the undermentioned nodes.

Large Mesenteric Lymph, which lie in the mesentery, forming a row parallel to the small intestine. Usually the intestine is removed before they are inspected, and they will be found, twenty or thirty in number, about 2 inches from the outer edge of the mesentery. Each is about 3 inches long and an inch wide. Small mesenteric nodes are found scattered through the mesentery. Most of the chyle passes through these and thence direct to the chyle cistern; but some, from the duodenal end, passes to the liver and thence to the

Portal (or *Hepatic*), two or three in number, situated in a ring of fat round the entrace of the portal vein to the liver; from these it passes to the chyle cistern. The pancreatic node lies among them.

The Gastric or *Rumenal* (miscalled Gastro-splenic), lie in the omentum along the edge of the spleen. As the omentum is always removed from the rumen and spleen before inspection these nodes are difficult to find, and are not usually inspected. They filter lymph from the walls of the four stomachs, and pass it to the chyle cistern.

The Thoracic Organs. Lymph from the heart and lungs all drains into the mediastinum, and is filtered by the *Mediastinal Lymph Nodes*. In practice, these are usually regarded as one group, but anatomically they are divided as follows:—

Anterior Mediastinal lie above the trachea between the two lungs. They receive lymph from the heart and bronchial lymph nodes and pass it to the thoracic duct.

Bronchial are situated (*a*) close to the origin of the left bronchus adjacent to the upward bend of the aorta, (*b*) on the medial surface of the right bronchus close to its origin, (*c*) at the bifurcation of the bronchi, (*d*) on the lateral side of the apical bronchus to the right lung. These collect lymph from the lungs and pass it to the anterior mesenteric lymph nodes for additional filtration. In many cases (*b*) or (*c*) or both are missing.

Posterior Mediastinal lie between the lungs but behind the bifurcation of the trachea and therefore rest on the oesophagus. These receive some lymph from the lungs, but most from the diaphragm and therefore some from the peritoneal cavity on its far side. They drain into the thoracic duct.

The Head. *The Submaxillary* lie on the inner surface of the lower jaw close to the angle. They may be found still attached to the jaw, or to the tongue if this has been separated, or the knife may have passed through them. They receive lymph from the nose and mouth and pass it to the Pharangeal nodes.

The Parotid lie under the parotid salivary glands immediately below the auditory meatus or ' ear hole '. The salivary tissue must be cut through to find them. They receive lymph from the upper part of the head and face and the cranium, and pass it to the pharyngeal nodes.

The Atlanteal lies under the wing of the atlas and receives lymph from the occipital regions and delivers it to the middle cervical nodes.

The Pharyngeal (or *Retro-pharyngeal* or *Upper Cervical*) lie on each side of the walls of the pharynx near the top adjacent to the uprights of the hyoid bone. They are found by placing the knife inside the pharynx and cutting outwards. They receive lymph from the submaxillary and parotid nodes, and also from the pharynx and larynx, and pass it by the two Tracheal Ducts to the thoracic duct.

These Abdominal, Thoracic and Head Nodes are examined as a matter of routine in all carcases. If found infected, the carcase lymph nodes are also examined.

The Carcase (Plate XI). The nodes shown in heavy type are those most frequently examined. The others are only rarely used.

Popliteal lies under the semi-tendinosus, close to the junction of the semi-membraneous and bicips femoris, about half way between the point of the ischium and the os calcis and about 6 inches deep. It is found on dividing the top side from the silver side if the cut follows the seam between the muscles or on taking off the ' leg '. It receives lymph from the lower part of the leg and passes it to both the sciatic and iliac nodes.

Sciatic (or *Ischiatic*) lies on the outer face of the sacrosciatic ligament, about half way between the medial corner of the ischium and the posterior end of the sacrum. It is found on separating the rump from the buttock. It receives lymph from the organs in the pelvis and also from the popliteal node and delivers it to the internal iliac nodes.

Superficial Inguinal, males only, lie in the back of the cod fat or just behind the inguinal canals in an entire animal. They receive lymph from the genital organs and the surrounding skin and also from the leg and deliver it to the internal iliac or (more rarely) the deep inguinal.

Deep Inguinal, males only, and frequently missing in castrates, lie at the inner end of the inguinal canal, and receive lymph from the superficial inguinal for delivery at the internal iliac. They are found when separating the rump and buttock. Both inguinal nodes should be examined as a routine measure, as they are liable to venereal infection, even in castrates. (Many castrated animals will mount their fellows.)

Supra Mammary, females only, behind the udder close to the abdominal wall. There are usually two on each side and they can be felt through the skin during life. They are found when removing the mammary or dug fat. They receive lymph from the udder and deliver it to the internal iliac.

Precrural or *Prefemoral* lies on the inner side of the patella fold of the panniculus muscle (the skin fold), and is found on taking off the hind quarter. It receives lymph from the skin and the superficial muscles of the thigh, and delivers it to the internal iliac.

External Iliac on the inner face of the ilium at a point level with the outer end of the first transverse process of the sacrum. It receives lymph from the abdominal muscles and delivers it to the Internal Iliac Node.

Internal Iliac forms a centre for the meeting of most of the lymph ducts of the hind quarter, and it delivers the lymph to the chyle cistern. It lies on the inner face of the ilium at the angle between the external iliac ureter and the aorta. It is found on taking off the hind quarter nearer the back bone than the external iliac.

The Intervertebrals. These are very small nodes, each about the size of a pea, and lying between the transverse processes of the vertebrae, close against the vertebral bodies. They are grouped, like vertebrae, into *Sacral*, *Lumbar* and *Thoracic* nodes. The sacral and lumbar nodes form a chain emptying into each other and finally into the chyle cistern, but each thoracic node empties direct into the thoracic duct. All intervertebral nodes receive lymph from the skin and muscles of the dorsal part of the trunk.

The Renal lies between the kidneys and the aorta, close to each renal artery. They receive lymph from the kidneys and deliver it to the intervertebral nodes.

Xiphoid lies in the heart fat above the junction of the xiphoid cartilage with the bony sternum in front of the diaphragm. It draws lymph from the diaphragm, pleura and ribs and their muscles and delivers it to the posterior suprasternal node.

Suprasternal (or *Sterno-costals*) lie on the inner surface of the intercostal muscles between the costal cartilages, and found by cutting into the sub-pleural fat about 3 inches from the border of the sternum and parallel to it. They receive lymph from the diaphragm and the abdominal and intercostal muscles and deliver it to the thoracic duct.

Presternal (or *Anterior Sternal*) lies on the inner face of the first sternal segment. It receives lymph from the adjacent muscles and delivers it to the prepectoral nodes.

Prepectorals (or *Lower Cervicals*), two or three on each side, lie over the anterior border of the first rib. They receive lymph from the neck, shoulder and axillary node and deliver it to the thoracic duct. The node in this group nearest the vertebrae is sometimes called the ' *Costo-cervical* ', and is often removed with the trachea.

Middle Cervicals lie on each side of the cervical portion of the trachea and receive lymph from adjacent tissues and the pharyngeal gland and deliver it to the prepectorals and prescapular nodes.

Prescapular lies between the point of the shoulder and ribs and 2 inches deep. It receives lymph from the middle cervicals and the musculature of the neck and shoulder and delivers it to the thoracic duct.

Axillary lies under the scapula at the trifurcation of the brachial artery and is found on removing the forelimb. It receives lymph from the forelimb and delivers it to the prepectoral nodes.

THE LYMPH NODES OF THE PIG

The Mesenteric lie in the thick bands of fat that fill the mesentery between the spiral coils of intestines, and are therefore easily found.

The Portal (or *Hepatic*) are six or seven in number, and lie round the entrance of the portal vein to the liver, but they are sometimes removed with the mesentery during disembowelling.

The Gastric, four or five, lie between the pancreas and the outer curve of the stomach.

The Mediastinal, close to the back bone, and may remain attached to it after removal of the lungs.

The Head. The submaxillary and parotid glands are numerous and are all separated by salivary tissue (Plate XII, T and R). Their general position is similar to that of the ox, but it is not easy to find them all. The pharyngeal gland (Plate XII, S) is further forward than in the ox, and there are usually noticeable ' *Tonsils* ' or collections of lymphoid tissue in the mucous membrane above them.

The Anterior Cervical lies on a level with the posterior end of the larynx, but is fairly near the skin. It is usually found on removing the head, and is normally covered with salivary tissue.

The Popliteal is usually missing, but the ' Hock Node ' (Plate XII, A), a few inches above the end of the os calcis, can sometimes be found just below. It is very rarely sought for.

The Precrural or Prefemoral (Plate XII, E) lies in the muscles of the abdominal floor below the sacro-lumbar joint and is best found by cutting through the whole peritoneal surface on a line at right angles to the back bone.

The Iliacs (Plate XII, F). There are several iliac nodes, some of which may be considered Internal Iliacs and some External Iliacs.

The Prescapulars (Plate XII, C) are six or seven in number on each side, and are placed more in the neck than the shoulder region. They are best sought for by deep cutting on the inside of the neck straight across from top to bottom, on a level with the junction of the axis and the third cervical vertebra.

The other nodes are similar in position to those of the ox.

In the sheep and goat the nodes correspond to those of the ox. In the horse, the nodes correspond in position to those of the ox, but each node is made up of numerous rather diffuse smaller nodes. They are not used in meat inspection.

HORMONES, ENDOCRINE GLANDS AND ENZYMES

HORMONES are substances that stimulate organs other than those in which they are produced. The organs that produce hormones are called Endocrine or Ductless Glands. The following are obtained from abattoirs for use in pharmacy.

Adrenalin, produced by the adrenal bodies lying at the inner anterior corner of each kidney. It is a strong stimulant to the sympathetic nervous system, and so stimulates the heart and white muscle. Applied locally, it checks bleeding by causing the arteries to contract.

Pituitrin, produced by the pituitary body below the brain. It also stimulates white muscle, especially that of the uterus, and is therefore used in obstetric cases.

Thyroidin, from the thyroid glands situated in each side of and below the larynx, is used to correct faulty growth.

Thymus Extract, from the thymus gland of young calves, is used to correct faulty growth.

Insulin, from the pancreas, is used to enable glycogen to be accumulated in the liver in cases of pancreatic disease. In the living animal, insulin is only produced under the influence of another hormone, Secretin, produced by the wall of the small intestine, but Secretin is not used in pharmacy. Testicular and Ovarian extracts are used to correct sexual abnormalities.

ENZYMES

Enzymes are substances that cause the breakdown of large molecules into smaller ones. Animal enzymes are not usually used in pharmacy.

Ptyalin in the saliva breaks down starch to sugar, but is not used commercially.

Rennet in the gastric juice, especially of sucklings, causes milk to coagulate. It is used commercially in the preparation of cheese, and is prepared from the abomasum of suckling calves.

Pepsin in the gastric juice partially breaks down protein. A vegetable preparation having the same effect is used commercially as a tenderiser.

Trypsin in the pancreatic juice continues the breakdown of protein. It is used commercially in the preparation of leather.

Lipase, in the pancreatic juice, breaks down fat.

Some six or seven enzymes occur in the small intestine, but are not used commercially.

Bile is not an enzyme, but may be mentioned here as it is used commercially in the manufacture of paints. It is also used in laboratories for testing for the presence of certain bacteria.

SUBSTITUTION AND DIFFERENTIATION

THE difference in appearance and texture of different meats is given on page 55, and the differences in the skeletons and internal organs in the various chapters describing them. A summary may, however, be useful for rapid reference.

The following carcases bear a superficial resemblance to each other after the skin, head and feet and viscera have been removed.

Sheep and Dog. The meat and fat of these two animals are indistinguishable by eye (though they can be differentiated by a ' Serum Test ' *), and carcases of large dogs have occasionally been found in consignments of mutton and lamb. In the dog there is no ' skin fold ' of panniculus muscle attaching the patella to the belly, but this is invariably present in sheep. The ribs and sternum of the sheep are broad and flat, while those of the dog are round in section. In the hind leg, the sheep has only one bone, the tibia, articulating with the tarsal joint, while the dog has both tibia and fibula. On dissecting the fore limb, it will be found that the sheep has a triangular scapula with a broad prolonging cartilage and the radius and ulna lie close together for their whole length, while the scapula of the dog has semi-circular posterior upper edges with practically no prolonging cartilage and the radius and ulna are widely separated along the greater part of their shafts. The xiphoid cartilage of the sheep is firm and grisly, that of the dog is softer and more fibrous, and is shaped like a dagger.

Sheep and Goats. The meat and fat of these two animals are indistinguishable by eye, and the proteins of the meat are so similar that no ' Serum Test ' * would be possible. Goats' fat is more sticky than sheep's, but it is doubtful if this would be of evidential value unless goats' hairs were actually adhering to it, and this, in fact, usually happens. The sheep's tail, whether docked or full length, contains very little muscle, but a large amount of subcutaneous fat, and it usually stiffens in rigor mortis in a depressed position over the anus; the goat's tail is very muscular, and stiffens in an erect position. The kidney knob of the sheep is nearly spherical, while that of the goat is more pear-shaped.

Actually in the United Kingdom and all Northern Europe the sheep are all short-legged, round-bodied breeds, and the goats are

---

* An outline of the Serum Test is given on page 110, Chapter VI.

all long-legged, flat-bodied breeds, so that, in section, the thorax is pear-shaped instead of circular; but in the warm-temperate and tropical zones both long legged sheep and short-legged goats are bred, and differentiation of their carcases is uncertain. Fortunately, in these areas the meat of both species is usually regarded as of equal value and errors in differentiation are not considered as of any importance.

Veal and Sheep or Goat. Mistakes in differentiating these carcases sometimes occur, owing to the similarity in size and the brighter red of the meat of the calf compared with that of the adult ox. A calf the size of a sheep or goat has accumulated very little fat in the large fat deposits, and its bones are cartilaginous and can be cut with a knife. A ' Serum Test ' * might be used, but it is difficult to believe that this would ever be necessary.

Born and Unborn or Foetal Veal. Foetal muscle does not develop rigor mortis. In cases of doubt a chemical test for the glycogen content of the muscle should be made, as this is very much higher in foetal muscle than in muscle of an animal that has been born alive.

Venison and Goat. Deer have mutton-like meat and beef-like fat, but attempts have been made to pass off the carcases of large but emaciated goats as those of small deer, such as roe-buck. The shoulders of a deer are flat, as the scapulae rise to the same height as the spines of the thoracic vertebrae and the space between is filled with trapezius and rhomboid muscle. Those of the goat present a sharp ridge as the thoracic spines stand well above the scapulae and, if the animal is so well fleshed that this ridge is rounded off, there is sufficient hard white fat present to show its species. The panniculus muscle (or ' bark ') of the deer covers the lumbar region of the back, while that of the goat covers only the flanks and belly. The tail of the deer, though muscular, is noticeably thinner with smaller bones than that of the goat. It is unlikely that a ' Serum Test ' * could be made as, in all probability, the proteins of both animals are similar.

Rabbit, Hare and Cat or Small Dog. There have been many attempts to substitute cat carcases for rabbits. Rabbits and hares have short, broad thoraces, with pronounced xiphoid cartilages and weak, short forelimbs; cats and dogs have long, narrow thoraces with soft narrow xiphoids and long and strong forelimbs. The tail of the rabbit (and hare) has very small bones, little more than cartilage, and practically no muscle, and the sacrum and anus are directed towards the ground. The tail of the cat (and dog) has

* An outline of the Serum Test is given on page 110, Chapter VI.

heavy bone and strong muscles, and the sacrum lies horizontally with the anus directed straight back. The kidneys of rabbits and hares have smooth, plain surfaces, and the right kidney is noticeably in front of the left or 'floating' kidney. Those of the cat (but not the dog) are covered with large blood-vessels, and lie nearly level. In the hind limb, the fibula of the rabbit and hare fuses with the tibia about half way down its length, so that only one bone, the tibia, articulates with the tarsal joint, while in the cat and dog there are two complete bones, tibia and fibula, freely articulated together. On dissection of the forelimb, the scapulae of rabbit and hare are found to be triangular, with large prolonging cartilages and sharp undercut acromion processes to which metacromions are fused, and the radii and ulnae lie close together. In cat and dog, the back edge and top of the scapulae form semicircles and the prolonging cartilages are negligible; the acromion processes are not undercut and there is a clear space between the shafts of the radius and ulna.

Adult hares have relatively longer hind limbs than rabbits, but in leverets or young hares the size of rabbits this difference is not so noticeable and carcases of leverets are frequently included with rabbits in error. It is unlikely that such an error would ever be considered as serious, but if necessary it may be noted that the carpus and metacarpus (or 'hand') of the hare is noticeably broader than the radius and ulna (or forearm), while in the rabbit the limb is much the same thickness from the elbow to the claws.

Pigs and Humans. Cannibalism has occurred in devastated countries of Europe after recent wars, and is still suspected to occur in certain recently civilised countries in other continents. No part of the human body anyway resembles that of any animal, so the meat would have to be cut away from the bones before being exposed for sale. Human red muscle is indistinguishable from pig's, but human fat is golden yellow and, compared with pig's, is scanty, even in fat persons. Human skin is noticeably thinner than pig's skin, and has soft hair instead of bristles. The hair follicles of human skin are minute and do not penetrate the dermis, but in pig's skin they are clearly visible and penetrate to the subcutaneous tissue. Human skin has numerous sudor glands, whose pores can be detected with a hand-lens. A 'Serum Test' * could be applied in case of doubt.

For the differentiation of the various meats, when separated from the bones, see the table on page 55 (Chap. III).

The internal organs of the different species can usually be

---

* An outline of the Serum Test is given on page 110, Chapter VI.

differentiated by the fat left on them, but the following table may be of use in memorising the more salient differences :—

KIDNEYS

	Av. Wt.	Right	Left	Remarks
Ox	1½ lb.	Pyramidal	Flat and floating	Twenty or thirty distinct lobes.
Sheep, Goat Dog	} 4 oz.	Nearly spherical	{ Nearly spherical and floating }	No visible lobes.
Pig	8 oz.	Flat and elongated	Flat, elongated and and fixed	Three poorly marked lobes. Very pale in colour.
[Human	—	Similar to sheep's	Similar to sheep's, but fixed	Yellow soft fat.]
Horse	1½ lb.	Heart shaped	Bean shaped	No visible lobes.
Camel, Deer,	6 oz.	Similar to sheep's	Similar to sheep's	Can be distinguished from sheep's by the soft fat.
Buffalo	1½ lb.	Similar to ox	Similar to ox	Can be distinguished from ox kidneys by fat.
Cat	—	Spherical	Spherical, fixed, level	Large blood-vessels in capsule.
Rabbit	—	Spherical	Spherical, floating	Left is always behind right. No visible blood-vessels in capsule.

LIVERS

	Average Weight	
Ox	10 lb.	One main lobe and small square caudate lobe. Flat.
Veal	—	One main lobe and small square caudate lobe. Thick owing to undeveloped rumen.
Sheep and Goats	1½ lb.	Main lobe partly divided. Small triangular caudate lobe. Flat.
Buffalo	10 lb.	Similar to sheep's (not ox).
Deer	2-3 lb.	Similar to sheep's.
Camel	8-10 lb.	Similar to sheep's, but no gall bladder.
Pig	4 lb.	Four main lobes. Small round caudate lobe. Very coarse and mottled.
[Human	—	One large and four small lobes. Not mottled.]
Horse	12 lb.	Three main lobes. Small triangular caudate lobe. Soft and dark red.
Dog	—	Five lobes of different sizes.
Cat	—	Seven lobes, all of different sizes.
Rabbit and Hare	—	Five lobes, all of different sizes.

8

SPLEENS OR MELTS

	Average Weight	
Ox	2 lb.	Oblong with rounded ends.
Sheep and Goat	4 oz.	Oyster-shape.
Pig	12 oz.	Long and thin, like a dog's tongue.
[Human	—	Oval.]
Horse	2½ lb.	Broad base, tapering rapidly, like very broad bladed sickle.
Camel and Deer	6 oz.	Similar to sheep's.
Buffalo	2 lb.	Similar to ox.

HEARTS

	Average Weight	Branches to Coronary Vessels	Os Cordis or 'Heart Bone' at Origin of Aorta	Remarks
Ox	6 lb.	3	Hard bone in adult Cartilage up to Three Years Old	
Sheep and Goat	3 lb.	3	Cartilage only	
Pig	12 oz.	2 large ones and usually 1 small central one	None	Very small and with very little fat.
[Human]				
Horse	9 lb.	2	None	More conical than ox
Camel	6 lb.	Similar to ox	None	
Deer	3 lb.	Similar to ox	More fibrous than cartilaginous	
Buffalo	6 lb.	Similar to ox	Hard bone at 5 years old	

LUNGS

	Right	Left	Trachea
Ox	5 lobes	3 lobes	Ends of rings upturned.
Sheep and Goat	Similar to ox	—	Similar to ox.
Pig	4 lobes	3 lobes	Ends of rings overlap.
[Human	3 lobes (no mediastinal)	2 lobes	Ends of rings do not meet.]
Horse	Lobes not clearly marked	—	Ends of rings overlap in the neck, but are wide apart in chest.
Camel	Lobes not clearly marked.	—	Ends of rings upturned.
Deer	5 lobes	3 lobes	Ends of rings upturned, but do not meet.
Buffalo	Similar to ox	—	

TONGUES

Ox	Short, pointed, rough upper surface, long piliform papillae at edges. Large prominence on dorsum, 20-30 vallate papillae.
Buffalo	Similar to ox, but black upper surface.
Sheep and Goat	Similar to ox, but upper surface relatively smoother.
Pig	Short, pointed, smooth upper surface. No prominence on dorsum. No piliform papillae at edge; 2 vallate papillae.
[Human	Short, spatulate, smooth upper surface, 20-30 vallate papillae, no piliform papillae.]
Horse	Long, spatulate, smooth. No prominence on dorsum. No piliform papillae, 2 vallate papillae.
Camel	Short and smooth.
Deer	Short, pointed, smooth upper surface. Short, soft, piliform papillae at edges. Small prominence on dorsum, 20-30 vallate papillae.

INDEX

INDEX

Oils, 55
Olecranon, 24
Olein, 54
Olfactory bulb, 82
Omasum, 141
Omentum, 66, 120
' Open ' side of carcase, 162
Orbit, 30
Ossa cordis, 95
  coxarum, 25
Ossification, 11
Osteology, 9
Osteomalacia, 132
Os uteri, 174
Ova, 175
Ovarian arteries, 101
Ovary, 175, 177
Oversticking, 105, 154
Oviducts, 124, 174
Oxygen, 6, 89, 155

PALATE, 30, 120, 148
Palmitin, 54
Pancreas, 126, 134, 205
Panniculus, 61, 67
Papillae, 71, 138
Paralysis, 85
Parasympathetic nerves, 87
Parchment, 78, 169
Parenchyma, 2
Parotid glands, 118
' Parson's nose ', 199
Parturition, 27, 59, 186
Patella, 25, 28, 201
' Patwack ', 21
Paunch, 140
Pectoral muscles, 60, 202
Pedestal of Camel, 79
Pelvic bones, 25, 40
  fat, 65
Pelvis, 25, 40
Pemmican, 214
Penis, 27, 61, 64, 170
Pepsin, 129
Pericardial fluid, 94
Pericardium, 81, 94
Perichondrium, 10
Periople, 75
Periosteum, 10
Peristalsis, 50, 122
Peritoneal membrane, 65, 81, 124
Peritoneum, 81, 124, 203
Peyers patches, 113, 122

Pharynx, 30, 120, 148
Phosphates, 12
Pia mater, 80
Pillars of kidney, 165
  of diaphragm, 59
Pin bones, 63
  in the heart, 94
Pineal body, 83
Pithing, 84, 202
Pituitary body, 82, 179
Placenta, 178, 183, 207
Placentation, 189
Plasma, 108
Platelets, blood, 107
Pleura, 66, 81, 153, 203
' Poisoned wounds ', 113
Pole axe, 43, 83
Polled cattle, stunning, 43
Pollution of air, 158
Pons, 82
Pores, 74
Portal vein, 102, 125
Posterior, 7, 64
Post-mortem movement, 209
Pot-belly, 112
Poulard, 207
Pregnancy, 179
  tests, 179
Premolar teeth, 31
Pre-natal influence, 198
Prepuce, 170
Previous sire, 198
Process, 14
Prolonging cartilage, 23
Prostate gland, 170
Protein, 6, 128
Prothrombin, 108
Psoas muscles, 56
Psyche, 3
Ptyalin, 127
Public symphysis, 25, 27
  tuberosity, 26
Pubis, 25, 26, 169, 201
Pulmonary vessels, 92, 98
Pulse, 50, 93, 96
Purring, 149
Purse, 169
Putrefaction, 212
Putrefactive bacteria, 73, 212
Pygostyle, 199
Pyloric valve, 121
Pylorus, 121, 139
Pyramids of kidney, 165